International Ocean Shipping

Other Titles of Interest

International Politics and the Sea: The Case of Brazil, Michael A. Morris

America's Maritime Legacy: A History of the U.S. Merchant Marine and Shipbuilding Industry Since Colonial Times, edited by Robert A. Kilmarx

Securing the Seas: The Soviet Naval Challenge and Western Alliance Options, Paul H. Nitze, Leonard Sullivan, Jr., and the Atlantic Council Working Group on Securing the Seas

The Year Book of World Affairs, 1979, edited by George W. Keeton and Georg Schwarzenberger

Contemporary International Law: A Concise Introduction, Werner Levi

Managing Ocean Resources: A Primer, edited by Robert L. Friedheim

About the Book and Author

International Ocean Shipping:
Current Concepts and Principles
Bernhard J. Abrahamsson

Intended as a basic text on ocean shipping, this book provides a basis for understanding how the industry functions and the problems and issues that arise because of its international character. Dr. Abrahamsson makes no attempt to judge the relative merits of various developments, arguments, or positions; rather, he explains concepts and principles and clarifies the interrelationships among various aspects of shipping.

The first four chapters include general concepts applicable to all modes of transportation, which are then applied specifically to ocean shipping. The book goes on to cover economic, technological, legal, political, and institutional developments and relationships in the ocean shipping industry.

Bernhard J. Abrahamsson is a master mariner and currently serves as associate professor in the Graduate School of International Studies at the University of Denver.

Published in cooperation with the
Canadian Marine Transportation Centre,
Dalhousie University, Halifax, Canada

International Ocean Shipping: Current Concepts and Principles

Bernhard J. Abrahamsson

Routledge
Taylor & Francis Group

LONDON AND NEW YORK

First published 1980 by Westview Press, Inc.

Published 2018 by Routledge
52 Vanderbilt Avenue, New York, NY 10017
2 Park Square, Milton Park, Abingdon, Oxon OX14 4RN

Routledge is an imprint of the Taylor & Francis Group, an informa business

Copyright © 1980 Taylor & Francis

Library of Congress Cataloging in Publication Data
Abrahamsson, Bernhard J.
  International ocean shipping.
  Bibliography: p.
  Includes index.
  1. Shipping. 2. Merchant marine. 3. Commerce. I. Title.
HE571.A27   387.5'44   79-26674

ISBN 13: 978-0-367-02219-8 (hbk)
ISBN 13: 978-0-367-17206-0 (pbk)

Contents

Preface

The purpose of this book is to provide a basic text in international ocean shipping and to serve as a basis both for an understanding of how the industry functions and for the problems and issues that arise because of its international character. No attempt is made to pass judgment on the relative merits of various developments, arguments, or positions. Rather, the effort is to clarify concepts and principles and explain how various aspects of ocean shipping relate to each other. Although the focus is on international shipping, the first four chapters include general concepts and principles applicable to all modes. These concepts are then applied to the specific mode of international shipping.

Statistics are not used in the main text except when necessary to illustrate a point. The reason for this is that the extensive use of statistics has a tendency to tie the text to the period of the data used. This is not desirable in the context of basic concepts and principles, the validity of which have no foreseeable time limit. However, the reader needs a frame of reference for magnitudes, in order to determine what is "big," "small," "large," or "little." Therefore, a statistical appendix is included.

This book—its organization and material—represents the accumulated experience of ten years' intermittent teaching of international shipping courses at both graduate and undergraduate levels throughout the world. That it finally goes to press is due to two circumstances for which I express my gratitude: first, to the Graduate School of International Studies at the University of Denver for granting me sabbatical leave for the 1978–1979 academic year, and second, to the Canadian Marine Transportation Centre at Dalhousie University for making it possible to spend the year with them and for generously supporting the project.

Special thanks are due to professors Graham Day and Edgar Gold for their support and comments at various stages during the writing of this book and to my wife for long hours spent at the typewriter.

Bernhard J. Abrahamsson

Acronyms and Abbreviations

AFRA	average freight rate assessment
BACAT	barges on catamaran
BCS	barge carrier system
bhp	brake horse power
BIMCO	Baltic and International Maritime Conference
B/L	bill of lading
BOB	barges on board
CAF	currency adjustment factor
cdwt	cargo deadweight ton(nage)
CENSA	Committee of European and Japanese National Shipowners' Associations
C&F	cost and freight
cft	cubic foot
C&I	cost and insurance
CIF	cost, insurance, and freight
CIRM	Comité International Radio Maritime
CL	carload
CMEA	Council for Mutual Economic Assistance (also known as COMECON)
CMI	Comité Maritime International
COGSA	Carriage of Goods by Sea Act

COMECON	Council for Mutual Economic Assistance (also known as CMEA)
CRISTAL	Contract Regarding Interim Supplement to Tanker Liability for Oil Pollution
dwt	deadweight ton(nage)
EEC	European Economic Community
ESC	European Shippers' Council
FAK	freight all kinds
FAS	free along side
FC&S	free of capture and seizure
fi	free in
FIATA	International Federation of Freight Forwarders
fios	free in and out and stowed
fiot	free in and out and trimmed
FloFlo	flow-in/flow-out
fo	free out
FOB	free on board
FPA	free of particular average
GATT	General Agreements on Trade and Tariffs
GESAMP	United Nations Group of Experts on the Scientific Aspects of Marine Pollution
GNP	gross national product
grt	gross register ton
H/H	house to house
H/P	house to pier
IALA	International Association of Lighthouse Authorities
IAPH	International Association of Ports and Harbors

IATA	International Air Transport Association
ICC	Interstate Commerce Commission (U.S.)
ICHCA	International Cargo Handling Coordination Association
ICS	International Chamber of Shipping
IGO	international governmental organization
IHO	International Hydrographic Organization
ihp	indicated horse power
ILO	International Labor Organization
IMCO	Intergovernmental Maritime Consultative Organization
INTERTANKO	International Tanker Owners' Association (1934–1969); International Association of Independent Tanker Owners (from 1971)
ISF	International Shipping Federation
ISO	International Standards Organization
ITF	International Transport Workers Federation
IUMI	International Union of Marine Insurance
JMC	Joint Maritime Committee (of the ILO)
LASH	lighter aboard ship
L/C	letter of credit
LCL	less than carload
LDC	less-developed country
LNG	liquefied natural gas
LoLo	lift-on/lift-off
LPG	liquefied petroleum gas
LTL	less than truckload
MNC	multinational corporation

MOT   Ministry of Transport (U.K.)

M/S   motor ship

M/V   motor vessel

NGO   nongovernmental organization

nrt   net register ton

OBO   ore-bulk-oil

OCP   overland common point

OECD   Organization for Economic Cooperation and
                Development

O/O   ore-oil

OSO   ore-slurry-oil

P/H   pier to house

P&I   protection and indemnity (clubs)

PIANC   Permanent International Association of
                Navigational Congresses

P/P   pier to pier

RoRo   roll-on/roll-off

SBT   seagoing barge train

S/D   shelter-decker

SEABEE   sea barge ship

shp   shaft horse power

spm   single point mooring

S/S   steamship

T/D   tween-decker

TEU   twenty-foot equivalent unit

thp   thrust horse power

TL   truckload

T/S	turbine ship
TOB	trailer on barge
TOFC	trailer on flatcar
TOVALOP	Tanker Owners Voluntary Agreement concerning Liability for Oil Pollution
ULCC	ultra large crude carrier
UNCITRAL	United Nations Commission of International Trade Law
UNCLOS	United Nations Conference on the Law of the Sea
UNCTAD	United Nations Conference on Trade and Development
USMC	United States Maritime Commission
VLCC	very large crude carrier
WS	Worldscale

International Ocean Shipping

Merchant Shipping in Transition: An Overview

International ocean shipping constitutes a highly significant aspect of world economic and political relationships. The rapid growth in world trade and the emergence of new national entities in the last thirty years have further emphasized the role of international shipping. Because of the generally free environment in which it has operated, the industry is highly mobile and flexible—factors that, together with technological progress, have facilitated the rapid growth in world trade.

In recent years, however, there have been several technological and institutional developments that are likely to have major effects on the industry. One of the latter is the aggregation of conventions and practices known as the Law of the Sea, which has been discussed in the United Nations Conference on the Law of the Sea (UNCLOS) since 1958. A new legal structure governing the oceans appears to be evolving, with traditional principles giving way to new concepts. Since the environment in which an industry operates determines its structure and mode of operations, international shipping has been molded by the conventional principles governing the use of the oceans as highways and will be strongly affected by shifts in the international climate and changes in the Law of the Sea.

Ocean shipping, as we know it today, has developed under the concepts of "freedom of the seas" and limited territorial waters with the right of "innocent passage." The "rules of the game" were formulated mainly by the maritime powers operating within private commercial relationships subject to specific national regulations governing fleet registration and corporate activities and to various international conventions. Clearly, a new Law of the Sea derived from a reinterpretation of these concepts will significantly change the atmosphere in which the shipping industry operates and, accordingly, dictate revised policies and practices for both industry and public authorities. A changing Law of the Sea will have an impact on all uses and users of the sea, but there are other technological and institutional developments that have already specifically affected the shipping of dry and liquid cargoes and will continue to do so.

In this overview, terms and concepts will be used with minimal explanation of their meaning. Further explanations and definitions will be given in the main body of the text.

Dry Cargo Shipping

Ocean shipping is divided into the carriage of liquid and dry cargoes. This is reflected in most maritime trade journals, which provide separate analyses and reporting of the tanker and dry cargo markets and the liner and tramp markets. For analytical purposes it is important to bear in mind that the first category of markets refers to the general kinds of cargo carried, while the latter refers to the types of service contracts and the terms on which the cargo is carried.

For example, dry cargo is carried in liners, tramps, bulk carriers, and specialty ships. Liners are operated as common carriers and are engaged on fixed routes according to published schedules. Most liner operators belong to international cartels known as shipping conferences. These conferences are formal agreements to control competition and avoid price wars through such means as fixed freight rates. The agreements can be of several kinds, from outright pooling arrangements—allocations of numbers of sailings or sharing the total volume of trade—to controlling the kinds of services offered. Because of the frequency, regularity, and reliability of liners, they primarily carry goods that move in relatively small lots —heterogeneous general cargoes, including manufactures and semimanufactures.

Tramps, on the other hand, go wherever and whenever their services are needed. Their freight rates are largely established by market forces and they carry primarily goods that move in large lots—homogeneous bulk cargoes such as coal, cereals, and ore. For various reasons (mainly general economic growth, economies of scale, and technological progress in shipbuilding), tramps carrying bulk cargoes have grown substantially in size. It is common to refer to these larger tramps as "bulk carriers." As the needs for raw materials increased, importers and exporters formed, respectively, purchasing and marketing organizations that have strongly affected the tramp market. To create a "countervailing" power, bulk carriers began in the late 1960s to pool their resources in order to coordinate the supply of tonnage and the freight rates.[1] This constituted a major development in a market that traditionally had been considered a "textbook example" of a free market. We will return to this topic later on.

Unitization

In the liner trade, the last twenty years have seen the introduction of new cargo handling methods and facilities, referred to as "unitization." This development, caused by the same factors affecting the tramps, led to the introduction of containerships, ranging from ships that carry containers in their holds to the LASH (lighter aboard ship) and SEABEE (sea barge ship), in which the containers are loaded into lighters and barges that are then stowed in their respective ships. At the same time, other special kinds of vessels like refrigerated ships and carriers of fruit, automobiles, lumber, newsprint, chemicals, and other so-called neo-bulk cargoes have been developed. Therefore, although ships engaged in tramp and liner services may have similar technical characteristics that might allow them to move from one type of service to another, recent innovations and modifications actually tend to make ships uniquely suited to only one type of service.

The containerization movement in the liner trade has had far-reaching effects. It is generally accepted that one containership can do the work of four to ten conventional vessels, depending on trade route and size. Because of this larger operational capacity, larger cargo volumes are needed in each port of call, and it is expected that in the future trade will be concentrated in a few ports on each route, with other ports being served by feeder ships. The fact that the con-

tainer can also be used in truck and rail transportation has resulted
in an integration of various modes into a truly international "transportation system." This integration movement has had inevitable effects on trade routes and shipping operations, facilitating the
development of the so-called land bridges. Cargo from Europe and
Japan, for example, can move in containers via the trans-Siberian
railroad to the Pacific coast of the USSR, then by ship to its destination. Alternatively, it might move by ship to the United States or
Canada, by rail across the continent, and on to Japan by ship again.
In cases where the destination of the shipment is on the rail segment, a "mini-bridge" has been used.

These rapid developments raise numerous problems and issues for
both the carriers and shippers. First, most shippers may benefit from
containerization, but what about those whose commodities cannot
be put into containers and cannot be moved as neo-bulk, or those
who want utilization in the form of pallets or pre-slings? Although
there are special pallet ships and a large number of conventional
vessels, such a shipper may one day pay higher rates as he becomes
an exception. This is particularly relevant to low-value cargo that
now, under the principle of "what the traffic will bear," moves at
rates lower than average cost. Second, although services in general
are faster, more regular, and more reliable, there are fewer ports
served by containerships than by conventional services, and the use
of feeder lines may cause hardships in particular cases. Third, in
door-to-door service, the containers are loaded by the shipper and
unloaded by the consignee, causing increases in labor costs that may
offset some of the savings on rates. The responsibility for proper
stowage in the container to prevent damage is shifted from the carrier to the shipper with added costs and manpower requirements.
Finally, the shippers must adapt their whole distribution network to
the use of containers. If this network involves areas that cannot be
serviced by containers, the resulting mixing of container and conventional shipping methods detracts from the benefits of containers.

Through Transport

From the carrier's point of view, containerization poses problems
of coordination of services. To derive the full benefits of containers,
containers should move from door to door—the so-called through
service concept of transportation. This necessitates interchangeable

containers, a tracking system, new rates, a system for the division of rates between different carriers and modes of carriage, and a uniform "through bill of lading." Most of these problems have been at least partially resolved, but much remains to be done. For example, although the International Standards Organization (ISO) has published standard dimensions for containers, and most ship classification agencies have formulated construction specifications, containers are still not completely standardized. While several international legal conferences have been held on the subject, no agreement has been reached on a uniform through bill of lading.

Marine Insurance

These various problems carry over into the insurance field. Insurance rates are based on actuarial experience, and it appears that this experience has not been sufficient to affect rates as much as was once expected. Also, before insurance rates can be assessed on container cargo, the containers must be uniformly classified as to their insurable characteristics and acceptable methods must be agreed upon to verify the containers' declared content. The legal aspects of who is liable, when, and where, for the cargo must be settled under a through bill of lading since commercial terms—free on board (FOB), free along side (FAS), and the like—become ambiguous when containers are used. There are further problems in finding a method to assess each shipper's share of general average[2] and salvage charges. Similarly, the Hague Rules pertaining to the carrier's liability need to be revised to include containers.

Effects on Labor

Labor also feels the repercussions as containerization makes a port capital intensive while conventional port handling is labor intensive. Thus, problems arise as port labor becomes redundant.[3] It is doubtful that overall land-based labor requirements in the transportation system decrease as much as the immediate impact on ports indicates. Since containers must be loaded and unloaded at points of origin and destination, labor requirements at these points increase compared to previous methods. Thus, to some extent, the demand for labor shifts from the intermediate points in the transport process (ports) to the beginning and end of that process.

Aboard ships, the increased size of the ship and its increasingly

sophisticated automated equipment have resulted in proportionately fewer crew members with higher technical qualifications. This
has brought about in many countries a reevaluation of present maritime manpower policies and reorganization of training curricula. A
current trend, notably in England and Norway, is toward "general
purpose" crews. Modern training and certification is expensive and
usually government supported; thus, there is a need for selection
criteria to ensure that the trainees spend sufficient time in the field
to justify the public expense. Research on this subject is being pursued in many shipping nations.[4]

The problems of labor redundancy did create conflicts throughout
the world as unions of both port labor and seafarers resisted the introduction of containers. However, these problems appear to have
been surmounted by policies based on principles formulated by the
International Transport Workers Federation (ITF).[5] In essence,
these principles stress that every effort should be made to maintain
employment at existing levels. Should this not be possible, the labor
force should first be decreased by natural attrition, and further
reduction should be accompanied by employer-provided retraining
schemes and financial assistance to those too old to benefit from retraining. ITF suggested lowering the retirement age of seafarers and
providing for their sharing, while aboard ship, the amenities of life
ashore.

Customs Clearance

Change has also been necessary for customs clearance procedures
as these have not generally been flexible enough for container shipments. Throughout the world, customs inspections have traditionally been made on piers and in ports. Although the arrival of air
cargo transportation broke this pattern by requiring customs inspection of exports and imports at inland nonwaterfront locations, inspections are still primarily made in ports. A container, if it is to
achieve the utmost efficiency in reducing costs, must be able to go
through ports without being delayed for customs inspection and
should be opened at the ultimate point of destination. The adjustment of customs procedures to accommodate containers involves,
therefore, additional inland inspection facilities. Much has been
done in this area in the major shipping countries, but there is further
need for action.

Ports

Of great importance is the obvious fact that ports are affected by changes in shipping. Ports require large, long-term investment. At the time the investment is made, the port facilities are adapted to the existing or immediately foreseeable shipping technology. Since no major innovation was introduced in the shipping industry until very recently—the late 1950s—ports were constructed to serve conventional ships. The ships, on the other hand, although requiring large capital investments and having a life of about twenty years,[6] are, relative to ports, small short-term investments. A shipowner who builds his ships after port facilities have been established, therefore, adapts the ships' design to these facilities. The long life of port investments and the heavy expenditures necessary for major innovation in established ports deter such innovation and this, in turn, holds back innovative shipowners.

This circle was broken by the development that led to modern bulk carriage and containerization as new bulk and container ports have been constructed. Since containers constitute only one possible solution to unitization in shipping and there is no reason to believe that the technological revolution has come to an end, port planning for future developments has become important. Any major port investment must consider the present uncertainties posed by the rapidly changing shipping technology as well as economic and political factors affecting trade flows. It may be of value to establish accelerated depreciation schedules for new port investment, so that the long book-life of existing facilities should not pose an obstacle to innovation. The effects of such a course of action and other port and ship innovations on the structure and level of port fees must be considered. It appears that shipowners and port authorities need to be in closer communication than ever before in order to provide rational bases for decisions.

Conferences

Concurrent with the specific operational problems recounted above, the carriers are faced with numerous other institutional and political developments. The large capital requirements necessary to keep at the forefront of the containerization movement have led to structural changes in liner operations. Since few individual com-

panies have the financial resources or the expertise required to
organize container traffic on an international scale in a highly competitive environment, they have depended on cooperation. International shipping consortia, designed to operate joint container services under joint management, have been formed among large liner
companies. The step from international consortia to multinational
corporations (MNCs) is small and is likely to be taken in the foreseeable future.[7]

These developments have had repercussions on the shipping conference system. In the past, there was a consensus that conferences
were precluded from assuming and abusing monopoly power by certain forces, including competition between conferences and real or
potential competition from tramps and nonconference liners. Further, it was assumed that the large number of members in most conferences would prevent effective collusion and add an element of
competition within the conferences. Should the conferences nevertheless become effective monopolies, in spite of these restraints, the
shippers could form "shippers' councils" or "users' associations" and
use their collective power to counteract the conference, and, as a
last resort, the possibility or threat of national legislation to control
conferences would act as a deterrent to monopolistic abuse.

Most of these countervailing forces, however, have been weakened by recent developments. First, there are the "super conferences," which appreciably reduce interconference competition.[8]
Second, the increased differentiation between tramp and liner
markets removes much of both the real and the potential threat of
competition from tramps. The high capital barriers to entry and the
formation of international consortia remove the threat from nonconference liners in container trades. At the same time, consortia
reduce the number of members serving a particular trade, elimi-
nating the major obstacle to collusion. Shippers' councils appear not
to have been able to carry countervailing power alone. Therefore,
potential national legislation for the control of international shipping
has become a major issue in the industry. This has long been the
case in the trades of the United States and some South American
countries, but the issue is now becoming worldwide.

National Merchant Marines

Apart from these events, which may be attributed to technological and economic changes, there are historical developments and problems that have the same political implications. With the exception of the major "flag of convenience" countries – Liberia, Panama, Singapore – the less-developed countries (LDCs), as a bloc, account for only a small share of total world tonnage – 7 percent in 1975. However, about 45 percent of the world tonnage consists of tankers, and since LDCs (except the Arab oil producers) operate predominantly dry cargo carriers and few tankers, their operational capacity in dry cargo carriage is greater than the 7-percent share indicates. Even so, for various reasons, including balance of payments, trade promotion, and defense considerations, many LDCs are actively promoting the expansion of their merchant marines.[9] As the available trade volume often does not justify the introduction of more tonnage, there is a growing tendency toward flag discrimination manifested in bilateral shipping agreements. Such bilateralism is likely to become the backbone of future shipping.

Liner Code of Conduct

One basic reason for the emergence of national merchant marines is the widespread feeling that nonshipping nations are treated unfairly and arbitrarily in terms of both services and freight rates by the shipping conferences. The problem is not new; it arose shortly after conferences were first established a century ago. At that time, shipper's councils were considered the appropriate solution, and in the post–World War II period, these organizations again became prominent. They have been effective, however, only when backed by governments, and a conflict situation has developed, with conferences and traditional shipping countries on one side and the less-developed, emerging shipping nations on the other. The concept of a "conference code of practice" evolved from this conflict, and such a code, with implementation on a voluntary basis, was issued by the Committee of European and Japanese National Shipowners' Associations (CENSA) in 1971. The following year, the United Nations Conference on Trade and Development (UNCTAD), issued its own code, reflecting more closely the stand of the less-developed countries. This code, certain to have a major effect on shipping, called for a system of international controls of liner shipping, based on the principles that (1) government will have a predominant role in all relations between shippers and shipowners; (2) admission to conference membership will include noncommercial criteria, one of which would be the development of national shipping lines; and (3) flag discrimination to aid national shipping lines will be acceptable in principle.

Meeting in Geneva in March 1974, UNCTAD adopted an international convention along these lines.[10] To come into force, the convention requires ratification by twenty-four countries accounting for at least 25 percent of world total liner tonnage. By June 1978, the first of these conditions had been satisfied, but only slightly less than 6 percent of the qualifying tonnage was represented. This situation may change rapidly, however: In the late 1970s, the traditional shipping nations had lost much carriage to state-owned fleets, particularly that of the USSR.[11] It is evident that this trend will continue as the Soviet fleet expands with modern, technologically advanced ships. In an attempt to maintain their shipping position, the traditional maritime nations may prefer a secure cargo base and, therefore, accede to the UNCTAD code. This would quickly bring the convention into force.[12] While the code specifically refers to liner shipping, its acceptance of bilateralism is certain to bring about changes in the employment of bulk carriers and other tramp ships and to facilitate international control of all ocean shipping.[13]

The most important aspect of the convention is the guideline suggesting that countries trading with each other have the right to carry 80 percent of that trade, with only the remaining 20 percent open to other flag carriers. This is known as the 40-40-20 rule and has for a long time been the norm in trade between the United States and Brazil and Argentina. Applying the rule to all trade means that bilateral agreements may be the main determinant of carriers' activities, and such agreements will decrease the international mobility of ships, which is one of the outstanding characteristics of the industry. Because the given volume of trade is restricted to the trading partners' tonnage, which in all cases is smaller than the world supply of shipping, there will be upward pressure on the freight rates. To prevent this, rates are likely to become part of the trade agreements and to come increasingly under government control. Since this would remove much of the basis for the existence of conferences, this system may well be on its way out. In any event, the general environment for transport of dry cargo has changed and will continue to change. Strategic managerial decisions relating to the type and kind of ships and services, scale of operations, and trade routes will be increasingly affected by governmental bilateral agreements. The industry is likely to lose much of its international character and mobility as markets are subdivided on a preferential basis.

Liquid Cargo Shipping

Liquid cargoes carried in tankers, mainly crude oil and its products, are normally homogeneous and move in large quantity lots, though some, such as vegetable oils, wines, latex, and various chemicals move in small quantities. A recent development is the movement, in special ships, of liquified natural and petroleum gases (LNG and LPG).

The typical tanker in the post–World War II period was the T-2 of about 16,200 deadweight tons (dwt). However, the rapid change from coal to oil-based energy in most parts of the world, coupled with accelerated worldwide economic growth, provided the transport volume needed to reap the economies of scale inherent in larger ships. At the same time, political events such as the closure of the Suez Canal and technological progress in shipbuilding made it possible to realize these economies. As a result, we now have crude oil carriers of some 500,000 dwt and even larger ships within the range of possibility.

Although the carriage of liquids is different from that of dry cargo, the distinction between tanker and nontanker shipping is becoming rather blurred. Because of their constructional characteristics, tankers are well suited for and have always engaged in the transport of grains. Recent years, however, have seen the advent of combination carriers that can carry both oil and dry bulk cargoes, and these bulk carriers are becoming increasingly important.

The structure of the tanker market is quite different from the dry cargo situation. Liner services, in the sense of common carriers, do not exist, and there are, consequently, no conferences. Instead, the major part of the world's tanker fleet, about 80 percent, is controlled by the oil industry, which either owns the ships or charters them on long-term contracts. (About 35 percent of the fleet is owned by the oil companies and another 45 percent is normally on long-term charter.) The remainder of the tonnage is available for spot charter-

ing and can be considered tramp service. Because of the concentrated control, the homogeneous product, and the similarity of conditions of carriage, tanker shipping management is faced with a less
complex environment for strategic decision making than is the case
in the liner market, but there are other problems of a more technical
than structural nature whose resolution may introduce tanker
management to a decision environment similar to that existing in the
dry cargo sector.

The draft of the very large crude carriers (VLCCs) excludes, at
the present, their passage through the Suez Canal and limits them
severely as to which ports and other sea-lanes they can use. Some
lanes are only partially located in international waters, or jurisdiction over a route may be shared by several nations. An example of
the former situation is the VLCC route to Finland, which partially
transits Swedish waters; an example of the latter problem is the
Malacca Straits. In addition, the traffic density and the maneuver-
ing of VLCCs may cause difficulties in narrow waters and may
necessitate traffic control. International cooperative efforts are obviously necessary to come to grips with these problems and the
crucial international legal problem of protecting the marine environment from pollution.[14]

Marine Pollution

Protection of the marine environment is rapidly becoming one of
the most important issues in ship operation. In this respect, the
tanker market, like the rest of ocean shipping, is governed by existing international conventions, except in relation to liability for oil
spills. Here the tanker operators have developed their own schemes.
Traditionally, insurance covered claims for damages in the shipping
industry. In the case of oil spill damages, however, insurance companies have claimed insufficient actuarial experience and have been
unwilling or unable to assume full liability. As a result, and particularly after the *Torrey Canyon* incident in 1967, some nations require evidence of financial responsibility for damages for tankers
entering their territorial waters. To meet such demands, oil companies and tanker owners have arranged their own compensation
funds on a voluntary, private cooperative basis. Two such schemes
exist: the Tanker Owners Voluntary Agreement concerning Liability for Oil Pollution (TOVALOP) and the Contract Regarding In-

terim Supplement to Tanker Liability for Oil Pollution (CRISTAL). In addition, the industry is subject to two international liability conventions. One, the 1969 Civil Liability Convention, which entered into force in 1975, assigns strict, but not absolute, liability to the shipowner; the other, the 1971 Compensation Fund Convention, which is not yet in force, is an international fund financed by the contracting nations and is intended to give compensation in cases where the first convention is inadequate. (See Appendix C.)

The major part of ship-originated marine pollution is not caused by accidents, but by intentional oil spills in the course of standard operational procedures. The control of these will have the greatest impact on the pollution problem, and efforts to effect such control are underway. The implications for the shipping industry of the various efforts to control marine pollution will depend on the final formulation of the Law of the Sea, which will determine the legal framework in which solutions are implemented.

If multiple standards develop in such a way that very strict rules might apply to some ships while others were allowed more liberal treatment, then bilateral arrangements for preferential treatment may become a major feature. In such a situation, the tanker market may move in the same direction as the dry cargo market—toward subdivided markets based on bilateral agreements and government controls—and that will affect the allocation of shipping resources and efficiency.[15]

On balance, it seems clear that the various technological and institutional developments toward increased ship sizes and specialization in both general cargo and bulk trades must work in the same direction. Specialization necessarily means less flexibility in operations while the traditional worldwide mobility of ships in search of employment is being constrained.

Notes

1. T. Rinman and R. Linden, *Shipping—How it Works* (Gothenburg, Sweden: 1978), p. 45; and H. P. Drewry, Shipping Consultants, Ltd., *Organization and Structure of the Dry Bulk Shipping Industry*, Study no. 63 (London: 1978).

2. General average refers to the voluntary and intentional sacrifice of

some cargo in order to save the ship or the rest of the cargo. Traditionally, general average is governed in marine insurance by the York-Antwerp Rules, which need reformulation to take containerization into account. The Hague Rules were revised in the 1968 Brussels Protocol, but, at that time, containerization was too new to be sufficiently reflected.

3. See A. A. Evans, *Technical and Social Changes in the World's Ports* (Geneva: International Labor Office, 1969).

4. National Research Council, *The Sea-going Work Force: Implications of Technological Change* (Washington, D.C.: 1974); J.M.M. Hill, *The Seafaring Career* (London: Center for Applied Social Research, Tavistock Institute of Human Relations, 1972); and *Journal of the Israel Shipping Research Institute,* December 1972.

5. Evans, *Technical and Social Changes,* chap. 2.

6. For modern containerships life expectancy is no more than seven to ten years.

7. There is a definite distinction between "international" and "multinational" firms, although the terms are commonly used interchangeably. Some outstanding characteristics of MNCs, quite apart from their large sales, are that they operate in many countries (shipping operates *between* countries), they are likely to engage in research and development in these countries, and their ownership as well as management are typically multinational. An international company, by contrast, is simply one that derives most, or a large share, of its revenues from international sales. See Sheldon Stahl, "The Multinational Corporation: A Controversial Force," *Monthly Review* of the Federal Reserve Bank of Kansas City, June 1976.

8. U.S., Congress, House, Joint Economic Committe, *Discriminatory Freight Rates and the Balance of Payments,* 89th Cong., 1st sess., January 6, 1965; and U.S., Department of Justice, *The Regulated Ocean Shipping Industry,* Report, January 1977.

9. UNCTAD's objective for the Second Development Decade is a 10-percent share for LDCs by 1980. See Chapter 10 of this volume.

10. UNCTAD, "Convention on a Code of Conduct for Liner Conferences," UN Doc. TD/CODE/11/Rev.(1974), April 6, 1974. Of the 84 countries attending, 72 voted for the convention, 7 against, and 5 abstained. For a description of the code and analysis of its objectives and principles, see M. J. Shah and S. G. Sturmey, "Code of Conduct for Liner Conferences," *Swedish Shipping Gazette* 12 (1975), and S. G. Sturmey, "The Development of the Code of Conduct for Liner Conferences," *Marine Policy,* April 1979.

11. See U.S., Congress, House, *Third Flag: Hearings* before the Subcommittee on the Merchant Marine, 94th Cong., 1st and 2d sess., no. 94-35, 1976.

12. The fifth UNCTAD met in Manila in May 1979, when the European Economic Community (EEC), the USSR, the Scandinavian countries, and the German Democratic Republic announced their acceptance of the convention, thus ensuring that it will enter into force in the near future. The EEC acceptance has certain reservations: While the group recognizes the LDCs' rights to a 40-percent share, the share for the developed nations should be open for competition among the lines of the EEC member countries. This is extended to any country in the Organization for Economic Cooperation and Development (OECD) that grants similar rights to EEC operators. However, if an EEC member does not have a "fair" share of its liner trade, others must negotiate for participation in that nation's share (*Fairplay International Shipping Weekly*, May 17, 1979).

13. According to *Norwegian Shipping News* (September 19 and October 10, 1975) the observed development patterns of merchant marines indicate at least four distinct stages of development. First, a liner fleet is established and expanded. Second, operations with tanker and bulk carrier fleets begin, leading to the third stage, which is participation in cross trades. The final stage would be vertical and horizontal integration of shipping with other transport as well as nontransport activities. Except for the oil exporting countries that have begun directly with tanker and bulk operations, most LDCs are in the first stage.

Although the LDCs' capacity is mainly in liner shipping, they have a great potential for bulk carriage because a large share of the world's seaborne trade in bulk commodities originates in these countries. The realization of this potential, however, may hinge on the implementation of cargo preference policies for these commodities. The extension of the UNCTAD convention to cover bulk carriage may, therefore, be only a matter of time. Indeed, the fifth UNCTAD meeting passed proposals to extend the cargo-sharing principles of the code to bulk trades and to restrict or phase out open registries. A major part of the world's bulk carriers are in these registries.

14. What actually constitutes pollution is largely a matter of definition. "When we say that something is polluted, we are in fact making a value judgement about the quantity of foreign matters present which may vary with social and economic circumstances." ("Identification and Control of Pollutants of International Significance," UN Doc. A/Conf. 48/4, quoted in J. Barros and D. M. Johnston, *The International Law of Pollution* [New York: Free Press, 1974]).

The most widely accepted definition is that of the United Nations Group of Experts on the Scientific Aspects of Marine Pollution (GESAMP): "The introduction by man, directly or indirectly, of substances or energy into the marine environment (including estuaries) resulting in such deleterious effects as harm to living resources, hazards to human health, hindrance to marine activities including fishing, impairment of quality or use of sea water, and reduction of amenities." (UN Doc. A/7750, Part I, p. 3, November 10, 1969).

15. For a more elaborate discussion, see B. J. Abrahamsson, "The Marine Environment and Ocean Shipping: Some Implications for a New Law of the Sea," *International Organization*, spring 1977.

Transportation Economics 2

Introduction

The *mode* of transportation refers to the general form of transport. There are five modes: railroad, highway, air, water, and pipeline. Any mode can be used in both domestic and international transport. The *means* of transportation are the specific vehicles used for the movement. For example, within the mode of highway transport, the means may be bus, van, or truck, while the water mode may employ the means of barges, containerships, tankers, and the like. Although each mode has its own unique economic, institutional, and operational characteristics, they all perform the same function, namely, to move people and goods from place to place. Hence all modes respond to the same basic economic factors and this makes it possible to derive basic and general concepts and principles applicable to all modes. The purpose of this chapter is to provide the overall context of transportation economics within which such concepts and principles are examined and analyzed by economists.

Transportation is at all times a very visible activity, and, therefore, nearly every transportation issue quickly becomes a public and political issue. We need only consider the impact, on the local level, of a strike by bus or taxi drivers. On the regional, national, and international levels, strikes by the crews of ships, trains, airplanes, or trucks can easily have devastating effects on a particular country's economy. The more complex and segmented the structure of the labor force engaged in transport is, the more vulnerable the system will be to disruption by the actions of a few. For example, airplanes may be grounded by separate, but equally effective, actions by pilots, flight attendants, machinists, air controllers, or fuel truck drivers.

In addition to service disruptions by strikes, other important and

17

more common issues involve increases in passenger fares and freight rates. In most countries such increases, whether local, national, or international, are not undertaken without much public debate and discussion. With respect to international air fares and ocean freight rates, these increases are often the subject of commercial policy debates and high level government action. In most countries there is substantial government involvement in the transportation system, from outright ownership and operation, particularly of railroads, to regulation of safety, economic, and legal matters. In brief, modern society cannot escape from transport issues. Transport is necessary to allocate and utilize resources and to exchange goods domestically and internationally. This is where economics enters, because it is the science of allocating resources among competing ends.

The economist's interest in transportation was aroused by the development of railroads. For some seventy-five years beginning in the mid-nineteenth century, economists focused on the problems of monopoly regulation because these were the problems manifested by the railroads at the time. By the time these problems had been extensively treated and a framework for regulation established, monopoly abuse was no longer the issue and regulatory concern was directed more toward control of competition than monopoly. New concerns had emerged due to technological progress that brought in the new modes of air transport and pipelines as well as modern water and highway transport. These developments created problems different from those of railroad monopolies because they centered on complex operational and managerial aspects within already existing regulatory frameworks in most countries. Such problems have proved to be manageable with the aid of computers and mathematical models that have opened up new vistas as a result of their application to traffic flows, scheduling and monitoring, coordination, and general management of transport activities.

A new era began with vigorous competition between modes, intermodal coordination and cooperation, problems of major capital needs, and adjustments of the railroads to the new developments. At the same time, shippers were presented with an intricate and bewildering array of new alternative modes, routes, services, and rates to meet their transport needs. Transportation, as a business management function, became more important and demanding than before, and today, the areas of logistics and physical distribution are of major importance to larger corporations.

As a consequence, the focus of transportation economics – or, rather, the application of economic theory to transport problems – has changed several times. The first focus was prompted by a concern for the economic and social evils perceived as coming from the railroad monopolies. This led to an emphasis on the understanding of the general principles of transportation, which would provide a grasp of the basic role of transport in the economy and allow for the formulation of national policies and a regulatory framework. The next focus was to examine how the different modes operated, within the constraints of policies and regulations, to achieve their objectives as businesses. That is, how did they solve specific problems of operations in the given environment? The logical next step was to look at the logistics of industries and firms that were the customers of the transport industry – i.e., how they availed themselves of the many transport alternatives – and this has led to a focus on operations research and systems analysis.

As a rather natural consequence of these shifting focuses, the teaching of and research in transport economics at universities has been in different disciplinary departments. General principles and regulatory theory are commonly taught in economics, while logistics, physical distribution, and operations research are usually housed in the business school. It is also common to find in geography departments courses in regional analysis with emphasis on location theory.

The main areas for inquiry into transportation are shown in Figure 2.1. The interest of the academic economist is today centered on the general role of transport and project appraisal techniques. This is a reflection of a changed social atmosphere that demands a greater concern for social and environmental effects of major public actions. On the whole, technology is such that continuous investment in transportation is both necessary and large scale. Since the location of transportation activities affects the location of other economic activities, any change in transportation has effects on other activities as well. Hence, there is concern for the social and economic consequences of transport investment. Similarly, there is concern for the environment as new transport facilities may add noise and other pollution as well as congestion.

Because of these concerns, one of the major issues today is the de-

Fig. 2-1

AREAS OF TRANSPORT ECONOMICS

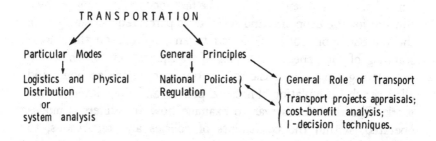

TRANSPORTATION

Particular Modes   General Principles

Logistics and Physical   National Policies   General Role of Transport
Distribution   Regulation
    or   Transport projects appraisals;
system analysis   cost-benefit analysis;
                                                     I-decision techniques.

cision process in transportation investment. This process, involving investment decision ("I-decision") techniques, must be able to assess both public and private costs and benefits likely to accrue from a given investment. Therefore, a great deal of effort is being devoted to cost-benefit analysis, which involves the two basic aspects of identifying the costs and benefits and evaluating, or pricing, them.[1] These aspects, in turn, involve the usual investment problems of choosing between present and future consumption, that is, which techniques and rates of discounting are to be used. In addition, the inclusion of social costs and benefits poses problems because these are not reflected in the market forces that normally determine the prices of private costs and benefits used in the calculation. The economist then has to resort to shadow pricing which, again, presents its own morass of theoretical and practical pitfalls whose importance carries over to the problem of resource allocation in transport. Suppose an investment can be made in trucks or in a railroad and that a private cost-benefit analysis favors trucks. Now the social costs of increased pollution and highway congestion are included. Whether this will swing the calculation in favor of the railroad depends on the prices set on these social costs and benefits—a thorny task susceptible to many subjective constraints. One way to avoid this problem is to attempt an evaluation of the time saved by investing in the alternative modes. The rationale is that transport achieves its function better the quicker the movement is performed. Therefore, there should always be an element of time involved in a transport investment.

Although much intellectual effort has gone into the evaluation of time and much insight and practical knowledge have been gained, this is still an area fraught with difficulties. There are many variables to consider: Who gains the time? When? Where? Why? Often the time saving involves higher speeds and, if this increases the probability of accidents and loss of life, questions arise concerning the values of accident prevention and of life. These, in turn, raise the issues of speed and safety regulations and the sensitive question of government participation in general.

Broadly speaking, transportation economics today is primarily concerned with three main areas:[2]

1. Investment decisions in transport, including techniques for cost-benefit analysis and discounting
2. Allocation of resources in transportation, including problems of pricing principles and shadow pricing
3. The role and impact of government in transportation, including questions of regulation and long-term planning for adequate infrastructure

Spanning all three major areas are efforts and problems connected with the values of time, life, and accident prevention.

These concerns are also reflected in current ocean shipping research where two general trends are clearly discernible. One line of research, seen in the works by UNCTAD, the Organization for Economic Cooperation and Development (OECD), and some agencies of various governments, is toward a basic understanding of the importance of ocean shipping in economic development and growth. It deals with policy issues such as levels and structures of freight rates, flag discrimination, the effects of conference behavior and its possible control and regulation, balance of payments effects of national versus foreign ships, and the expansion of national fleets. The other research direction is toward topical managerial issues concerned with operational aspects of shipping. This is the main focus of various shipping research institutions throughout the world. It includes such topics as cost and financial analyses, port turn-around times and costs, and specific feasibility studies. The continuing need for efficient transport within and among nations ensures a future interest in teaching and research in these areas.

Conceptual Overview of Ocean Shipping*

One of the major features of the post–World War II era has been the worldwide experience of rapid industrial and population growth that has resulted in large, concentrated centers of production and consumption. This has led to an increase in demand for transportation in general and, with world trade rapidly growing, for ocean shipping in particular. As indicated in Chapter 1, attempts to increase the efficiency of shipping have resulted in technological progress and change in shipbuilding, cargo handling, and management. The most visible manifestations of these developments are the very large and automated ships used today for the transport of oil and bulk cargoes and the introduction of various concepts of containerization and other forms of unitization in specialty ships.

Increased ship sizes and new, sophisticated cargo handling equipment have far-reaching effects on port facilities, transportation patterns, and labor requirements–all of which have repercussions on economic activities and social patterns as well as on international political institutions. The more dependent a country is on shipping, the greater is the significance of these repercussions, and the more imperative it is to be aware of and prepared for the problems likely to be encountered so that proper policy responses can be taken. This, in turn, requires an understanding of some basic transportation concepts and the structure and environment of the shipping industry. As a first step to such an understanding we will draw upon the exposition given in Chapter 1 to formulate a conceptual framework that will allow us, if we so desire, to look at the shipping industry in discrete segments and to broaden or narrow the scope and level of analysis as required.

The movement of seaborne foreign trade involves a *total transportation system* consisting of five components. The first of these constitutes the *land carriers* serving the *domestic* ports. In a broad sense, this component encompasses the whole domestic transportation system. The second component consists of the *domestic ports* with all of their facilities: piers, tugs, warehouses, storage, cargo handling

*This section draws upon B. J. Abrahamsson and M. A. Singer, "A Shipping Research Program with Particular Reference to Smaller Nations," *Journal of the Israel Shipping Research Institute,* April 1972.

equipment, and the like. In the port, the goods are transferred to the third component, the *ocean carriers*. These include domestic as well as foreign flag ships that can be owned or chartered and engaged in liner, tramp, special, and tanker carriage. Unloading takes place in *foreign ports*, which, with their facilities, make up the fourth component. The *land carriers* serving the *foreign* ports—that is, the receiving country's transportation system—are the fifth and final component of the system.

Of these, the *ocean transportation system* comprises the three middle components: the ocean carriers and the domestic and foreign ports. This system operates in an *environment* determined by complex and numerous sets of relationships that involve both domestic and international economic, technological, social, and political factors influencing world trade in general. The environment is affected by the major trading and shipping nations as they effect changes in the conditions under which seaborne trade is moved. Smaller nations, on the other hand, are affected by these changes, but have little scope, if acting alone, in influencing the worldwide course of events. However, as a group, i.e., UNCTAD, the smaller nations have considerable impact, particularly in affecting international institutions and the general political environment.

Shipping policies are likely to be different for different countries depending on the country's role and participation in world trade and shipping. The larger the country is in these respects, the more likely it is that its policies are directed toward the initiation of change rather than passive acceptance of the status quo. For example, the U.S. Merchant Marine Act of 1970 provides for a technologically advanced rejuvenation of the U.S. Merchant Marine.

The components of the ocean transportation system can also be described in terms of *areas of activity*. From the earlier overview, these can be summarized as:

1. the carriage of goods;
2. activities supporting the carriage, such as port operations, manpower, customs procedures, and other similar activities; and
3. institutions and policies affecting both the carriage and the support activities, such as labor unions, government regulations, and international agreements and conventions.

Fig. 2-2

CONCEPTUAL FRAMEWORK FOR THE
OCEAN TRANSPORTATION SYSTEM

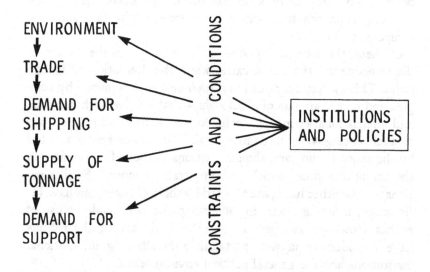

This leads to the conceptual framework illustrated in Figure 2.2. Here the environment generates trade resulting in demand for shipping. This demand brings forth a supply of domestic and foreign tonnage, which, in turn, gives rise to demand for supporting activities. Superimposed on that sequence of events are constraints and conditions exerted by existing domestic and international institutions and policies. It is important to have a clear view of these conceptual relationships so that at least the broad ramifications of major events in one activity area can be traced through the whole system.

In this book, however, the focus is on the carriage of goods. This does not mean that the other two activity areas are unimportant; as the overview clearly shows, the three activities are closely integrated and related, and it is impossible to discuss one without introducing some aspects of the other two. But an extensive treatment of support activities and institutions, which is merited by their economic and political importance, is deemed to be beyond the scope of this book—as the following reflections should indicate.

The seemingly simple task of listing all the support activities turns out to be, in reality, a rather complex exercise in trying to identify what degree of relationship to shipping is necessary to qualify an activity area as essential for the carriage of goods. A nonexhaustive list of activity areas would definitely include manpower and training for seafarers and port labor; ports; naval stores and ship chandlering; freight forwarding and brokerage; customs clearance and documentation; marine insurance for cargo, ship, and crew; ship and trade financing; shipyards; navigational aids; and facilities. A reasonably solid understanding of any of these activities would require identification and description of its processes and procedures and the links between these and the carriage of goods. That is, for each activity it would be necessary to examine the institutional framework and the factors determining demand and supply. For instance, to understand a particular port, we would, at the minimum, need an initial survey of its capacity, utilization, lay-out of facilities, feasibility for expansion, and possible plans for such expansion. Next, we would need an analysis of current and projected cargo flows and the port's linkages with its hinterland. In addition, something must be known about the port's competitive relationships with other ports; its administrative, economic, and fee structures; and the relationships between port and ship designs.

The picture is equally complex and difficult when we look at institutions that are both domestic and international and affect both carriage and support activities. Included here would be government regulations, particularly those pertaining to subsidies; taxation; financing; registry; manning, training, certification, and work rules; labor union practices; shippers' councils; export and marketing associations; and international conventions and agreements such as General Agreements on Trade and Tariffs (GATT), OECD, and various UN agencies, particularly the International Labor Organization (ILO), the Intergovernmental Maritime Consultative Organization (IMCO), UNCTAD, and the regional economic commissions. For each of these, understanding requires identification, description, and analysis of the particular institution's structure, objectives, means, and activities as well as its relationship to, and effects on, the shipping industry, support activities, and other institutions.

These complex aspects are integral parts of the ocean transportation system, and their pervasive interactions can be gleaned from the general overview. As we proceed, the broad conceptual view given here should be kept in mind: Ocean shipping is only one activity area of the ocean transportation system, which, in itself, is merely one part of a total (global) transportation system.

Notes

1. A. R. Prest and R. Turvey, "Cost-Benefit Analysis: A Survey," *Economic Journal*, December 1965.
2. See C. H. Sharp, *Transport Economics* (London: Macmillan Press, 1973), chap. 1; and J. M. Thomson, "Some Reflections on Transport Research in Europe," in *Research Seminar Series*, spring 1978 (Ottawa: Canadian Transport Commission, 1978).

Basic Concepts and Principles

Demand

Demand for transportation is derived demand, arising as a substitute for, or complement to, the demand for something else. (Some passenger travel, however, is undertaken for sheer enjoyment. In such cases, the demand is for transportation as a final good or service.) A simple example of derived demand is the demand for transportation of small cars from Europe to Canada, derived from the demand in Canada for small imported cars. Hence, the demand for transport is also a complement to the demand for the final good, which is the car. As another example, take a particular city that is desirable for both working and everyday living. As people flock to the city, its capacity to accommodate the influx reaches its limits and it becomes expensive and difficult to find work, housing, and other services—a common enough situation. However, the suburbs now become both feasible and desirable substitutes for the city if there is good transportation between them. In this case, the demand for transportation arises as a substitute for demand for space in the city proper. But it also arises as a complement to the demand for space in the suburbs. The cost of transportation—in a broad sense, time and money—imposes a limit on the extent to which a distant area can be linked to a given center. Beyond that limit, the demands for space and transportation become divorced, and where the limits are depends on transport technology. Hence, technological change translates into changing limits with attendant economic and social adjustment problems.

The simple concept of derived demand allows us to make several general statements with respect to the price elasticity of demand for transport. In the short run, that is, with a given technology, *overall* demand for transport of goods is relatively inelastic. This is because it is derived from the general level of economic activity that pro- duces the goods and services for which transportation is demanded. Lower transport costs can act as a stimulus to the economy, but these costs are generally only a small part of the final price. There- fore, even a relatively large decrease in freight rates may result in a relatively small decrease in the final prices. As demand for transport is derived from the demand for the final products and that demand now responds to a proportionately much smaller price change, it is not likely that the transport demand will show any elastic response. This does not mean that the level of freight rates is irrelevant. Since there are many ways in which both passengers and goods can be moved, the demands for particular modes (*modal* demand) and means of transportation tend to be relatively elastic in the short run. It also follows that in those instances in which transportation is a final service, demand elasticity is greater than is the case for derived demand. A case in point is the lowering of trans-Atlantic air fares in 1977, which resulted in a sharply increased passenger flow, thus in- dicating a high price elasticity of demand. It should be remembered that this response was from tourists for whom the flight itself may be part of the final consumed service. But, more importantly, in most tourist travel the air fares and other transportation costs make up a very large, and in some cases major, part of the total expense, so that a reduction in the fare affects the final overall cost substan- tially. While lower transport costs are desirable, as will be discussed shortly, care must be taken in the analysis of possible demand re- sponse to lower rates. Some effects should obviously be achieved from lower freight rates in the various modes, but there is little reason to expect the spectacular response seen in air travel.

In the long run, when technology changes, demand is expected to be relatively elastic. More transport is needed as the economy grows, and new technologies provide more efficient, lower-cost transportation, promoting further economic growth. The very generation of these technologies provides new industries, such as for cars and airplanes, that have a powerful impact on the economy and consequently, on demand for transport. There are some prob- lems, though, when looking at the long term, since most modes necessitate costly, enduring infrastructures. Decisions to locate roads, ports, railroads, and airports in particular places lead to the establishment, over time, of specific social and economic patterns. Once established, there is a tendency to resist technological change in transportation that may affect these patterns, and this in turn affects long-term demand elasticities.

Demand tends to be more inelastic if increased rates can be shifted forward to the final consumer or backward to an earlier supplier. The same is true if there is room for the shipper to absorb the increase himself. It is easier for him to do so if freight costs are a small proportion of his final price, or if the increase is from a very low level. In the reverse conditions, demand would be more elastic.

The fact that transport demand is derived means that a producer must relate his transport needs to his final product. That is, the costs of transporting raw materials, or inputs, to his plants, as well as the transport of the final products to his markets, must be considered in the context of his whole production process. He therefore must consider more factors than transport costs alone in his physical distribution system. Among these factors are:

1. Inventories: Considering the costs of interest and insurance, how much of the raw materials and products may be held in inventories and shipped in large lots, as opposed to a continuous flow of small lots? Where should the inventories be held considering location of markets, the plant, and production scheduling?
2. Purchasing: The buying of inputs is closely related to and affects the inventory decision on inputs. Are there savings to be had from the ordering of large quantities?
3. Packaging: This relates to the problems of packing the final product, considering market acceptance, storage characteristics, and transportation needs.
4. Transportation: With consideration of the whole production and distribution process, the problem here is to provide input and output in proper and timely sequences.[1]

For the firm, the objective is to minimize the total of these costs. Therefore, a higher transportation cost may be accepted if it contributes to a larger decrease in one or more of the other items, and vice versa. More will be said about this in the next section.

We have seen that transportation is provided in the form of a system with several components, each of which is an industry in itself with numerous independent operators. The supply, by different operators, may be by truck or rail to the port, then by ship overseas, and then by truck again. Demand, on the other hand, is for one ser-vice only: from the origin, or exporter, to the destination, or im-porter. If demand and supply are to meet, the supply must be coordi-nated. This *coordination* is one of the main issues in transportation, domestic or international.

Coordination requires a well-developed commercial infrastructure to allow the goods to change from one carrier to another and across borders. It includes documentation, financing, insurance, and clearance procedures. Technological progress in transport together with closer and expanded economic transactions between countries, puts increasingly stronger demands on the transport system, and, hence, increases the need for coordination. In the less-developed countries the commercial infrastructure is most developed in the ex-ternal sector. Their problems of coordination are therefore more evi-dent in domestic than in international transport. For the developed countries the problem exists on both levels. Its cause is not lack of a basic infrastructure, but, rather, insufficient adaptation and devel-opment of the existing structure. Much has been done to facilitate coordination, but there is still room for action. Given the need for coordination, it may be expected that financially strong operators like ocean shipping consortia will seek integration with other modes of transportation. We may, in the not too distant future, see the development of "transportation systems companies" rather than in-dependent, one-link operators.

Significance of Transportation Costs

As mentioned earlier, the level of freight rates is not irrelevant. Lower transport costs can have tangible general effects on the economy as a whole as well as on a particular firm. Cheaper trans-port makes it possible to draw raw materials from and provide the final products in more and distant markets. As these conditions hold for everyone, there are likely to be more producers and sellers in any given market, so that *competition* increases. Overall *employment* may rise, *alternative goods* are made available, and *consumer welfare* in-creases. *Prices* are stabilized and, to some extent, equalized, as the cheap transport allows goods to flow from low-price areas to those where prices are higher. This has both long-term and seasonal effects on prices. *Land values* are obviously affected as the advantage of being close to a market decreases while, at the same time, that of distant land increases. The existence of the large, suburban shopping centers would not be possible without relatively cheap private transport. That transport makes distant, "low-value" land very valuable. In the same manner, urban areas have grown with the assistance of cheaper transport. Since both raw materials and final products are brought more cheaply to their respective users, *production costs* are also affected. A product is of use to a potential consumer only if it is made available to him at the proper place and time. Therefore, transportation to the place of use is said to create *space utility* while the physical production of the good provides *form utility*. Production costs are then the sum of the costs for creating form and space utilities. Depending on whether the production process is such that the final product gains or loses weight, the plant generally locates closer to the sales market or to raw materials sources, respectively, and this has an effect on the role of transport costs in the overall production cost.

In general, transportation costs act as a barrier to trade both domestically and internationally. Analogous to a reduction in customs tariffs, lower transport costs make possible *regional specialization* by lowering prices on components and enabling the exchange of finished products. *Large-scale production* is also facilitated as larger markets become accessible. A pertinent example of the latter is the Swedish car industry, in which inexpensive sea transport in specialty ships has opened up a worldwide market allowing large-scale production that would not otherwise be justified.

As economies grow and develop, transportation becomes an increasingly important activity. More regional specialization and the consequent need for exchange results in more transportation. This, in turn, means that transportation costs are, in part, being substituted for other production costs (proportionately more is being spent to create space utility). Consider the following example:

	Producer	
	A	B
Physical production costs	$6	$3
Transportation costs	2	6
Total production costs	$8	$9

A customer will buy from A although the physical production costs are lower for B. If transport costs are reduced by 50 percent, the situation will be reversed. In that case, B will spend proportionately more on freight than he did before while total costs are lower.[2] In other words, as rates are reduced, more resources are spent on the creation of space utility (transport), and relatively less on form utility (physical production). There has been a *reallocation of resources*. But as B, the distant producer, replaces A, the near producer, sales are diverted from A to B. If the trade flow from B is greater than that previously coming from A, then trade or sales creation has occurred. Similarly, if both A and B are able to compete and participate, and trade is greater than before, there has been trade creation. The arguments are the same as those used in the theory of economic integration. In sum, lower freight costs lead to the substitution of transport costs for physical production costs, which is a reallocation of resources. New sources of supply emerge with the effects of trade diversion and creation. The reality of these concepts can be seen quite readily in, for example, the competition between ports in both Canada and the United States, and, internationally, between the ports of these countries as well as in other parts of the world.

It is clear that an efficient transportation system is essential for economic development and growth. This explains why most decisions on transport investments in developing countries and regions are made mainly on the basis of their impact on the development of the area or country.[3] In this context, there are a few basic considerations to take into account. Given that the government commonly provides and maintains the basic facilities such as roads, ports, and airports, the taxpayer rather than the user pays part of the cost of transportation. The question is whether these facilities should be paid for by society or if they should be financially self-sustaining. This opens the issue of user charges such as license fees for cars, weight fees for trucks, and port fees.[4] One interesting aspect of this pertains to technological change in ocean shipping. The unitization development, particularly containers, together with specialization in bulk carriage, creates heavy demands for new port investments. But who reaps the benefits from these investments? If the port improvements result in a faster turn-around for the ships, carriers' costs decrease and these benefits should be passed on in the form of lower freight rates. But lower freight rates tend to accrue to *all* shippers on a trade route that may include many ports and countries. Those shippers who use the improved port may not benefit sufficiently to justify the investment. This raises the issue of how to structure port charges so that the benefits of improvement accrue to the improving port or country.[5]

The Modes of Transport

The five modes of transport can be divided into three groups: land, air, and water carriers. Each group can be engaged in domestic or international transportation. The land carriers consist of the railroads, trucks, and pipelines. Domestic water transport, known as *cabotage,* can be *coastwise* — shipping along a coast or, put differently, between ports located on the same coast — *intercoastal, interisland,* or through *inland waterways.* International shipping is between two countries even if they are adjacent and very small ships are used. International *ocean* shipping, or deep sea operations, usually connotes longer hauls and larger ships.

The carriers in each mode can also be identified according to legal characteristics. They can be *for-hire* or *private* (not-for-hire) carriers. Delivery trucks of the local dairy or department store are examples of private carriers. These carriers are usually subject to regulation in public matters such as safety and licensing. This is different from economic regulation, which imposes on the carriers certain rules and procedures concerning financing, accounting methods, inspections of books and operations, and restrictions and obligations as to business activities and services. This is the type of regulation usually applied to the for-hire carriers. Such a carrier is either a *common* or a *contract* carrier. The latter offers his services to selected customers on a contractual basis, while the former has a standing offer to serve the general public.

There is competition between the modes (*intermodal* competition) as well as within each mode (*intramodal* competition). The competitive situation depends on whether we refer to long or short hauls and the short or long term. In the short term, a firm's competitive position depends on its cost structure. The short term is defined here in the common economic sense in which fixed costs are inescapable.[6] This means that for a firm whose fixed assets are relatively permanent (such as a railroad), the short term may last a very long time. The fixed costs are incurred whether traffic is carried or not. Hence, it is rational for a firm to accept a rate that may not cover all costs as long as it covers the direct costs and makes some contribution to the fixed costs. The situation, under perfect competition, is illustrated in Figure 3.1. Output is where MC = MR. In both parts of the figure the loss is given by P-A-B-D and total fixed costs by the shaded area. In the left figure, total fixed costs are less than the loss from continued operations; therefore, the rational action is to close down. In the right figure, the opposite holds.

The greater the proportion of fixed costs is, the greater the range over which the rates or price, can fluctuate and still cover direct costs (or average variable costs). In the short run, such a company can be very competitive. Rates can fall to very low levels and it is still rational to stay in operation. This cost structure often leads to

Fig. 3-1

COST STRUCTURE AND MAXIMIZING BEHAVIOR

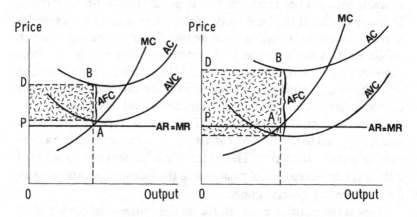

AC = Average cost = Average variable costs + Average fixed costs
AVC = Average variable costs
AFC = Average fixed costs
MR = Marginal revenue
AR = Average revenue
MC = Marginal costs

"cutthroat" competition and price wars and makes it possible to practice *price discrimination* between both shippers and commodities. The public policy problem here is the extent to which such pricing policies are justified. This leads to the complex issues of rates and rate setting.

Factors in Rate Determination

The freight rates depend on the services being offered and demanded. Both shippers and carriers have to consider at least five factors that for the shipper affect demand and for the carrier affect rates. These are, for each mode: the area covered; frequency, reliability, and speed of the service; and extra services available.

With respect to the *area covered,* trucks are clearly the most flexible mode, while water and pipelines rank at the bottom. Coordination between railroads and trucks and barges have resulted in piggyback and "fishyback" concepts. More appropriately, the former is known as trailer on flatcar (TOFC) and the latter as trailer on barge (TOB).

Concerning *frequency of service,* fixed time schedules allow the shipper to plan his transport needs. The frequency of departures and arrivals depends on the speed of loading and unloading and this, in turn, depends on the *size of the transport unit* and the *volume of freight* available. It may be necessary to arrange for consolidation of cargo at the origin and dispersion of consignments at the destination. In ocean shipping, the units are normally large, giving rise to a need for consolidation, which would argue for relatively infrequent service. But here, as in other modes, shippers require a certain frequency to be maintained, and this leads to overcapacity that undoubtedly is reflected in the rates. Provided that loading and unloading are fast, it becomes important to have sufficient *speed* in transit between origin and destination, and this makes the mode more *reliable* with respect to prompt departure and arrival.

Extra or *auxiliary services* are those that are provided over and above the simple transport of the goods, with an extra rate usually charged. Such services include pickup and delivery, storage, weighing, and loading and unloading, if not included in the terms of transport. Two very common services used in ocean shipping are diversion and reconsignment. The former makes it possible to specify a new receiver, in a different port, while the goods are still in transit. Under reconsignment, a new receiver is specified after the goods have arrived but before delivery.

In the determination of rates it is recognized that they should compensate the carriers for their services while facilitating the shipper in moving his goods. From the carrier's point of view, the costs of providing the service sets the lower limit for the rates, while the upper limit depends on the value the shipper attaches to the service. The question arises whether rates should be set on the basis of the *cost of the service* or the *value of the service*. The latter principle implies a recognition of different demand schedules for transportation and allows differential rates for different products and shippers. This is also known as charging "what the traffic will bear." It means that some commodities of high value, which can carry a higher freight rate without major effects on the final price, will be charged rates higher than the cost of providing the service. Low-value goods, on the other hand, will be carried at rates below average cost. One major argument for this procedure is that high-value goods cost more to transport because they require more care in handling. In addition, the carrier's liability is higher and this should be reflected in the rates. However, containers present a new perspective by occupying the same space and requiring the same handling regardless of the content's value. Hence, the care-in-handling argument is weakened and this is reflected in "freight all kinds" (FAK) rates.

This cross-subsidization is shown in Figure 3.2, in which an average rate based on cost is shown. Low-value goods are charged lower and high-value higher rates, the surplus of the latter subsidizing the deficit from the former. This procedure obviously assumes that the proportions of low- and high-value traffic are such that the carrier recovers his total average costs. If the composition of traffic changes, then the rate structure must change as well. The dotted line in the figure indicates the structure when the proportion of low-value traffic increases. It is clear, then that the value of the commodity is of primary importance in rate setting.

Although the principle of charging according to the value of service is commonly considered to be the same as the principle of charging what the traffic will bear, the two are not strictly equal. The former implies that only the shipper's situation is considered. For example, a producer in port A has physical production costs of $1 per

Fig. 3-2

<u>CROSS — SUBSIDIZATION</u>

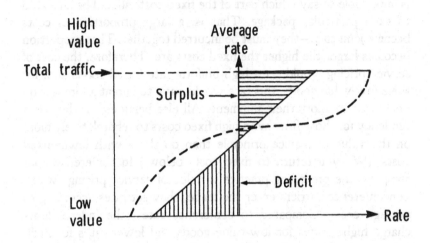

unit and can sell in port B only by charging a maximum unit price of $1.20. In this case, the value of transport to him is $0.20 per unit and this is what the rate should be according to the value of service principle. But this may or may not be what the traffic will bear. If the traffic in the commodity does not move freely and in growing volume, then the rate is higher than the traffic will bear, notwithstanding that it may reflect the value of service to the shipper. Behind the value of service principle is a consideration mainly of the shipper's position in existing markets and the setting of rates to maintain that position. But in charging what the traffic will bear, a more dynamic element enters into rate setting that will progressively expand the volume of traffic to be carried. The focus is more on the carrier's objectives and the rate setting, below or above average costs, reflects his opportunity costs. By giving a certain rate to a product in accordance with what the traffic will bear, the carrier's opportunity costs with respect to other goods have been considered. It therefore seems more appropriate to use the term "what the traffic will bear." Although there is a difference in the precise meaning of the two expressions, we will use "value of service" and "what the traffic will bear" interchangeably.

Under the cost of service principle it is argued that some low-cost commodities would not move. The argument is that once a transport unit, say, a ship, has been committed to a particular run (put on the berth), the marginal cost for each package is small and it is impossible to say which part of the fixed costs should be allocated to each particular package. That is, a large proportion of costs become *joint costs*—they must be incurred together. That proportion becomes larger the higher the fixed costs are. Therefore, the cost of service pricing would set a high uniform rate for all goods and, for some low-value goods, this rate would have too great an impact on final price to allow their shipment. All else being equal, there is a tendency for those firms with high fixed costs to rely relatively more on the value of service principle than do those with lower fixed costs. (We will return to fixed costs below.) In conference liner shipping, the prevailing practice is value of service pricing. When nonconference carriers enter the trade, they set rates according to average costs. Compared to conference rates, the independents charge higher rates for low-value goods and lower rates for high-value commodities. Consequently, the independents are able to "skim the cream" off the traffic.

Discussion of the relative merits of these principles has, through various court decisions in the United States, given rise to a concept of "reasonable" rates that should give carriers a "fair" return while allowing the goods to move. But what is reasonable is a matter of interpretation, and it is clear that aside from costs, demand and competitive conditions play a major role in the process of rate setting. However, rates for domestic transportation are only partly established by market forces. They are subject to elements of public policy, and welfare considerations influence these rates substantially.

This element of public policy and welfare has not yet reached ocean transport, mainly because it is not subject to any one sovereign authority—it is international in the extreme. Active attempts at regulatory controls of international shipping have been instituted only by the United States and the results are questionable.[7]

But there are several aspects concerning the cost of transportation that must be considered because they do affect the setting of rates. We have seen that the higher the proportion of fixed costs is, the stronger are both the short-term competitive position and the tendency toward the value of service principle. It therefore is important to establish what these costs really are.

Fixed costs are those that are inescapable.[8] Under this general definition there are four categories. First, there are costs that are inescapable in the short but not in the long run. An example of such costs is a contractual arrangement covering a specific amount and time period. This would include labor agreements or a firm's contract to purchase a certain volume of raw materials. Once the contract is signed, the cost is inescapable and fixed for the duration of the contract. In transportation such costs are incurred when a ship, truck, airplane, or rail car is committed to a certain trip. The costs for that trip, excluding cargo handling expenses, are fixed.

Second, there are costs that are inescapable because they are *common* or *joint costs*. These costs usually, but not always, result from *joint supply*. Two commodities or services are in joint supply when the supplying of one necessarily provides a supply of the other. The classic example of this phenomenon is the supply of beef, which also provides hides. It is important to note that hides are supplied because of the demand for beef. Hence, at any one time, demand for and supply of hides do not respond to each other. A railroad can be used for transport of both passengers and freight, and the costs of providing the facilities are common, or joint, but there is not joint supply. That is, the supply of transport for freight does not necessarily also supply transport for passengers, because we certainly have exclusive passenger and freight trains. On the other hand, an airplane with a freight and mail compartment has both joint costs and joint supply of transport for freight and passengers.

Suppose forty rail cars are needed to carry cargo from point A to point B, while only twenty are required from B to A. By carrying the freight from A to B, the carrier also supplies back-haul capacity, which includes twenty empties to be returned from B. The costs of these empty cars are joint with the forty full cars and are inescapable. It follows that the marginal cost of using the empty cars is small. Consequently, *back-haul capacity* is always in both joint supply and cost, resulting in low marginal cost for back-hauls. The trip was prompted by the cargo available at A. Therefore, the rate from A to B should cover the cost of the round trip, and the rate from B to A may be much lower as it needs to cover only direct costs. This situation has been documented in United States–United Kingdom trade. The major trade flow from the United States to the United Kingdom created much back-haul capacity and lower rates on the return trip.[9] At the same time, the search for back-haul cargoes appears to have been a prime mover in the technological progress we have seen in bulk shipping, and particularly in the development of the ore-bulk-oil (OBO) carrier.[10]

The third category constitutes those costs that are inescapable for small, but not large, changes in output. In economic jargon this refers to the size of the indivisible unit. In order to carry freight that occupies half a car, a whole car must be supplied. Once the decision is made to send that car, certain inescapable costs are incurred, as explained earlier. To add a few packages to the half-empty car – a small increase in output – does not change these costs. When the car is filled, however, the carrier has a choice as to whether or not to add one more car, incurring additional fixed costs. Hence, for a small change in output, costs are inescapable, while for a large change – more than half a car – there is a choice. What constitutes small or large changes depends on the size of the transport unit, in this case, the rail car. The smaller the unit is, the smaller are, presumably, the corresponding fixed costs, and the more often the carrier has the choice of supplying additional units. This means a generally smaller proportion of fixed cost, as well as greater flexibility with respect to these costs.

The fourth category of fixed costs includes those that are inescapable in all instances, such as costs for equipment, legal and other expenses in forming the firm, real estate taxes, and license fees.

These comments on fixed costs indicate that there are different concepts of these costs depending on the time horizon, mode, demand conditions, and output level. A thorough understanding of this will provide a clearer picture of the often baffling pricing practices encountered in transportation. For example, the existence of stand-by and other low-priced airplane fares are easily understood in terms of the size of the indivisible unit. In this context it should be noted as well that technological improvements that increase the divisibility of the units also decrease fixed costs, and vice versa. The actual level of fixed costs for a firm depends on its equipment and scale of operations, both of which clearly must be geared to the expected demands. The total expenses of the firm can be divided into two groups, *fixed charges* and *operating expenses*. Only those fixed costs included in the fourth category are fixed charges at all times. The other fixed costs are more properly constant operating costs that together with variable costs make up total operating expenses. In ocean shipping these constant operating costs are usually referred to as running or standing costs and include expenses for capital (interest and depreciation), administration, crew, ship's stores, surveys and repairs, and insurance.

The main factors accounting for variable operating costs—that is, costs that vary with output—are terminal costs, cargo handling expenses, and hauling costs. Terminal costs are independent of the length of the haul, but do depend on length of stay at the terminal, services used (such as storage and warehousing), and terminal fee structures. These costs vary with the modes. They tend to be relatively low for trucks, higher for air and railroads, and of major importance in ocean shipping. Since a transport unit performs its function only when on the way between two places, efforts to decrease terminal stays are prominent. In shipping, modern cargo handling equipment and the unitization development have had substantial impact in decreasing the turn-around time in ports.

Cargo expenses depend on the kind of cargo, cargo handling equipment, and the volume. After terminal and cargo handling costs have been incurred, costs increase more or less proportionately with the transport distance. Total average variable costs, however, do not increase proportionately with distance. Terminal charges and cargo handling costs are the same whether the cargo moves one mile or a thousand. As these charges must be spread over the total transport distance, the charge per mile becomes smaller the greater the mileage. The same holds for average total costs when the constant operating expenses and fixed charges are included. Therefore, a larger transport unit means a less proportionate increase in costs as distance increases. A striking example of this is the use of VLCCs and large bulk carriers. A long haul is able to absorb higher terminal costs than a short haul because the per-mile costs are smaller. As a consequence, these costs must constitute a larger proportion of a short-haul rate. Within a certain distance, the terminal charges may be higher than the hauling costs, with the result that many low-value products do not move at all except by private means in the proximity of the source. The low terminal costs of trucks compared to railroads is a major explanation of their competitive strength on short hauls. For the same reason, economic air transport requires a minimum distance, the length of which depends on the type of aircraft used.

There are several other aspects that must be considered in the setting of rates. Every transport unit has a certain capacity to carry volume as well as weight. The ideal cargo should utilize both capacities fully. This is rarely the case except where the transport unit is specially constructed for only one specific kind of cargo such as crude oil, coal, a chemical, or other homogeneous cargo. Although there are many other cargoes that could fill any unit in terms of both volume and weight, the value of the good must also be such that it is worth moving given the existing rates. Therefore, various modes are more or less suitable for different kinds of cargoes. Of course, each mode carries all kinds of goods, particularly in international transport, but in very general terms, water and railroads are suitable for bulk carriage, trucks for general cargo, and air for high-value general cargo and perishables.

Notes

1. E. W. Smykay, *Physical Distribution Management,* 3rd ed. (New York: Macmillan, 1973).

2. This example, in different form and context, is given by J. Dupuit, "Public Works and the Consumer," in *Transport: Selected Readings,* ed. Denis Munby (Baltimore: Penguin Books, 1968), p. 33.

3. See J. Lansing, *Transportation and Economic Policy* (New York: Free Press, 1966); and W. Owen, *Strategy for Mobility* (Washington, D.C.: Brookings Institution, 1970).

4. Alan Walters, *The Economics of Road User Charges* (Baltimore: Johns Hopkins University Press, 1968).

5. E. Bennathan and A. A. Walters, *Port Pricing and Investment Policy for Developing Countries* (Oxford: Oxford University Press, 1979).

6. A classic treatment of fixed costs is W. Arthur Lewis, *Overhead Costs* (London: Allen & Unwin, 1949).

7. R. Larner, "Public Policy in the Ocean Freight Industry," in *Promoting Competition in Regulated Markets,* ed. A. Phillips (Washington, D.C.: Brookings Institution, 1975).

8. Lewis, *Overhead Costs.*

9. See E. Bennathan and A. A. Walters, *The Economics of Ocean Freight Rates* (New York: Praeger, 1969).

10. See Erling Naess, *Autobiography of a Shipping Man* (Colchester, England: Seatrade Publications, 1977).

Freight Rates and Tariffs

Given that value of service pricing predominates, we should, theoretically, list each good separately and assess the rates to be charged under different conditions. This is obviously impossible. In order to obtain an overview of the traffic and to make it possible to set rates, carriers have grouped together goods with similar charac-teristics into classes and then assessed rates to the different classes. The value of the goods is also considered because the major deter-minants of the level of the rate are the goods' value and physical characteristics. The major determinant of the actual freight cost is the distance moved. In determining the class, "what the traffic will bear" thus plays the major role.

To find the rate for a particular good, it is necessary first to find out to which class it belongs. This is found in the *classification,* which refers to a *tariff* (for each class), which, in turn, quotes the rate for the commodity. As each mode has its own characteristics, classifications and tariffs differ. This may also be true for individual carriers in a particular mode and certainly applies to different parts of a country with respect to trucks and railroads. In ocean shipping, each conventional liner conference has its own, often confidential, classification and tariffs. The unitized segment of shipping indicates, however, a trend toward simpler classifications and rates. For in-stance, roll-on/roll-off (RoRo) services often charge per square foot occupied by the vehicle and ignore, unless unusual conditions apply, both kind and weight of cargo. In container shipping, FAK rates are not uncommon. International air transport is subject to a worldwide tariff agreement among lines belonging to the International Air Transport Association (IATA). The multiplicity of classifications and rates both among and within modes, as well as regional differ-ences, makes rate comparisons on different routes and among modes virtually impossible, particularly in an international context.

There are generally three kinds of tariffs: *class, commodity,* and *service.* The first gives the rates for shipping classes of goods. The second shows the rates for shipping specific commodities, usually goods that move in large quantities. The third tariff gives rates for special services. We have, generally, class, commodity, service, and all-kinds rates. When some commodities are excluded from the class in which they would otherwise be found, we have exception rates.

Within these general categories, rates are based on quantities shipped, routing characteristics, previous or future shipments, agreements, and special conditions.[1]

Examples of rates in the first group are minimum rates, rates for carloads (CL) and less than carloads (LCL), rates for truckloads (TL) and less than truckloads (LTL), and rates for trainloads and multiple cars.

Depending on how the goods are routed, we can have *local rates* or *joint rates.* Local rates are charged when the good moves on the line, or route, of one carrier only, and joint rates involve more than one carrier. A *through rate* is quoted from origin to destination and may be local or joint. When several rates are added together, we have a *combination rate.* A *proportional rate* is the same as the combination rate except that only a certain proportion of subsequent rates is added. When a certain differential is added to or subtracted from a standard rate, we have a *differential rate.* For example, a standard rate is given between port A and port B. Between A and C the rate is the standard rate plus or minus a certain percentage of that rate. This type of rate is used in the tanker market in the form of World-scale quotations. More will be said about this later.

Transit rates are based on previous shipment. Here the goods are allowed to stop during the transit for processing. Since this means that there is a different good inbound than outbound, there is a rationale for charging two different short-haul rates. The transit rate avoids this by allowing the shipper one long-haul rate that is less costly than two short-haul rates.

Types of transit rates are the *export* and *import* rates given by railroads in the United States. These rates have evolved as competitive devices to attract volume to and from ports served by the railroads. They are usually substantially lower than the domestic rates between the same points. These rates are powerful means in fostering competition between ports and hinterlands, because their effects are to equalize the cost advantages of various ports and coasts with respect to different trade sources. Thus, the author has seen examples of plywood being imported from Taiwan through San Francisco for U.S. East Coast customers in competition with Italian plywood through New York.

In essence, an export rate is an export bounty while the import rates constitute a real decrease in trade barriers. From the land carriers' point of view, these rates mean that those serving the port obtain more traffic both to and from the port. Carriers who do not serve the port are excluded from direct participation in this traffic and lose volume as domestic traffic suffers from the increased foreign competition using import rates. For these reasons, many countries prefer, as a matter of policy, outright export subsidies and customs tariff reductions.

The tendency of these rates is to equalize the advantage of ports and coasts. In Figure 4.1, the ocean rates are equal from a foreign country to two ports, A and B, but inland transport to C is cheaper from A than from B. As a port, A has an advantage over B. Hence, more export and import traffic will move through A with adverse effects on carriers serving B. To maintain and expand their role, these carriers will reduce the rate from B to C to equal that between A and C. Should the rate not be lowered, the ocean freight volume to

Fig. 4-1

EXPORT AND IMPORT RATES

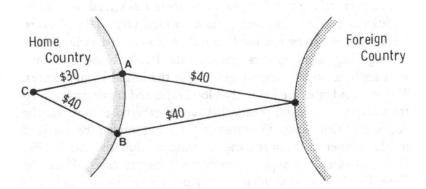

and from B would be likely to decrease with ocean rates becoming relatively higher than those to A. This would further the decline of B, and the necessary adjustments in economic activities could cause serious problems of both economic and political scope. The opposite situation may also occur. There may be equal domestic rates, while the ocean rates are unequal. In this case, domestic rates would be raised or lowered to equalize the combined transport cost. Lower ocean rates would prompt higher domestic rates, and vice versa.

In the United States, competition for port traffic resulted in price wars among railroads in the late 1800s. Finally, in 1877, the railroads reached an agreement to control port differentials and rates. It is interesting to note that the first effective ocean shipping conference was formed on the United Kingdom–Calcutta trade only two years earlier and for the same reasons, namely, to control rates and to prevent further price wars.

The early port differentials continue to have a strong influence on the pattern of export and import rates. The main reason is that the earlier low inland rates promoted economic activity and growth in areas that would face readjustment difficulties if relative rate patterns were drastically changed. It appears that the U.S. regulatory authority, the Interstate Commerce Commission (ICC), follows a course of action that recognizes this situation. However, the ICC has set guidelines for minimum levels, below which export and import rates may not go. In these circumstances, shipping conferences have taken up the former role of railroads. They have structured other rates that do what export-import rates do, namely, originate cargo to and from inland points. For example, the Pacific Westbound Conference, which covers the trade from U.S. and Canadian Pacific ports to the Far East, has two sets of rates in addition to its traditional tariff. These sets pertain to local and overland rates. *Local rates,* not to be confused with those mentioned earlier, apply to cargo originating in areas close to the Pacific Coast. *Overland rates* apply to commodities originating in the inland United States. The overland rates are lower than local rates and are designed to attract cargo from inland points that would otherwise move via the Atlantic or Gulf ports. The rates do this by absorbing the overland freight differential between the Atlantic or Gulf and the Pacific. Overland rates are applied similarly for import trade. Here the Trans-Pacific Freight Conference of Japan covers the inbound trade from Japan and Korea to Pacific Coast ports. This conference has one set of rates for local cargo and one for overland common point (OCP) cargoes. OCP rates are the import complement to overland rates. They apply to cargoes destined for inland points in the United States and are lower than local rates. It appears that most conferences, at least in U.S. trades, employ similar rates.[2]

Shippers and carriers also often make formal contracts for carriage. The shipper commits his freight, or part of it, to be exclusively transported by specific carriers. This arrangement is very common in ocean shipping where the "dual rate" system is extensively used by liner conferences. We will return to this point shortly.

Other rates are in the category of "piggy-back" or TOFC rates, of which the ocean shipping version is the container rate. There are several types depending on whose container it is, where it is picked up or delivered, and by whom. *Space available rates* are lower than others, but delays may be very long (although sometimes a time limit is imposed). This procedure is most often used when the shipper wants time to sell the goods. *Weight-volume, carrier's option rates* are mainly used in ocean transport. The carrier will charge a rate according to either volume or weight of the shipment, whichever gives him the highest freight. A common relationship between weight and volume for these rates is a measurement ton of 40 cubic feet versus a short (2,000 lbs.) or long (2,240 lbs.) ton or 1,000 kg. versus 1 cubic meter. Also common in ocean shipping is the *ad valorem rate*, which explicitly relates the rates to the value of the cargo. These rates are usually applied when the declared value of the good is greater than the limit on value given in the bill of lading. In such cases the ad valorem rate both increases the carrier's liability and compensates him for this added responsibility. An *arbitrary* is exactly what the term implies: an arbitrary sum added to another rate. It is used in cases where the traffic is small and the establishment of a special rate is not considered worthwhile. For example, a common conference rule may be along these lines: "Container cargo destined for Bremen and Hamburg may be reforwarded between these ports at no cost to the cargo. However, between Antwerp and Hamburg an arbitrary of $20 per metric ton will be assessed subject to a minimum of *x* tons per 20-foot container. Break-bulk cargo for shipment on a conventional vessel and delivered to the carrier's loading terminal will be assessed an arbitrary of $35 per metric ton." Some commodities are listed in the tariff as being shipped under *open rates,* that is, exception rates. These apply to commodities for which there is relatively keen competition so that adherence to fixed rates by the conference would result in loss of traffic. Thus, open rates are set by the individual carriers in accordance with their competitive circum-stances.

The conference tariffs give detailed rules for the calculation of rates, how to measure the cargo and in what units to express these measurements, surcharges for specific characteristics of the cargo (such as unusually long or heavy commodities), and minimum bill of lading charges. In addition, the currency in which the rates are ex-pressed is specified together with stated exchange rates for other ac-ceptable currencies. When actual exchange rates depart by a certain percentage (commonly 4 percent) from those stated in the tariff, cur-rency surcharges, given in the tariff, go into effect.

In container tariffs it is common to give three different rates for the same commodity depending on the service required. In order of decreasing rates, these services are *house-to-house; house-to-pier* or *pier-to-house;* and *pier-to-pier.* The last service is essentially break-bulk and applies to conventional vessels when operations in-clude both conventional and container ships. In addition, most rates are offered on a contract or noncontract basis. As mentioned before, those shippers who sign a contract to ship their cargo with the members of the conference obtain the contract rate—the rate nor-mally given in the tariff. Those without such a contract are assessed the contract rate plus a certain percentage of that rate. The percent-age addition in Canadian and U.S. trades is commonly 15 per-cent, which is also the maximum differential legally permitted by the United States.

The terminology used in a tariff is commonly specific to the mode and trade. Some common abbreviations particularly relevant to ocean shipping, but also used in other modes, are given in Table 4.1.

We have seen that the various factors that go into the determina-tion of freight rates give rise to many different kinds of rates. On the most fundamental level, rates are structured with reference to the carrier's cost of service and consideration of what the traffic will bear. On a more specific level, the rate structures depend on the commodities' characteristics with respect to value, volume, and nature of the shipment; how it is to be routed; agreements between shipper and carriers; and competitive and special conditions and ser-

TABLE 4.1
Common Abbreviations

Abbreviation	Meaning
Ad. Val. or A.V.	Ad valorem, or according to value
Bbl(s)	Barrel(s)
Bdl(s)	Bundle(s)
B/L	Bill of lading
CAF	Currency adjustment factor
CBM or CM	Cubic meter
CL	Carload
Ctn(s)	Carton(s)
Cft	Cubic feet
Ea.	Each; per item
Ft.	Feet
KD(F)	Knocked down (flat)
Kg(s)	Kilogram(s)
Lb(s)	Pound(s)
LCL	Less than carload
LTL	Less than truck load
Max	Maximum
Min	Minimum
N.E.S.	Not elsewhere specified
OCP	Overland common points
Pkg(s)	Package(s)
SO	Ship's option
Std	Standard
SU	Set up
TL	Truckload
Ton(s)	Ton(s) of specified weight in lbs. or kgs.
TEU	Twenty-foot equivalent unit for container
TW/M	Ton weight or measurement. 1,000 kgs. vs. 1 cubic meter; or 2,000 lbs. vs. 40 cubic feet as explained in the tariff
H/H	House-to-house
H/P	House-to-pier
P/H	Pier-to-house
P/P	Pier-to-pier
SITC	Standard international trade classification

vices. But the rate structure is also strongly affected by the distance of the shipment.

We can perceive four basic rate structures based on distance.[3] First, a rate that does not change at all with distance is the so-called *postage stamp* structure. At the other extreme is a rate that varies directly and proportionately with distance, the *straight mileage* structure. Between these extremes are the *modified mileage* and the *blanket* structures. The former takes into account terminal and cargo handling expenses that, being independent of distance, make the cost per mile smaller as distance increases (see Chapter 3). The blanket is a combination of the modified mileage and the postage stamp structures. In this case the same rate applies for a certain commodity from a given origin to all points within a specified geographical area; that is, the area has been "blanketed." In effect, a postage stamp rate prevails within the blanket. But if the good moves through a series of blankets, each with a higher rate than the preceding one, then the total rate shows a modified mileage structure. Blankets are also known as group, or zone, rates and usually group together points of origin or points of destination – origin and destination blanket, respectively. A major argument for this structure is that it simplifies rate setting. It also allows feeder services by which small cargo lots from within the blanket or from close outside areas are consolidated into major shipments benefitting from both quantity and blanket rates. Blankets exist in all modes, but are particularly prominent in railroads and ocean shipping. In the latter mode the blankets are known as *ranges* and are often very large.

So far we have dealt with general and basic concepts and principles applicable to all modes. As such, the preceding chapters have attempted to provide the reader with a foundation for the understanding of transportation and its role in the economy and as a business. The public interest in transportation requires a more informed public to facilitate optimal policy formulation and implementation, and the overall utilization of and provision for efficient transportation requires transportation managers with a solid understanding of the many facets of the sector as well as specialized knowledge of particular modes. In the following chapters we will attempt to provide at least the main features of such knowledge with respect to ocean shipping.

Notes

1. See R. Sampson and M. Farris, *Domestic Transportation: Practice, Theory and Policy*, 4th ed. (Boston: Houghton Mifflin, 1979), chap. 12.

2. U.S., Department of Justice, *The Regulated Ocean Shipping Industry*, Report, January 1977, app. E., p. 4.

3. See Sampson and Farris, *Domestic Transportation*, chap. 13.

The Elements of Ocean Shipping

—————————————————————————— **5** ——

The ship is the means of transport in ocean shipping and, as such, must be designed to provide its services as efficiently as possible. Because it must meet the needs of the intended service, there is constant work and research to achieve optimal ship designs but there is no one standard design. Given the ship operator's requirements, new ship construction is closely related to the technical limitations of naval architecture. These limits have expanded rapidly in recent years, providing the shipowner with a wide choice of ship sizes and types. In the not too distant past a new ship design was usually a modification of earlier ones, and the operator's basic decision was the relatively simple one of whether or not to build a ship at all. Today he must add to that decision what type of ship to build.

The financing of ships is becoming increasingly complex as well. The huge capital needs of modern ships make it very difficult, if not impossible, for most operators to continue to rely on retained earnings. Moving to external financing, they rely on a worldwide market affected by government support programs for both shipping and shipbuilding in the form of investment grants, low interest loans, tax relief, accelerated depreciation, and other subsidies, all of which must be evaluated in the light of differential rates of inflation in a system of floating exchange rates. The final evaluation of these factors determines not only how to finance the ship, but also where it will be built and under what flag (and therefore corporate structure) the ship will be operated. Increased sizes and specialization of ships limit their flexibility so that correcting a wrong decision by entering a different service is difficult. As in all economic activities, the investment decision process is becoming increasingly complicated as the scope for making a poor investment has increased. While there are unique aspects to shipping investments, the techniques used in the decision process, such as discounted cash flows, are not very different from those used in other industries.[1]

Assuming that a basic decision has been made to build and where and when to do so, the next step is to decide what to build. Basically, this entails finding the design and size that provide maximum profitability over the life of the investment and requires specific data and assumptions as to operations, such as trade and traffic, operation costs, financing and currency conditions, and various tax and subsidy arrangements. Underlying such specific data are general considerations. From the operator's viewpoint, decisions must be made as to *what* services he will offer to *whom, where,* and *how.* "What" refers to what type of freight, or perhaps passengers, to carry. "To whom" is a question of type of service to be offered. "Where" is a choice of trade routes, and "how" raises the question of specialization versus flexibility, that is, type of ship.

As passenger traffic is today insignificant, except in the cruise trade (which is not strictly part of the international transport system), the focus here is on freight. The question is whether to carry *dry cargoes* or *liquid,* and whether to serve as a *common* or *contract* carrier. A common carrier in shipping provides liner service while the contract carrier operates a tramp service.

Having made a basic decision on these, four technical aspects must be considered: (1) type of ship and hull construction, (2) machinery, (3) weight and volume capacity (i.e., tonnage and cubic space), and (4) cargo handling equipment. The decisions on these aspects, in turn, depend on analyses of *navigation conditions* on the intended trade routes–draft in ports, canals, distance between ports, bunkering facilities, ice and general weather conditions–the potential *volume* and *kind of cargo,* and *competition.* With respect to cargo volume, it is important to know how fast it accumulates on the route because this affects the number of ships needed and their sizes and speeds. These needs are also affected by the existing competition, which has further effects on the frequency of service, shore organization, and shipboard cargo handling equipment. Experience in the various ports as well as knowledge of port expansion and investment plans also affect the decisions on shipboard cargo gear.

Until the post–World War II period, these decisions were considered more an art, with heavy elements of luck and intuition, than rational management procedure. Today, as mentioned, the scale of modern trade requirements and technology demands different skills and sophistication. Students of the industry, as well as management, must have a more analytical understanding of the industry than in the past.

The overview in Chapter 1 touched upon the elements that make up a total picture of ocean shipping. At this point, however, and drawing upon what has just been said, we will attempt a more

Fig. 5-1

ELEMENTS OF SHIPPING

	Dry Cargo				Liquid Cargo		
Types of cargo	Gen'l cargo	Special cargo (cars, paper, etc.)	Bulk (ore, coal grain, etc.)	Oil Crude Products		Gas (LNG, LPG)	Other (chemicals, wine, etc.)
Type of service ind. markets and market structures	Liner	Industrial (private)	Tramp	Tramp			Industrial (private)
Type of legal contract	Common carriage	Contract of Affreightment (COA)	Time Voyage charter charter	Time Voyage charter charter			Contract of Affreightment

Functional types of ships	Dry gen'l cargo ships
	
	Multipurpose
	Conventional
	Ro-Ro
	Containership
	Palletships
	Barge carrier
	  a) cellular (Lash)
	  b) horizontal shelf (Seabee)
	Carriers for:
	  cars → cars
	  fruit → fruit
	  refrigerated → refrigerated
		Specialized dry cargo ships	Dry bulk carriers
			
			Multipurpose
			Combination
			  carriers
			  (O/O; OBO; OSO)
			Carriers for:
			  gypsum
			  cement
			  coal
			  grain
			  ore
			  sugar
			lumber
			paper
			woodchips
				Liquid bulk carriers for:
				
				Crude oil
				Products
				Comb. ore-bulk-oil
				Multiple grade oil
				LPG
				LNG
						Slurry (minerals)
						Wine
						Milk
						Chemicals	

Structural types of ships		Single Hulls
		Full bodied hulls
		Bulkers
		  Tankers
		  Barge
		  carriers
		  Cargo-
		  liners
			Displacement Ships
			
			Fine Hulls (high speed)
			
			Containerships
				Multiple Hulls
				Catamaran Trimaran
						Submarine Ships
						Semi-submerged Submerged	

systematic presentation and discussion of these elements. Figure 5.1 outlines the structural relationships between the main analytical components of shipping. The questions of what service to provide for whom, where, and how have been reformulated in the figure and are given in the left column. As an example, if the interest is in the shipping of dry cargoes in general, we enter the vertical flow originating from the "dry cargo" heading. To obtain a proper picture we must examine the *types of cargo* moving by sea and, on the next level, the *types of services* offered for their carriage. A particular type of service such as liner or tramp implies a certain market structure that must also be considered. Other major considerations are the *types of legal contracts* under which the carriage is performed and the *types of ships* used, both with respect to their service characteristics and their construction. To summarize, the general types of dry cargo to consider would be general cargo, special cargoes, and dry bulk. Three types of services enter the picture—liner, tramp, and in-dustrial—and each leads to different legal contracts. A vast array of different ships with different functional characteristics is at the next level, followed by various structural types of ships. Both of these levels embody technological progress. A similar process exists for liquid cargoes.

The analytical focus becomes narrower if we move horizontally. For example, if the interest is on types of service, it is necessary to look at liner, tramp, and industrial carriage in either dry or liquid carriage, or both, recognizing that liner services do not exist in the latter trade and that industrial carriage is usually private. Or, look-ing at functional types of ships, a multitude of types must be con-sidered for each major cargo group. But important features become apparent at this level: First, there is a connection between general and special carriage; second, the dry and liquid bulk markets are connected by the use of combination carriers such as the OBO ship, and this has effects on the market structures examined on the sec-ond level. Moving vertically provides a similar narrow focus. If the interest is in dry bulk carriage in general or of a specific kind of cargo, the primary service to consider is tramp, with various possi-bilities of contracts and ships to be used.

It is readily conceded that no industry can be divided into neat, unambiguous components and segments. This is particularly true when, as in shipping, the operations are part of a wider system.

However, the figure should provide a useful frame of reference for and identification of the main elements and relationships that make up ocean shipping. Within each element there are at work various practices, customs, and institutions, the proper analysis of which requires substantial specific and specialized knowledge. In the chapters to come, we will not undertake the impossible task of providing that knowledge; we will, however, sketch out the more important and basic features that must be considered in any informed discussion about shipping.

Technological Change

Technological progress in shipping, as in other industries, follows a logistic curve with three distinct phases. The first, early development, is characterized by research, feasibility studies, and some pilot operations. This is followed by a second state of implementation of proven techniques with large new investments. In the final state of maturation, techniques are refined and investments taper off.[2] On this scale, most of the ship types dependent on single hull displacement construction (see Figure 5.1) are in various degrees of implementation and rapidly moving toward maturity.

In a basic sense, ship technology is related to the needs of commodity flows. The structure, composition, and direction of these flows depend, in turn, on many factors, both economic and political (see Figure 2.2). But given that the characteristic of the trade are considered in the design of the ship, there is an obvious close relationship between ports and ship technology that must be kept in mind. This relationship raises the question of causal direction: Do ship designs affect port facilities or vice versa? The causal relationship that actually dominates is of interest, because if ships are dominant, port planning must be based on reliable assessments of future technological developments in shipping. If, on the other hand, ports are dominant, then port planning is independent of external shipping decisions and can to some extent affect these decisions. A closer look at these relationships is, therefore, desirable, especially since they are also relevant to the carrier's decision to begin operations.

Some of the most important relationships between ships and the technical planning and operation of a port depend on the ship's dimensions, carrying capacity, frequency and regularity of call, shipboard cargo handling equipment and design, and various special features. The dimensions of the ship–length, width, and draft–determine the necessary depth, width, and turning radius of the approaches to the port as well as the depth along quays, width and depth of basins, and, to some extent, anchorages. The carrying capacity, assuming a reasonably high capacity utilization, determines the width and size of the dock apron, storage, and back-up areas. It also affects the need for crane capacity and transportation facilities to and from these areas, because the larger the carrying capacity is, the larger the flow of goods will be per unit of quay length. The frequency and regularity of calls affect the length of docking space required and random arrivals necessitate reserve or excess capacity to prevent congestion.

Ideally, shipboard cargo handling equipment should be complemented by that of the port. As far as hoisting facilities are concerned the ideal situation rarely holds since this equipment is usually duplicated, but there is the possibility of using both the ship's and the port's equipment if outside lighters can be used for ships docked along a quay. For roll-on/roll-off ships with stern or bow ports, minimally specialized docking facilities must be available. The recent development of angled stern ramps further minimizes the need for special facilities. For other specialty ships such as those for containers, frozen cargoes, and bulk, special facilities are needed.

To repeat the obvious, ports and ships are closely related, although it is difficult to say unequivocally which is the causal factor. Until the late 1950s, it could be said that the port dominated the relationship. As already mentioned in Chapter 1, ports require large, long-term investments. At the time the investment is made, the port facilities are adapted to the existing or immediately foreseeable shipping technology. Since no major innovation was introduced in shipping until relatively recently, expectations as to possible innovations were small. Therefore, the immediately foreseeable shipping technology was perceived as not materially different from the existing technology, and ports were constructed accordingly. Ships, on the other hand, require smaller and shorter-term investments. A shipowner who builds ships after port facilities have been established has a tendency to adapt the ship's design to these facilities, other conditions being equal. The heavy investments necessary for major innovation in established ports deter such innovation and this, in turn, holds back innovating shipowners. There are also in-stitutional factors in various countries that have prevented innova-tions in shipping. For instance, labor unions in many countries have resisted the containerization process and, in some trades, actually prevented its introduction for some time. Also, as mentioned in Chapter 1, procedures for customs clearance and documentary work, which are adapted to traditional ways of shipping and not readily changed, pose obstacles to innovation.

Indirect evidence for the above argument is the fact that while modern freighters in the late 1950s had better hulls and engines, navigation aids, and winches and cranes, their basic characteristics were not materially different from those existing in the pre–World War II period. That is, the arrangement and type of hoisting equip-ment (derricks and king posts), hatch covers and hatch arrange-ments, structure of tween decks, and the location midships of the engine were basically unchanged. On the other hand, tankers, ore and other bulk carriers, and a wide variety of specialty ships carry-ing such commodities as cars, various liquid gases and hazardous chemicals, wine, orange juice, and bulk cement changed rapidly in size and design after World War II. These latter ships were mainly engaged in new kinds of trade and were built for these special trades, and new ports and equipment were constructed specifically for them. Hence, ports were developed with reference to the par-ticular ships they had to serve; the causal direction had shifted and now was from ships to ports. However, too strong a claim should not be made for such strict causal sequences. In a dynamic world there must be mutual interactions between port and ship designs. The choice of a particular ship is always highly dependent on the capacities for loading and unloading in the intended ports. The more specialized the ship is with respect to both cargo carried and ports of call, the better are cargo handling facilities utilized aboard ship as well as on shore. As a consequence, turn-around time and costs decrease, and there is an incentive for both sides toward specializa-tion. In conventional trades, change was slower to come and was, together with bulk and specialty shipping, facilitated by technologi-cal development and research in shipbuilding, cargo handling, pro-pulsion machinery, and navigation.

In shipbuilding, the use of new materials such as aluminum and fiberglass, together with improved welding techniques and effective

antifouling bottom paints, has made possible lighter, larger, and
stronger ships requiring less maintenance than before. It is now
possible to build so-called open ships—those with hatch openings
that cover almost the whole deck. This arrangement makes it possible to place cargo directly into its allotted space and thus minimizes
time-consuming horizontal movements in the hold. With the
machinery placed midships, part of the space in the aft lower holds
is taken by the propeller shaft. Therefore, to obtain the full advantage of the open-deck arrangement it is desirable to move the bridge,
crew quarters, and machinery from midships to the stern. This
seemingly simple rearrangement of features was a major break-
through in ship construction. A ship should draw a somewhat
greater depth at the stern, enabling the propellers to exert maximum
power. This difference in draft measured at the stern and at the fore
is known as the trim. In a conventional ship, the proper trim is obtained by distributing cargo between the fore and aft parts of the
ship and by the use of water ballast tanks. When the machinery and
other quarters are moved to the stern, there is greater need for
ballast tanks in the fore, and as a consequence, the ship's construction and materials are subjected to greater stresses than in a conventional vessel. These problems have been solved, and the new
arrangement makes stowage easier and increases cargo space.

It also has been possible to provide side, stern, and bow ports as
well as to increase cargo cubic space by increasing the width of the
ship without impairing stability and seaworthiness. An increase in
width will normally affect the ship's speed, but this problem has
been solved by improved machinery and hydrodynamic designs,
notably the bulbous bow. This bow reduces wave action and saves
propulsion power.

Cargo handling equipment both aboard ships and ashore have
become more mechanized, efficient, sophisticated, and expensive in
response to the unitization of cargo in barges, trailers, containers
and pallets. More will be said presently about this equipment.

Computers have become integral parts of shipboard equipment
and operations, and have facilitated many developments both on
deck and in the engine room. With respect to machinery, to which
we will return shortly, the overall tendency is toward automation
with remote control of major functions. In the sphere of navigation,
introduction of satellites and expansion and improvement of the

DECCA, LORAN, and OMEGA computer systems allow for un-precedented accuracy that, together with better weather fore-casting, have made possible weather routing, said to save up to 5 percent of voyage time. Also, precise navigation will facilitate the introduction of traffic control schemes, should that decision be made in the future. The scope for on-board computers is wide. Not only can they be used for hyperbolic navigation systems (DECCA, LORAN, OMEGA) but they can also be used for "dead reckoning" and star fixes. Other uses, excluding the engine room, would include store records, accounts, hull strain measurements, and cargo control and monitoring.

Shipbuilding techniques have changed. Modern yards use assem-bly lines on which components, built in different places in the yard, are put together. These components are completed sections of the ship weighing several hundred tons. Computers are used to design and cut frames, plates, and girders, thus replacing the old methods of using specially built templates and mock-ups in a molding loft. These older methods, which had a high skill content, are now replaced by high technology methods requiring different skills that are more easily transferred than were the older ones. This may be one explanation for the expansion in recent years of modern ship-building capacity to countries not traditionally thought of in these terms, such as Korea, Spain, Portugal, Greece, and Brazil.

Classification Agencies

Naval architects and shipyards are concerned with fitting the commercial requirements of the owners with those required for sea-worthiness. That is, the consideration of trade route and cargo characteristics and the owner's need for cargo capacity, speed, economy, and earning power must be reconciled with the demands for stability, buoyancy, and maneuverability. This reconciliation is helped by and must conform to the rules and guidelines of various classification agencies. Based on their own research and interna-tional conventions these agencies issue rules and standards for material, construction, and maintenance. They supervise the con-struction of hull and machinery, assign load lines, measure tonnages and capacities, and issue required safety certificates. At the comple-tion of the new ship, it is assigned a certain class by the agency and listed in the latter's register of ships.

The commercial importance of classification is that the class of a ship is analogous to a credit rating—it is a shorthand description of its functional worthiness. Highest class means that the ship is suitable, and seaworthy, to carry goods ("dry and perishable cargoes") to and from all ports. Hence, the classification serves insurance companies as a risk indicator both for the insurance of the ship itself and for the cargo it carries. Similarly, it serves as a basic source of information for ship brokers and charterers. If, therefore, a shipowner wants to maximize his business opportunities, he will build his ship to the highest class and maintain it there by undergoing major surveys every fourth year as well as annual surveys of the hull.

There are several classification agencies, some of long standing in the traditional maritime countries and others of recent creation in developing countries such as India, Taiwan, and South Korea. In addition, there are classification agencies in the USSR and in Poland serving the needs of Eastern bloc shipping.[3] The American Bureau of Shipping is recognized as the official U.S. agency in the Merchant Marine Act of 1920. Lloyd's is probably the best known of these agencies. Although established in its present form in 1834, it began

TABLE 5.1

Major Classification Agencies

Year of Origin	Name	Country
1824	Bureau Veritas	France
1834	Lloyd's Register of Shipping	England
1861	Registro Italiano Navale	Italy
1864	Det Norske Veritas	Norway
1867	American Bureau of Shipping	United States
1867	Germanischer Lloyd	West Germany
1899	Nippon Kaiji Kyokai	Japan

formally in 1760. At that time insurance underwriters used to meet at Lloyd's Coffee House in London to exchange information on the merits of various ships as insurance risks. This involved the pooling of information on ships' construction; where and by whom built; age of ship; and names of owners, masters, and crews. This type of information became institutionalized when a committee was formed in 1760 to issue a shipping register, the first of which came out in 1764. Another register emerged in later years, and competition between the two registries was resolved when they merged and became Lloyd's Register in 1834. The most widely recognized agencies are listed in Table 5.1.

The objectives of classification agencies are (1) to provide information on ships' owners and construction of hull and machinery, (2) to prepare rules for the construction and maintenance of hull and machinery, and (3) to provide for the testing of ships' materials and to establish standards. Classification agencies also supervise construction and periodic surveys. These agencies are obviously very important vehicles for the application of technological progress and safety. Before building a 500,000-ton tanker, the appropriate agency would be asked for rules, standards, and approval, since without these it may not be possible to insure the vessel and its cargo—or, it follows, to employ the ship. In this sense, it is appropriate to regard classification agencies as supervisors of technology and technological change. Although each agency has its own rules and standards, there is much conformity, with Lloyd's exerting a heavy influence on the others simply because of its size and long-standing experience. Each agency publishes an annual register of its ships. Lloyd's Register includes all of the world's nonmilitary vessels.

Notes

1. See, for example, J. W. Devanney, *Marine Decisions Under Uncertainty* (Cambridge, Md.: Cornell Maritime Press, 1971), and R. O. Goss and C. D. Jones, "The Economies of Size in Dry Bulk Carriers," in *Advances in Maritime Economics*, ed. R. O. Goss (Cambridge, England: Cambridge University Press, 1977).

2. See S. Lawrence, *International Shipping: The Years Ahead* (Lexington, Mass.: Lexington Books, 1972).

3. These are, respectively, the USSR Register for Shipping and the Polski Rejestr Statkow. The Hellenic Register is in Greece.

6

Functional Types of Ships

The Ship

The most important development within shipping in the post-World War II period has been the pronounced tendency toward specialization of services and ships. The technological advance that has made possible this development, and which can be seen today in the numerous types of ships in operation, has affected the ship's machinery, hull, and cargo handling equipment.

Machinery

The hull and the machinery are the two main components of the ship. Choice of the proper engine is made only after the ship's trade or service has been defined and hull design determined. The first objective is to acquire machinery as small and light as possible given the required horse power. A second objective is to achieve maximum efficiency from the engine–that is, to transfer as much as possible of the power generated by the engine to the propeller. In this context there are several measures of engine power that are important. *Indicated horse power* (ihp) is the driving force of the piston. *Brake horse power* (bhp) is the power that comes from the engine measured at the connection to the propeller shaft. The power going through the connection and actually transferred to the propeller is the *shaft horse power* (shp), and the amount of power that actually drives the ship is the *thrust horse power* (thp). Ihp shows the highest value of power, with each succeeding expression indicating lower values as power is lost at each step. The ratio thp/shp is an expression of the propeller's efficiency. Clearly, to improve the propulsion machinery, development had to be directed to the engine itself and to the propeller–i.e., to the two objectives mentioned above–and this brought us through a succession of engines. Reciprocating steam engines were introduced in ships in the 1860s followed by turbines in the 1890s. The diesel, invented in 1897, went to sea in 1912 and is today the main type in use.

Several specific considerations, apart from weight and space, enter the engine selection process. These would include the reliability of the machinery and service facilities as they affect the evaluation of initial cost and maintenance, as well as availability of trained personnel and fuel consumption. Vessels that use steam engines burn either coal or oil and are known as *steamships* (S/S), and *turbine ships* are always in this category (T/S or S/S). Those using diesels are *motor ships* (M/S or M/V) and burn only oil. Most ships in the world today are motor ships, as the diesel has low fuel consumption, is reliable, and is thoroughly familiar to crews around the world. However, the use of the steam turbine, and the more recently developed gas turbine, has increased because of the larger power needs of fast container ships. The gas turbine in particular has advantages in weight, space, and maintenance, but fuel consumption is high. In light of the current oil situation it is possible that coal-fired steamships in general may come back. However, a problem with the old steam engines was the need for manual stoking and coal trimming. With today's emphasis on automation, in the engine room particularly, it is inconceivable that crews could be found to do this type of work. There have been reports of trials with slurried coal, but there are no specific indications of future directions.

At present, the main manufacturers of diesel engines are Sulzer Brothers (Switzerland) and Burmeister & Wain (Denmark), each with about one third of the market. The German firm Maschinenfabriek Augsburg-Nurnberg (M.A.N.) comes third, followed by Doxford (England) and Götaverkan (Sweden). In steam turbines, the major companies are Stal-Laval (Sweden) and General Electric (U.S.). Gas turbines are produced by Rolls Royce and Pratt & Whitney, both of England.

Nuclear power has been used for a long time in naval vessels, and the USSR uses it in ice breakers. There have been applications to merchant ships in the United States, Germany, and Japan, showing that safe operations can be expected. Although, from time to time, there are press reports that nuclear power will be economically feasible if the required horse power reaches this or that level, its commercial future remains uncertain, in spite of the fact that the stated horse power requirements have been reached time and again.

Automation has progressed far in the engine room; systems are commonly devised so that it can be left unattended for the night. Such systems have been approved by several of the major classification agencies, including Lloyd's and those in Norway, the United States, and Japan. Progress in machinery can, however, be lost by the propeller. Questions arise concerning the number and site of propellers: Should there be one, two, or more? Should propellers be placed in the bow to improve maneuverability? Should the pitch of the propeller be fixed or adjustable? All of these considerations of machinery are closely connected to the shape of the hull which, in turn, depends on the many factors and requirements of the trade.

The Hull

Each functional ship type has cargo carrying characteristics given by various measurements common to all types. It is important to know the ship's capacities in terms of carrying weight and volume.

The *cubic capacity* of the ship simply tells how much space is available for cargo and is expressed in cubic feet or cubic meters. Depending on how this space is measured in the hold, there are *grain* and *bale* cubic capacities. The grain measurement is based on the fact that a grain cargo would fill all available space in the hold by trickling into all the small and narrow spaces between frames and girders. When loading baled cargo, these spaces cannot be used and are, therefore, excluded when measuring bale capacity – that is, the hold is assumed to have smooth and reasonably straight sides. The difference between the two is often substantial in conventional ships, and therefore important to the shipper when demand is for space rather than weight capacity. The latter, *weight capacity,* is given in metric tons. But when dealing with tonnage measurements in shipping it is important to keep in mind that there are both weight and space tonnages, with the former referring to cargo carrying characteristics. The first *weight measurement* is the *light displacement* tonnage, which is the weight of the ship unloaded. Next, the ship is loaded to the designed draft with crew, provisions, and bunkers aboard as well; this gives the *loaded displacement.* The difference between the two displacements is the weight carrying capacity or *deadweight tonnage* (dwt) of the ship. Deducting the weight of non-earning loads such as bunkers, stores, and water gives the *cargo deadweight tonnage* (cdwt), an expression rarely used in day-to-day business. (The dwt and various space tonnages are those in common use.) Only naval ships are characterized by displacement tonnages.

The connection between the cubic and weight measurements and the cargoes carried is given by the *stowage factor* for each commodity. This factor gives the number of cubic feet (or metric units) needed for one ton of the good with its packing. One effect of unitization is to change these factors so that past, stable stowage factors cannot always be assumed today. Another relationship between space and weight is given by the *block coefficient*. This is the ratio of the volume of the ship, excluding superstructures, to the volume of a box with the same dimensions as the ship. Hence, if the ship were a box, the coefficient would be one. The more the hull form departs from the box shape, the smaller is the block coefficient. It is, therefore, an expression for how full-bodied the ship is. Tankers and bulk carriers have large block coefficients of .70 to .85, while general cargo ships are less full-bodied with values of .50 to .75. Containerships would fall in the lower range since their high speed requires sleek hulls. As hydrodynamic and machinery research progresses it may be possible to achieve higher speeds with fuller hulls.

Space tonnages appear in all documents pertaining to the registration of the ship. The basic unit is, therefore, the *register ton* of 100 cubic feet (2.83 cubic meters). There are two such measurements, the *gross register ton* (grt) and the *net register ton* (nrt). There is no single, universal set of rules for measuring these tonnages, but it may soon come. In 1969, IMCO proposed an International Convention on Tonnage Measurement of Ships. The convention will come into force two years after ratification by at least twenty-five states representing at least 65 percent of the world's grt. Meanwhile, register measurements do follow, as in the past, some general guidelines. Gross tons measure the entire internal cubic space except areas that are integral parts of the ship's construction. That is, the measurement will exclude only those spaces that, because of the construction of the ship, must at all times be used for the running of the ship. Examples would be the bridge, anchor box, and steering gear—spaces that can never be used for cargo. Net register tons are derived from gross register tons by deducting certain specified non-earning areas such as galley, crew quarters, stores, and engine room—that is, spaces that need not necessarily, and for the life of the ship, be used for the same purposes. The register tonnages are used to determine manning scales and fees for registration, ports, pilots, and canal transits. However, the authorities for the Suez and Panama canals assess fees according to their own measurement rules resulting in Suez and Panama tonnages. When the measurement convention enters into force these tonnages will presumably disappear.

It should be clear from the above that registered tonnages are important to the shipowner because they affect the fees and charges he pays on a particular trip. Similarly, they are important to authorities whose revenues depend on these fees. For the shipper, on the other hand, they are irrelevant. For him it is the carrying capacities in terms of dwt and grain and bale cubic capacities that are important—a problem because official shipping statistics are commonly given in grt and nrt. In this context, it must be remembered that *there is no fixed relationship between register tons and deadweight.* There is a trend toward more relevant official shipping statistics, prompted by the Shipping Division of UNCTAD's Trade and Development Board and several shipping research institutes around the world. Privately, a number of ship and chartering brokers provide relevant data to their customers.

Cargo Handling Equipment

Shipping is an international business with many opportunities for the shipowner to transfer the ship from one trade to another in response to market conditions. The more flexibility he wants for his ship, the more self-sufficient the ship should be with respect to loading and unloading. But the technological developments that have occurred in shipping tend to make trades more specialized, and this has resulted in both greater dependence on port facilities, such as container and bulk ports, and specialization of shipboard equipment, such as gantry cranes and self-loading systems. Hence, while there has been great progress in cargo handling, the net effect is one of decreased flexibility with increased specialization of ships and ports. As a result, some ships rely entirely on the port's equipment and have no cargo handling equipment at all, while others carry very sophisticated gear.

As trade and seaborne traffic grows, the technical concern with cargo handling equipment and facilities on ships and in ports will naturally continue and will be closely related to the types of ships, present and future. To attempt an enumeration, description, and discussion of the many cargo handling systems available would tax both reader and writer beyond acceptable levels. Instead, we will give the broad categories of shipboard equipment.[1]

First, there are the conventional systems of *derricks and winches*. There are two kinds of these: the *regular lift* with capacities of 2 to 10 tons and the *heavy lifts* that are capable of handling up to 100 tons. Derricks and winches are commonly used in the "union purchase" arrangement. Here one derrick is positioned over the hold, the other over the pier, and the lifting wires are connected to the same hook. If the ship is loading, the derrick over the pier lifts the cargo while the other derrick pulls it horizontally over to the hatch and lowers it into the hold; for unloading, the procedure is reversed. While very efficient, this system has been largely replaced on newer ships by *cranes* that may be *stationary* or *mobile*. The latter are usually gantry cranes of great lifting capacity and speed and are used on container and other specialty ships. In an interesting incident several years ago, the author was asked to arbitrate a labor dispute that arose from the use of stationary cranes. The question was whether the longshoreman who operated the equipment should be paid the rate of a winchman or a crane operator – a substantial difference. In that particular case it was clear that the skill required to operate the ship's crane was actually less than that required for handling a winch in a union purchase arrangement. Since it was the skill content that was reflected in the different wage rates, the decision had to be made accordingly. The new mobile, high performance cranes do, however, require very substantial skill and training to operate.

A third group includes *cargo elevators* used in containerships and barge carriers to transport the units into place. The fourth group consists of various types of *conveyer belts*, which can be continuous or intermittent and can be power driven or operate by gravity flow. They are used in general cargo ships, specialty ships, fruit carriers, and some self-loading bulk carriers.

The next category, used on the various types of roll-on/roll-off ships, consists of *ramps*. These provide access to all decks on the ship from ports in the bow, sides, or stern. A recent development is the angled stern ramp, which allows the ship to dock alongside and still be able to use the ramp. However, only the side toward which the ramp is angled can be used for docking—which is not much of a constraint unless approaches and basins pose obstacles to necessary turning maneuvers. Ramps that are movable sideways, i.e., slewing ramps, overcome these problems.

A final category is *liquid* and *slurry* pump systems, used in tankers, bulkers, and combination carriers. It is important for a tanker to discharge quickly; consequently, the growth in tanker size was accompanied by pumping systems of increasingly greater capacity. The transportation of various ores in slurry form is a recent development. In one system, used in New Zealand, the ship takes slurried iron ore through an underwater pipeline at a single point mooring (spm) buoy. The water is removed from the slurry within twenty-four hours and, at port of discharge, is either unloaded by grabs or reslurried and pumped out.[2]

Types of Ships

Ocean shipping is based on the transport of raw materials and goods in various stages of manufacture. As these commodities initially moved in small lots to and from many ports, the need were for general cargo ships, which were able to accept numerous parcels of different shapes, sizes, and weights in many ports for many destinations. Over time, these needs resulted in the *shelter-deck* ship with many hatches, derricks, and tween decks. It is useful to briefly trace the development of this ship as it also allows the introduction of some further terminology.

The first steamships were much like the sailing ships—basically a box with a deck separating the hold into the upper and lower hold. For stability and reasons of trim, the engine was placed midships and protected by a casing. Soon a superstructure was built around the casing to house the galley, stores, and the bridge. Next, living spaces were separated so that officers moved from the stern to the midships, the engine crew moved to the stern, while the deck crew remained in the fore. In due time, the crew quarters were protected by superstructures—the forecastle head at the fore and the poop in the stern. Seen from the side, the ship's profile showed three "islands" and two "wells." Appropriately, they were called *"three-island"* ships. A practice evolved of carrying cattle and low-fare passengers in the wells between the islands and a light deck was built for their protection. This became known as the *shelter* or *weather deck*. As cargo volumes grew and the need increased for more volume capacity, the shelter deck was strengthened and became permanent to allow cargo to be carried in that space. The *shelter-decker* had emerged.

However, for purposes of registration and the assessment of fees, it was desirable for the owner to exclude the shelter-deck space. This could be done by counting it as deck space. On the other hand, he wanted to attract cargo and charge appropriate rates by counting the shelter deck as bona fide under deck space. This dilemma was solved by providing access from the shelter deck space to the open deck. This access, known as the *tonnage hatch,* can be closed, in which case the shelter deck becomes "under-deck" space and we have a *closed shelter-decker*. If left open, the ship operates as an *open shelter-decker* and the space does not count. It is the operator's decision, for each trip, whether the ship will be closed or open, but the decision carries implications for the closing of tween-deck hatch openings and freeboard as well as for cargo insurance and freight rates. The new Load Line Convention of 1966 has introduced rules making freeboard the factor that determines whether the ship is to be considered a closed or open shelter-decker. A new load mark in the form of an inverted triangle has been introduced; if the ship is down to that mark it is closed; if on its regular marks, it is open.

Despite the impressive changes of the last twenty years, the shelter-decker (referred to also as the tween-decker, although this term applies technically to all ships with tween decks) is still the most common type in operation. It is a multi-purpose ship and is used for dry bulk as well as general cargo. But the needs of the trade are changing and so are the ships.

Dry Bulk Carriers

The conventional shelter-decker poses difficulties for bulk carriage because the tween decks and propeller shaft tunnel often lead to uneven distribution of the cargo, resulting in stability problems and underutilization of capacity. Loading and unloading are costly and time-consuming because trimming—i.e., evening the distribution of the cargo in the hold—must be done by hand. The configuration of the holds makes it difficult to unload by clamshell grabs, still the

most common method. Hence, there is a move toward specialized
bulk carriers with self-loading and unloading equipment, self-
trimming holds, and no tween decks. A number of these specialized
bulk carriers have emerged and are listed in Table 6.1.

The sizes of the ships have changed in response to needs. For one,
there are significant economies of size. Building cost per deadweight
ton falls as size grows. Therefore, capital charges—depreciation and
interest—as well as insurance per ton of cargo carried at full capacity fall. Also, the required size of the engine and, therefore, fuel consumption, increase less than proportionately to deadweight capacity. The overall result is lower average costs. In terms of the market,
the need for bulk ships depends on the usual sizes of the lots of a
particular commodity that are being shipped. The lot size, in turn,
depends mainly on the shipper and the nature of his or his customers' production and marketing processes into which the material
is an input (see the comments about physical distribution in Chapter
3). Basically, it is a question of whether an even flow of inputs is
preferred to the building up of stockpiles and the holding of large inventories. In the former case, frequent but smaller shipments are
generally needed, while the latter implies less frequent and larger requirements. In either case, the decision must take into account the

TABLE 6.1
Main Differences between Bulk Carriers

Type of Ship	Main Characteristics
Tanker	"Closed" deck. No hatch covers
Bulk Carrier	"Open" deck. Large hatches with large volume in the holds for low density commodities
Ore Carrier	Same as for bulk carrier, but the holds are small and shallow to allow for proper stability with high density cargo
Ore/oil and ore/slurry/ oil	Basically a tanker with hatches. The center tanks, used for ore, are narrow and shallow
Ore/bulk/oil	Basically a bulk carrier with small and large holds arranged, and structurally reinforced, to carry ore and oil and lighter bulk cargoes

storage costs both before and after the shipping has taken place. As will be seen in Chapter 7, there are several ways in which the shipowner can meet these needs with a contract of affreightment. However, as a general rule, the more expensive the commodity is, the higher the storage costs are in terms of interest and required storage facilities, such as, for example, covered storage areas. The consequence is that ship sizes are affected in such a way that, generally, high-value commodities tend to require smaller ships with more frequent service, and the opposite for relatively low-value goods. The transport distance affects this relationship as well: the longer the distance, the larger the optimal ship.

The movements of dry bulk cargoes reflect these aspects. Thus, the five major cargoes—iron ore, coal, grain, bauxite/alumina, and phosphate—move in lots from 20,000 tons to well over 100,000 tons. Other, minor, bulk commodities like cement, clay, gypsum, manganese ore, potash, pyrites, salt, sugar, and sulphur move in small as well as large lots ranging from a few thousand tons to the 20–30,000-ton range. As a result, bulk carriers also range from the mini-bulker of 3000 dwt, through the handy sizes of 20–30,000 dwt and the 60,000 tonners (known as Panamax ships when built specifically to fit the Panama Canal's lock dimensions) to the large carriers of 150,000 dwt and the combination carriers of close to 300,000 dwt.

While the general cargo ship has many disadvantages in bulk carriage, it still has flexibility and can carry many products. The specialized carrier loses this flexibility and, particularly, the ability to pick up back-haul cargoes. Attempts to provide more employment flexibility and to minimize ballast trips resulted in the development of combination carriers.

For years tankers had been engaged in the carriage of grain. Then why should a bulk carrier not participate in the oil trade, especially if it could alternate between the two types of cargo and thus avoid much of the voyaging in ballast? The first combination carrier was the *ore-oil* (O/O) carrier in the range of 100–250,000 dwt. Because of differences in densities of oil and ore, the ship carried a relatively small volume of ore when fully loaded. The ship therefore was basically a tanker with a tight hatch provided on top of the central tank. This type of carrier offers flexibility and, while not avoiding all ballasting, provides the owner with alternate choices for employment. A typical voyage could be: iron ore from Peru to Japan, ballast to Indonesia for oil to the U.S. West Coast, and ballast to Peru to repeat the route. A variant of the O/O is the *ore-slurry-oil* (OSO) ship, or mineral tanker, ranging up to some 140,000 dwt. This ship can receive the ore in either dry form or as slurry and can also transport coal.

Even more flexibility was gained by the OBO ship, roughly in the 70–150,000–dwt range. Technically, this was a more difficult design because the low density bulk cargoes such as grain and coal had to be considered. The result is a ship with many different hold sizes and oil-tight hatches. The holds are usually arranged so that larger and smaller holds alternate. In this way, heavy ores can be loaded in the small holds, thus distributing stresses more evenly, while the others are used when carrying lighter bulks. A possible OBO voyage would carry grain from the United States to India and ballast to the Persian Gulf for oil to the United States. Or, coal from the United States may be loaded for Japan, after which new oil cargo is picked up in Indonesia for Brazil, with a return cargo of iron ore to Japan.[3]

Table 6.1 summarizes briefly what the main differences are between the various types of bulk carriers. In this context, the tanker is included to make the comparison complete.

Liquid Bulk Carriers

Liquid bulk typically moves in large quantity lots, and the sizes of carriers have developed accordingly. There are, of course, cargoes that move in relatively small quantities – vegetable oils, wines, milk, latex, and various chemicals – but the most important carriers at this point are the *oil tankers,* which divide into crude and products carriers with a recent specialization into liquid gas carriage. The carriage of *crude* oil in large quantities is a relatively recent phenomenon tied to the post–World War II economic recovery and large-scale oil production in the Middle East. The markets for oil products in the early postwar years were small and the needs did not justify the building of refineries in these markets. Instead, large refineries grew up in the Persian Gulf[4] area where the British presence at the time provided the political stability for a perceived good investment climate. The same favorable atmosphere was perceived in Venezuela and, again, refineries were built close to the source—the main ones on the Dutch islands of Aruba and Curaçao.

As a result, oil trade was mainly in *refined products,* which re-quired relatively small ships of about 12–20,000 dwt. The existing crude oil trade was also in small tankers and there was little dif-ference, if any, between crude and products carriers. It was quite common for a tanker to carry crude, or dirty cargo, on one trip and, after cleaning the tanks, carry products, or clean cargo, on the next. In the 1950s several factors operated to change this picture. The Abadan crisis in 1951 shook the confidence of both consumers and oil companies in the security of Middle East supplies of refined prod-ucts. The 1956 closing of the Suez Canal had a similar effect. At the same time, world oil demand was reaching levels that could justify the development of market-located refineries. The need for the transport of large quantities of crude oil had arrived and, as transport economies could be achieved by using large ships, the movement toward large tankers accelerated. This trend toward market-located refineries and large crude carriers has continued, with a distinct difference developing between crude and products tankers, the latter decreasing in importance.

However, as demand grows, more refining capacity is needed. In much of the Western world, there is environmental opposition to new refineries, and new refining capacity is exported, so to speak, to places outside the main consuming areas. As a result, transportation of products is again becoming important. This tendency is reinforced as the main oil exporters, such as Saudi Arabia, further develop their resource base, since they are likely to meet their consumers' in-creased demand for oil by exporting products rather than crude. Product carriers range from about 15,000 dwt to 50–60,000 dwt, while crude is carried on ships of any size up to the 500,000-dwt range. While the product carrier is much smaller than the crude tanker, it should be clear that this is the outcome of demand factors. Although there are ships carrying several kinds of products in dif-ferent tanks at the same time, most carry one particular product. Demand for such a particular product must be less than for crude oil from which a number of products can be made, meeting a number of consumer demands. Over time, however, larger shipments of specific products will be required, and product tankers will grow in size. Crude carriers over the 150,000-dwt capacity are referred to as *very large crude carriers* (VLCC) and become, somewhat arbitrarily, *ultra large crude carriers* (ULCC) when they surpass 300,000 dwt.

Another recent development is the carrying of *liquefied petroleum gas* (LPG) and, even more recently, *liquefied natural gas* (LNG). Liquefied petroleum gases are propane and butane produced in re-fineries from petroleum and natural gas, made into liquid form to allow them to be marketed and used in this form for heating, cook-ing, camping, car fuel, raw material for the petro-chemical industry, and, lately, as a substitute for natural gas. LNG, on the other hand, is natural gas, a primary fuel, which has been liquefied only to allow it to be transported. Before use, it is reconverted to gas. Petroleum gases turn into liquids at either very high pressure with unchanged temperature or at low temperatures with normal pressure. Combi-nations of pressures and temperatures are possible. For butane the temperature must be below 0° C to keep it liquid, while propane requires it to be below −40° C. LNG, however, requires a temperature below −160° C to remain liquid; pressure will not af-fect the form of natural gas.

The two gases respond to different demand factors and require different shore facilities as well as ships. Both types of tankers have high pressure, *cryogenic* (low temperature) tanks, but those for LNG require higher capacity freezing plants and insulation. Since they respond to different demands—that is, LPG is for a final product while LNG is for a primary fuel—the shipped quantities differ, as do the ship sizes. LPG tankers range from 1,000 to 75,000-cubic-meter capacity and LNG ships are commonly 125,000-cubic-meter capac-ity (4,417,000 cubic feet). Considering that one cubic foot (cft) of LNG converts into about 600 cft of gas, the capacity of such a tanker is truly impressive.

Dry General Cargo Carriers

The events leading to new types of general cargo carriers are com-plex, but, in very simplified terms, can be perceived in the following manner. Some of the bulk commodities shipped in special bulk car-riers, such as forestry products, cement, some oils, and latex, were previously shipped as parcels in the conventional cargo liners. As the trade grew, and as old ships used for bulk cargoes were scrapped, new specialty ships came into operation and meant better utilization of special cargo handling equipment with shorter turn-around time and lower overall costs. This, in turn, meant loss of

base cargo for the general cargo ships and had two major consequences. First, the liners lost revenue from cargo that required
relatively small outlays for stevedoring because the good stowed
easily and required no special care. As a consequence, the remaining
revenue was earned from a highly heterogeneous cargo, the handling of which entailed relatively higher stevedoring costs and
longer turn-around times. The result was that the ratio of cargo handling costs to revenues increased and rate increases as well as attempts to control costs were necessary. Efforts to control costs
were two-pronged: reduce actual cargo handling costs, and, con-
comittantly, shorten the turn-around time. Facilitated by the
various technological advances in shipbuilding, machinery, and
cargo handling equipment, two basic types of general cargo ships
developed. They were the *roll-on/roll-off* and the *lift-on/lift-off*
types, commonly known as RoRo and LoLo ships, respectively.
Within each type there are several kinds of ships. Although, as we
shall see, there are other forms of unitization, these two types are
both based on the carriage of cargo in containers; they have
developed rapidly and are now in the stage of maturation carrying a
major part of the general cargo trade.

Containers come in several types and sizes. There are containers
for regular cargo as well as for refrigerated, perishable, and hazardous cargoes. The ISO has done much to standardize sizes and fit-
tings, but there is still much variation. The usual dimensions are
twenty or forty feet long with the height and width at eight feet
each. The *container capacity* of a ship is given in *twenty-foot
equivalent units* (TEU). Hence, a forty-foot box equals two TEU.
The hold of a containership is known as a bay, and the container's
place on the ship is given by its slot in a certain tier in a given cell of
a specified bay.

Where the two types differ is with respect to the principle of
loading and unloading. The RoRo principle is to handle cargo by
horizontal movements through side, bow, and stern ports. The units
are brought aboard as or by vehicles and are rolled on and rolled off.
The LoLo is an "open-deck" ship, and cargo moves vertically in and
out. That is, shipboard or shore-based cranes are used. Both principles have proven to be both fast and efficient, and turn-around
times have decreased drastically. The most important advantage of

the RoRo is that terminal facilities are relatively simple and inexpensive because no cranes are needed. Therefore, the RoRo becomes more attractive on short runs where terminal costs are relatively more important than hauling costs. The utilization of RoRos in short trades has mainly been a combination of passenger and cargo operations—i.e., ferries. In long trades, they are used purely as cargo ships, the most common of which are the *car carriers* and *trailer ships*, both of which do exactly what the names imply—carry cars and trailers, respectively.

Both types of ships have one problem in common, but it is more pronounced for the RoRo. Because of the difficulty in stowing big units in some parts of the ship, there is much loss of cubic space. The stowage factor is particularly high in the RoRos. One aspect of this is that a given amount of cargo requires either more frequent service by a RoRo than a conventional ship or, if the frequency is the same, the RoRo must be considerably larger than the ship it replaces. Attempts to minimize the loss of cargo space by increasing the width of the ship has led to a more full-bodied hull and also to a limited adoption of catamaran hulls for RoRos. Such ships draw relatively little water, so the use of double hulls could conceivably enable shallow ports to develop into RoRo container ports.

In a strict sense, the term "LoLo ship" ought to refer to those ships that are not RoRos, but accepted usage reserves it for *cellular containerships* and combination container–general-cargo ships, so-called *partial containerships* or *combo ships*. The main advantages of containers are the integration of the whole transport function from producer to consumer into one coordinated operation and the shorter turn-around time. Specifically, the container, a large unit of about twenty tons, can be loaded and unloaded in one single movement, in many places, and the short time in port means low terminal costs. The disadvantages following from this are that the available cargo volume suitable for containers must be very large and must accumulate at a fast rate. Since this is true in relatively few trades, such as on the North Atlantic, some Pacific, and Mediterranean trades, containers cannot be used on some routes. To overcome this problem regional container ports have developed with feeder services to the smaller trading centers.

But where there is not sufficient base cargo for a container feeder service, as well as in some other traditional trades, the *pallet* ship can provide unitized service. The pallet is simply a wooden platform approximately four feet square on which cargo is loaded and secured into a uniform unit for loading in the ship and transporting to its destination as one unit. The ship itself is very little different from a conventional break-bulk carrier. It usually has side ports and flush tween decks to allow the operation of forklift trucks, but no other special equipment is needed. Without pallets, the ship operates as a conventional carrier; conversely, conventional carriers can easily handle pallets. The pallet ship is very flexible and its impact on ports and labor is small.

The simplest form of unitization is the *pre-sling* used in a conventional ship. Here cargo is loaded in a rope or net sling that, with the cargo in it, is left as a unit aboard the ship. There are other situations in which containers can be used, but not to the extent that even a small RoRo or containership is justified. To meet these needs, the *barge carriers* were developed. There are several systems of these, the most well known being the LASH (lighter aboard ship), SEABEE (sea barge), and BACAT (barges on catamaran), and others such as the European barge carrier system (BCS) and barges on board (BOB). The barge carrier concept is an extreme form of unitization that paradoxically provides much more flexibility than do the RoRo or LoLo. Containers are loaded into barges that in turn are loaded onto the carrier. Their importance and flexibility lie in their use in areas where the next transport link is along inland or coastal waterways, or where deep, well-equipped ports are absent. The barge carriers can offer a large range of lot sizes for shipment to several ports. They can call on a number of ports and discharge the required number of barges, which are brought into port by tugs, unloaded, and reloaded, to be picked up when the carrier calls on the return voyage. The carrier itself spends little time in port and the barges can carry containers or break-bulk. In this way the containers on the barges can be moved upriver and into very small ports, and container technology becomes flexible and feasible even for relatively small-volume trade.

As seen in Figure 5.1 (p. 55), there are two main barge carrier systems. In the cellular system, used on the LASH, the barges are lifted into place, or cell, by a gantry crane; in the SEABEE, which uses the horizontal shelf system, the barge is floated into the carrier hull to the proper place and then elevated for stowage. The latter may well be called a *flow-in/flow-out* vessel (FloFlo).

To complete the picture, we ought to mention two concepts that are not in use but are discussed from time to time, both relating to the problems that barge carriers appear to have solved successfully. The first is the *seagoing barge train* (SBT), which simply would consist of barges towed, or pushed, across the ocean. It appears that the barge carriers provide a more feasible solution both in economic and technological terms. The other concept, aimed at the problem of shallow ports, is the *sealift*. Its basic design would be that of a self-propelled floating dock equipped with a bow. The ship enters the lift, which is raised just as a floating dock is. The sealift draws less water than the ship and can, therefore, bring it into ports too shallow for the ship to enter on its own. It is interesting to note that this concept, known as the "camel," was used from 1842–1849 in the port of Nantucket. The sandbar across the harbor prevented the passage of whaling ships over 300 tons and these larger ships therefore tended to use New Bedford. To maintain the competitive position of Nantucket, the "camel" was used to bring the larger ships over the bar. With increasingly larger ships, the "camel" became insufficient and its use was discontinued in 1849. Twenty years later, Nantucket sent out its last whaler and disappeared from the list of whaling ports, as New Bedford took over.[5]

Notes

1. See E. Frankel and H. Marcus, *Ocean Transportation* (Cambridge, Mass.: MIT Press, 1972), p. 147, for a diagram summarizing existing systems.

2. United Nations, *The Application of Modern Transport Technology to Mineral Development in Developing Countries* (New York, 1976). This publication also has an excellent description of the most used and promising slurry system, the Marconaflo System.

3. The prime mover in the development of these ships was Erling Naess, a Norwegian shipowner. In his *Autobiography of a Shipping Man* (Colchester, England: Seatrade Publications, 1977), he gives a fascinating account of the importance of back-haul considerations in his operations

and particularly as the motivation for his search for a specific type of ship, which materialized in the combination carrier.

4. The Persian Gulf is the traditional name used in the West, but ship-ping circles now commonly call it the Arabian Gulf or the Middle East Gulf.

5. *Whale Fishery of New England* (no author given) (New Bedford, Mass.: Reynolds-deWalt Printing, 1968 [first pub. 1915]).

7

Types of Transport Contracts

In shipping, as in all other modes, the operator may serve as a common, contract, or private carrier. The concept of the common carrier means that he has a standing offer to serve the general public within the limits set by his equipment and area of service. The contract carrier has no such obligation. He offers his services to selected customers on the basis of a contract. These obligations determine what services and markets the respective operators will serve and this, in turn, will have decisive effects on the choice of ship design. The common carrier operates a scheduled service in a market where regular service is important. This is *liner* service that usually, but not always, serves the general cargo trade. The bulk trades, including both dry and liquid cargoes, are primarily served by contract carriers who operate *tramp* services, and by private operators.

Ocean Bills of Lading

The contract used in liner trade is the ocean *bill of lading* (B/L). Basically, it is similar to those bills of lading used in other modes, but there are important differences in its usage that properly make it, together with marine insurance, the very foundation of ocean-borne trade. Generally, a bill of lading, used by any mode, is a transport document giving particulars about the shipment. Each carrier is likely to have his own forms, but the standard information includes a description of the goods; the places of origin, destination, and routing; the freight charges; and the names and addresses of the shipper and consignee. Sometimes the value is stated if it is higher than the carrier's statutory liability, and the terms of carriage are given, usually on the back of the document. The bill can be directed to some specified person, who then is the only one to whom the shipment can be delivered; this is a *straight bill of lading* and is non-negotiable. If it is directed to the "order of someone" we have the *to-order bill of lading,* which is negotiable. The former is common in domestic trade and the latter in international trade and particularly in shipping.

The bill performs three main functions. Two of these are to serve as a *receipt* for goods shipped and delivered by the carrier. By signing the bill of lading and returning it to the shipper, the carrier or his agent acknowledges that the goods described in the bill have been loaded for shipment on a particular vessel. At the destination the signed bill is returned to the carrier in exchange for delivery of the goods. The third function is that of a *certificate of title,* and it is in this role that the ocean bill of lading plays such a fundamental role in international trade. Before turning to this aspect, we will look at the actual process by which the bill serves as a receipt.

Suppose a shipper has booked cargo space with a particular carrier. He obtains the carrier's bill of lading forms and enters the required information. At the proper time, several sets of the bill are brought with the goods to the carrier's stipulated delivery place, usually his waterfront terminal. The carrier has now received the shipment for loading and acknowledges this by one of several methods. The bill of lading may be stamped "received for shipment," or a special *dock receipt,* sometimes called *mate's receipt,* is given to the shipper. When the shipment is actually loaded, the name of the vessel is given in the bill and it is stamped "on board," thus signifying that the goods are now being shipped. The *received for shipment B/L* has now become an *on-board B/L,* also known as a *shipped B/L.* At the time of loading, the particulars on the B/L are checked and the goods inspected. Any exceptions the carrier makes against the goods, such as water-stained or damaged packing, are noted on the B/L. If such exceptions occur, the B/L is called "dirty"; otherwise it is "clean." One copy of each B/L is kept on the ship. From these the ship's *manifest* is prepared. This is an important document for the ship for insurance purposes and because it is necessary to document the ship's content whenever entering or leaving port. When the ship arrives at the destination, the carrier's agent sends a *notice of arrival* to all consignees, who now exchange their B/Ls for the carrier's *delivery order,* which allows them to receive the good at the terminal.

The process by which the consignees obtain their copies of the original B/L brings us to the role of that document in the financing of international trade. The basic principle is simple. As a negotiable instrument of title, the ocean B/L confers ownership on whoever holds the document at any particular time. (In actual practice the document is made out to "Mr. X or order" so that, until endorsed by Mr. X, it is his property.) During the time the shipment is in transit, the shipper can forward the B/L, through a bank, to the consignee. However, unless the consignee pays the shipper for the goods, he will not receive the B/L from the bank and, hence, cannot claim the goods. In the actual process, banks and marine insurance under-writers become crucial because the B/L is intimately connected with the letter of credit (L/C) and the insurance certificate.

The *letter of credit* is the most common method of financing inter-national trade. It ensures that the exporter receives his payment and the importer his goods. Assume that an exporter, A, receives an order for a tractor to be shipped abroad to B. A requests B to open a L/C in favor of A. But A wants to be sure that B cannot withdraw that L/C and specifies that it must be irrevocable. In ad-dition, A does not know conditions in B's country and therefore re-quests that a bank in his own country confirms the L/C. This means that B will commit himself irrevocably to the transaction and that a bank in A's country guarantees B's commitment. Naturally B will not make this commitment unless he is assured that he will receive the proper tractor in good condition at the right time. He therefore agrees to A's request only if A will supply evidence of shipment in good order with proper insurance and whatever other documents B may require. That is, he wants documentary assurances, with the main documents being a clean on-board B/L and the *insurance certif-icate.* The resulting L/C is then a confirmed, irrevocable, documen-tary L/C. B now proceeds to instruct his bank to open a L/C in A's favor and specifies under what conditions and against which documents the bank is authorized to pay A. The bank forwards these conditions to a correspondent bank in the exporter's country and guarantees that bank's confirmation to A. The correspondent bank now informs A who must comply with the given conditions.

The exporter delivers the tractor for shipment and in due time receives his *on-board B/L,* which must be clean. It is quite common for shippers to give carriers a *letter of indemnity* in return for a clean B/L, but there are also many conferences that do not allow this practice. With the B/L and the insurance certificate, and whatever other documents may be needed, A can draw upon the L/C. This is done by drawing a draft on the importer and presenting it together with proper documents to the bank that will pay A the face value of the draft less a certain discount. The exporter is paid at this time and drops out of the picture. The bank forwards all the documents and the draft to B's bank, which reimburses the correspondent bank—now also out of the picture. B's bank keeps the documents but sends the draft to B who accepts that order to pay by signing it and simply writing "accepted" on it. Against this *trade acceptance,* B receives the B/L and can claim the good when it arrives. At the stipulated date, the bank presents the trade acceptance to B for payment, and the transaction is completed. The process is illustrated in Figure 7.1, with the sequence of events indicated by circled numbers.

This lengthy exposition has been necessary to point out that the L/C is indispensable in the financing of international trade, and it is the B/L together with marine insurance that make its functioning possible. There is a system, consisting of the bill of lading, the insurance certificate, and the letter of credit, that integrates the financing of trade with its actual transportation—and this has some unexpected consequences. Assume that A sells steel from Europe to an importer in Indonesia. The importer does not want to open a L/C because the shipment will take about three months to arrive, the interest rate charged by his bank on the L/C is high, and he has no access to other sources of financing. The transaction can still take place. The exporter ships on a "transshipment B/L, discharge Singapore, option Djakarta." Sometime before the ship arrives in Singapore, say, ten days, the exporter again requests a L/C. If it is opened, he then exercises his option to discharge in Djakarta; otherwise the steel is unloaded in Singapore with the right to transship it when the L/C is finally arranged. In this case, financial conditions in one country have affected, through the bill of lading, the trade volume in a neighboring port.

A more tangible effect is seen in ports and the scheduling of liners. Letters of credit are valid only for a certain time period specified by

Fig. 7-1

THE BILL OF LADING — LETTER OF CREDIT SYSTEM

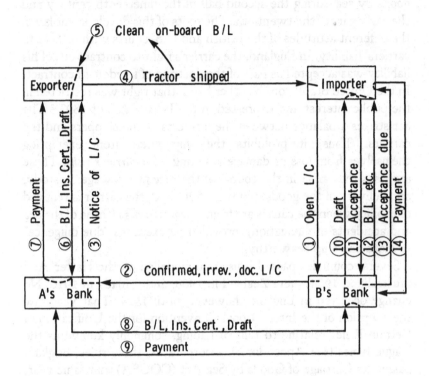

⑤ Clean on-board B/L

④ Tractor shipped

Exporter

Importer

Payment ⑦

B/L, Ins. Cert., Draft ⑥

Notice of L/C ③

Open L/C ①

Draft ⑩

Acceptance ⑪

B/L etc. ⑫

Acceptance due ⑬

Payment ⑭

② Confirmed, irrev., doc. L/C

A's Bank

B's Bank

⑧ B/L, Ins. Cert., Draft

⑨ Payment

the importer—unless the L/C is "open." Expiration dates commonly are at the end or beginning of the month. From the exporter's point of view, this is entirely acceptable because his needs for cash are usually most pronounced at that time. Therefore, the need to have the on-board B/Ls dated at a particular time results in a tendency for cargo to accumulate at a faster rate at the end of the month. Shipowners, responding to demand, schedule their ships accord-ingly. The final result is that port loadings tend to fluctuate, with peaks spanning the end and beginning of each month. In some cases, port congestion may be severe enough to cause delays and sur-charges.[1]

Until relatively recently, ocean bills of lading showed little inter-national uniformity. Different national laws allowed shipowners to insert into the bills clauses that virtually freed the carrier from any liability. The result was much difficulty, uncertainty, and litigation. In order to achieve some uniformity and to facilitate their trade, the major trading nations did pass domestic legislation for the carriage of goods by sea during the second half of the nineteenth century and the early part of the twentieth. The roots of this development lay in the different attitudes of the British and U.S. courts with respect to carriers' liability. In England, the carrier's right to contract out of his liability was accepted as part of the doctrine of freedom of contract. In the United States, on the other hand, that right was restricted in the public interest and expressed in the Harter Act of 1893.[2] The act strikes a balance between the interests of the shippers and the carriers. Thus, it prohibits the shipowners from exempting themselves from loss or damage resulting from *carrier's risks*. These are risks that arise in the course of the receipt, stowage, custody, and delivery of the goods. On the other hand, the carrier is relieved of liability when the causes are from *navigation risks* (those of the sea and accidents of navigation), provided he exercises "due diligence" to make the ship seaworthy.[3]

Several countries passed legislation modelled on the Harter Act: Australia in 1904, New Zealand in 1908, and Canada in 1910. No change occurred in England, however, until 1924. That year saw the adoption of the International Convention for the Unification of Certain Rules relating to Bills of Lading, commonly known as the Hague Rules (see Appendix B). Incorporating these rules, England passed its Carriage of Goods by Sea Act (COGSA) that same year, and the United States and Canada followed in 1936. The Hague Rules had three objectives: to standardize bills of lading, to set rules to expedite claims settlement, and to standardize the rights and obligations of both shippers and carriers. One important outcome was to specify the limit of the carrier's liability under the bill of lading, raising problems for cargo insurance, particularly when containers are used. The rules were amended in the 1968 Brussels Protocol to take into account recent developments, and UNCTAD is proposing a new Convention on the Carriage of Goods by Sea, the so-called Hamburg Rules. However, the basic principle of uniformity is accepted and there is today a high degree of uniformity in ocean transport contracts.

The *freight rates* used in liner trade are the same as in other modes—that is, class and commodity rates and "freight all kinds." These were discussed in Chapter 3, but some further comments are warranted. Liner shipping often quotes *open* rates, i.e., exceptions from class rates, for commodities for which there is keen competition. There is no fixed rule for the determination of such cargoes except that rates are opened or closed for different commodities on different routes depending on the competitive conditions.

As mentioned, *weight-volume, ship's option* are very common rates, and various surcharges are levied, after appropriate notice, for such things as entering congested ports or war zones and for carrying unusual cargoes. Agreed rates, however, are the most prominent feature in the rate structure and are manifested in the contract or *loyalty-incentive* rates. Here the shipper makes a formal contract with a carrier or a group of carriers to ship only with that carrier or group. He may contract to ship all his freight without specifying volumes, or he may specify a certain volume that may be his total freight or only part of it. The shipper is then charged a *contract* rate that is lower than the *noncontract* rate applied to other shippers. In U.S. trade, the maximum spread between the rates is set by law at 15 percent. This arrangement is also known as the *dual rate system.* One variant of this is the *deferred rebate system,* which is illegal in the United States and Canada but otherwise extensively used. Under this system, the shipper pays the noncontract rate but is given a refund at the end of a specified period, usually six months. The refund is the difference between the contract and noncontract rates or an agreed percentage of the freight paid. However, during the deferred period, the shipper must continue to ship exclusively with the contract carriers or lose the rebate.

The shipper is the one who is responsible for the payment of the freight cost. Whether this is the seller or buyer of the good is determined by the *terms of sale,* most commonly CIF or FOB. Under CIF (cost, insurance, and freight) the seller is the shipper; under FOB (free on board) the buyer has this responsibility. But how much freight the shipper pays depends on his agreement with the carrier, that is, the *terms of shipment.* Over the years, very specific terms have developed to show precisely who assumes responsibilities, when, and where with regard to the shipment. In general, the more the carrier does and the greater are his responsibilities, the higher is his rate. There are numerous such terms, some of which are shown in Table 7.1. These terms are often combined so that one applies to loading, another to unloading; for example, "ex ship's tackle/to ship's tackle," "ex ship's tackle/free out," "free in/to ship's tackle."

TABLE 7.1

Common Terms of Shipment

| Term | Costs and risks to be borne by: | |
	Carrier	Shipper
Ex ship's tackle (port of loading)	Provides slings; loads, stows in named port; carries cargo to destination	Loads into slings, brings sling to cargo hook and attaches it
To ship's tackle (port of discharge)	Brings goods on hook over the side of the ship	Settles the sling on dock and does all the rest
FAS -- free alongside (port of loading)	Handles goods from alongside of ship	Brings goods alongside
FAS (port of discharge)	Handles good until off hook along side	Removes goods from along side
fi - free in (port of loading)	Only transports goods at sea, but stows and trims cargo aboard the ship	Everything until in ship
fo - free out (port of discharge)		
fio - free in and out		
fiot - free in and out and trimmed		
fios - free in and out and stowed		

Note that the use of the word "free" in these terms means free of costs from the carrier's point of view.

Since the terms of shipment can be applied to any size shipment, their use on liners, which may carry thousands of shipments, would be unwieldy and costly both to administer and litigate, if the need arises. Therefore, these terms are used primarily in the tramp market, and tramp rates, agreed on in *charter parties,* must be understood in those terms. Most liner rates are on *liner terms,* which include everything connected with the handling and transport of the cargo from delivery to the terminal to pickup at destination.

Charter Parties

The contracts used in tramp shipping are known as charter parties and contracts of affreightment. It should be noted that these are contracts and that bills of lading, having different functions to perform, are also issued in the tramp market. There are two general types of charter parties, time and voyage, each of which offers different kinds of charters.

Time charters can be short, that is a few months, or long, stretching to twenty years. Over the years, practice and experience have resulted in standardized charter parties for various commodities on different trade routes; for example, "Cemenco" covers the cement trade between the United Kingdom and the Continent; "Baltwood" and "Benacon" are for wood to the United Kingdom from the Baltic and the United States, respectively; "Orecon" is for ore from Scandinavia to Poland; and "Gencon" is a general form used for grains, ore, salt, and wood. Shipper and carrier agree on a form and insert the freight rate and special terms and conditions that may apply, determining the obligations of the parties. The manner of payment may be, at one extreme, a *lump-sum charter* for the use of the ship for the specified period, with the shipowner taking care of all operations and costs. At the other extreme, the charterer rents the bare ship and takes care of manning and operations himself; this is a *bareboat* or *demise charter.* The rates on time charters are quoted per dwt carrying capacity and the utilization of the capacity is a matter for the charterer to decide.

Voyage charters are for ships hired for a specific trip or trips. These can be single voyage or consecutive voyage charters between specified ports. With these charters, the rates are not based on the chartered vessel's capacity, but on the tonnage of cargo actually transported. Hence, capacity utilization becomes the owner's concern.

Charter parties usually specify how long a time is allowed for loading and discharging. This time, known as *lay-days,* is carefully defined in each charter, because if the allowed time is exceeded, the charterer pays a penalty to the shipowner. This is known as *demurrage* and is usually related to the daily costs of the ship. In the opposite case, in which less time is used, the shipowner pays *despatch* money that is often a certain proportion of the demurrage rate.

Any contract for the transport of a good is a *contract of affreightment,* but in shipping the term has a specific contractual meaning. It is a contract that specifies a certain volume to be carried on a route within a specified period. Usually, but not always, it includes a schedule for both quantities and times of shipment. It may specify the exclusive use of a particular ship, but it is also common to allow the carrier to choose the ship, which may or may not be the same ship used for the whole contract. Rates are usually quoted per ton actually carried. Contracts of affreightment are often used in the carriage of major bulk commodities like iron ore, coal, and oil.

The contract of affreightment is used in areas where time charters were previously the rule. It is advantageous in situations in which there is no need for a steady flow of the commodity, but a certain volume delivered within a certain period is required. For example, a steel mill may draw down its stockpiles of coal and iron ore during the year. While there is no need for a steady replenishment, the stockpiles should be full again by the end of the year. In a case like this, there is no need to specify exclusive use of any ship; the ship-owner may be free to arrange the transport as he sees fit. Another case is a port that may have limitations as to how large a single shipment can be and how often a maximum shipment can be received. If the port can accommodate only one 60,000-dwt ship once a month, the shipper must "spot charter" such a ship every month or take a time charter. In the first case he faces uncertainty of rates and costs and in the second case scheduling problems, so it may be to his advantage to go for a contract of affreightment. This would give him certainty of both cost and delivery times and would shift the risks of market fluctuations as well as operational problems to the ship-owner. If the rates are for capacity rather than volume lifted—that is, the contract calls for a certain capacity to be made available to carry a certain volume during the specified period—then the problem is to ensure maximum utilization of that capacity. In this case the charterer may specify the exclusive use of one or more particular ships with minimum and maximum volumes to be carried each trip.

Notes

1. See "Technological Progress in Shipping," extracts from an

UNCTAD report, *Indian Shipping,* January 1972.

2. This description draws on E. Gold, *Canadian Admiralty Law: Introductory Materials,* 2nd ed. (Halifax: Dalhousie University, Faculty of Law, 1978), pp. 505–9.

3. That is, the absolute warranty of seaworthiness is replaced by "due diligence." See Chapter 8 in this volume.

Marine Insurance

The very foundation of modern international trade and shipping lies in the combination of the bill of lading, the certificate of insurance, and the letter of credit into a system, or mechanism, that allows goods to be financed and transported under acceptable conditions of risks to both shippers and carriers. While the use of any of these documents must draw upon areas of special knowledge and expertise, the field of marine insurance merits particular attention at this stage. It is based in antiquity and, as such, is extremely traditional and complex. Our purpose here is merely to present the major concepts necessary for a fuller picture of ocean shipping.[1]

Marine insurance is a very specialized business, the practice of which requires expert knowledge. Hence, there are insurance *brokers* to act as intermediaries between the *insured* and the *insurer*. The broker is the agent of the insured, but he serves both parties and receives part of the premium as his fee. The insured are the shipowners and those responsible for the cargoes.

Cargo insurance may be obtained for a single shipment on a particular voyage, in which case it is a *special policy*. A trader who ships often on various ships to many different destinations may have an *open policy*, which automatically covers shipments as they take place provided the insurer is properly notified. There are also other types of policies in use, each with specific characteristics to suit the purposes of the insured. Whether the seller or buyer is responsible for insurance depends on the *terms of sale*, which, as mentioned earlier, also determine who is the shipper. However, the shipper is not necessarily the one to pay for insurance, although under FOB and CIF terms this is the case. If the sales terms are cost and insurance (C&I), then the seller takes care of insurance, while the buyer is the shipper. The roles are reversed if the terms are cost and freight (C&F).

The importance of the bill of lading, in terms of cargo insurance, is that it proves that the goods really were aboard a specified vessel for which claims are made. Without such proof, it becomes difficult to claim reimbursement from the insurer. The amount of freight earnings the shipowner can insure is also determined by the sum of the freights given on the bills of lading for a particular voyage.

To obtain insurance, the responsible party will submit to the broker all particulars concerning the cargo and the required insurance coverage. The broker will relay the information to the insurer who, after assessing the risks involved, will either decline or accept the risk. Normally, he will specify under what conditions and for what premium he will assume the insurance. If the prospective insured party agrees to both the premium and the attached conditions, then the broker and the underwriter sign the original application, which now becomes a "binder" for both parties until an appropriate policy is issued creating specific bilateral obligations.

Since marine insurance represents a contractual obligation to both parties, the fundamental principles of contract law must be followed. This means that the contract must be the result of an offer and an acceptance, consideration must pass between the two parties, the intention must be to create legal obligations, the object of the contract must be legal, and the contract must be capable of performance. All of these requirements are generally considered to be fulfilled by the marine insurance policy. However, the contract is voided if these or some other conditions (insurable interest, good faith, and implied and expressed warranties) are violated.

Not only must the object of the policy coverage be legal, but the insured must have an *insurable interest* as well. While there is no conclusive legal definition of such interest,[2] the general concept is that the insured must "benefit from (the property's) safety or due arrival, or be prejudiced by its loss, damage, or detention, or incur liability in respect thereof."[3] Where the insured has a questionable interest, but still desires coverage, the underwriter may insure with the clause "policy proof of interest, full interest admitted." Under these conditions, known as *honor policies,* the underwriter agrees not to raise the question of insurable interest.[4] Even if all conditions of contract law have been fulfilled and there is an insurable interest, the policy can still be voided if the contract is not made in *good faith.* If one of the parties has withheld material facts that would affect the assessments of risks or benefits to the other party, the latter may void the contract.

Additionally, the injured party may void the contract if there is a breach of any of the implied or expressed warranties. *Expressed warranties* are clearly stated in the policy and are those conditions under which the policy is issued. *Implied warranties*, on the other hand, arise from the nature of the maritime venture. For instance, if a ship is insured for a trip across the North Atlantic in winter, it is implied that the insured will see to it that the ship is sufficiently crewed and equipped to be able to make the trip safely and speedily. Thus, there are two implied warranties, that of seaworthiness and that of no deviation. The underwriter has assumed responsibility based on normal risks associated with a seaworthy ship for a specific voyage expected to last a certain period of time. Therefore, if the ship is not seaworthy or departs from its expected route without justification, so that the time of exposure to risk increases, the policy may be voided. Normally, the underwriter can, by means of the policy, restrict the vessel's activities to, for example, specific ports, trade routes, or time periods. Since cargo owners have no control over seaworthiness or deviation, the practice is to waive these warranties in cargo policies.

Risks Covered by Insurance

The standard marine insurance policy contains a "perils clause" listing the principal risks that are covered:

> Touching the adventures and perils which [we the assurers are] contented to bear and do take upon us in this voyage, they are of seas, men-of-war, fire, enemies, pirates, rovers, thieves, jettisons, letters of mart and countermart, surprisals, takings at sea, arrests, restraints and detainments of all kings, princes, or people, of what nation, condition or quality soever, barratry of the masters & mariners, and all other perils, losses and misfortunes, that have or shall come to the hurt, detriment or damage of the said goods and merchandises, [and ship, etc.] or any part thereof.[5]

These perils can be restricted or expanded by additional clauses. A number of such clauses have developed over the years and are today integral parts of most policies. Among the more significant are the following.

The *sue and labor* clause entitles the insured, after a loss condition has occurred, to take whatever action is required to save the property without losing his insurance coverage. *Direct loss–proximate cause* holds the insurer liable only if the loss was a direct result of the peril insured against, i.e., direct loss, or there is a direct and unbroken chain of events that led from the peril to the loss, i.e., proximate cause. *Free of capture and seizure* (FC&S) excludes from the policy all coverage for war risks mentioned in the perils clause. Instead, special war risk policies are issued when required. The *Inchmaree* clause covers the insured for loss caused directly by negligence of the crew, accidents while loading or unloading, explosions aboard, machinery defects, and the like, provided the reasons were not because of lack of "due diligence" on the part of the owner of the ship. The name of the clause, which is properly a negligence clause, comes from a decision in 1887 pertaining to the steamer *Inchmaree*. A *collision and running down* clause covers damages to another vessel, i.e., collision, or to any other object, i.e., running down.

Loss Principles

There are two kinds of losses in marine insurance: partial and total. *Partial losses* are known as *averages* and there are two categories of these, *particular* and *general* average. Particular average, the most common reason for claims, occurs when there is a partial loss of the property of a particular interest. The loss is to be borne entirely by the particular interest that suffers it. Some cargo, by its very nature, suffers damage during transportation and would therefore constitute particular average. To avoid liability for such damage, insurers would insert a *free of particular average* (FPA) clause, or "FPA of less than x percent." This means that the policy does not cover particular average or does so only if it exceeds a certain percentage. This clause is also sometimes known as the "memorandum" clause. General average is also a partial loss, but it is borne by *all* relevant cargo interests; i.e., it is general rather than particular. It arises when there is a sacrifice by one interest for the benefit of all. For example, at a time of distress the cargo of one interest is jettisoned in order to save the ship and the remaining cargo.

In this case, the cost of the sacrificed cargo is to be shared by all those who benefitted from the action.

Total losses can also be of two kinds, actual or constructive. *Actual* loss occurs when the cargo is physically lost or destroyed. A *constructive* loss is more difficult to discern, but one example would be when cargo has been so extensively damaged that its repair would be greater than its original value. Although the cargo is not physically lost in this case, it will usually be considered a constructive total loss. For example, the ships trapped in the Suez Canal in 1967 were considered to be total constructive losses in 1972. For both actual and constructive losses, there may be total loss of a shipment or total loss of a part of a shipment. The former means that all the cargo on the ship is lost; the latter means that all the cargo of a particular interest is lost while the other shipments aboard are undamaged. Although in this case the loss represents the interest of one party, it is not particular average, but a total loss for that interest. When the underwriter pays a claim he takes over the insured's interest in the cargo and his rights to take action against third parties—that is, he has the right of *subrogation*.

Marine insurance is needed for the cargo and the ship to meet specific requirements, one of which is to cover contributions to general average. The coverage may be obtained from insurance underwriters, or, for the shipowner, from the self-insurance schemes entailed in the protection and indemnity (P&I) clubs, which will be discussed shortly. The general principles governing the definition and practice of general average are in the 1864 York-Antwerp Rules. These have undergone several revisions, the most recent one in 1974, and are usually incorporated in the bill of lading.

For the shipowner, there is a need to insure the profit he expects from a particular trip. This is *freight insurance,* the amount of which is determined from the bills of lading for the trip. The carrier must also insure the ship itself. Such *hull policies* are normally of the navigation type, that is, they give coverage only while steaming. They may be for a voyage or for a specific time, and may be for single ships or whole fleets. Hull policies may also be written to cover ships under construction and while undergoing repairs. *Voyage policies* normally contain specific expressed warranties as to the activities of the ship, whereas *time policies* have more standardized warranties relating to trade and loading requirements. *Trade warranties* may refer to the type of service of the ship and general trading areas and are important because they are relevant aspects in the risk assess-ment and, therefore, important for the setting of insurance rates. *Loading warranties* attempt to regulate quantities of certain heavy or dangerous commodities that may be carried.[6] The implied warran-ties of seaworthiness and deviation discussed earlier are also impor-tant obligations for the carrier.

Most hull policies contain deductible clauses for partial losses. These used to be in the order of 3 to 5 percent, but the proportion has steadily risen, and by 1977 the underwriters were trying to intro-duce 25-percent deductibles.[7] This has encouraged the development of cooperative self-insurance moves on the part of shipowners. In the past, a similar development led to the formation of the P&I clubs. Although hull insurance provides the shipowner with some protection against third party liability, the coverage is restricted. It gives only limited protection for collision damage and none at all for loss of life, personal injury, or cargo damage. In other words, while marine insurance covers ships and cargoes it does not insure against claims that can be made against the shipowner himself. To handle such claims, the shipowners formed protection and indemnity clubs that are basically self-insurance schemes run on a mutual basis. The clubs insure the members against liabilities to crews and others for injury or sickness and cover collision liability and damages done to ships, wharves, and cargoes. For example, the cargo owner who has insurance and has suffered a loss because of the damage done to his goods during the voyage will claim against his underwriters under the terms of his insurance policy, and when the claim is settled he will subrogate his rights in the claim to his underwriters. The latter will then claim against the shipowner to recover the loss paid under the insurance, and the shipowner will refer the matter to his protec-tion and indemnity club. If the damage caused is a liability of the shipowner, then either the shipowner will pay the claim to the underwriters or the claim will be settled directly between the club and the underwriter.

The most recent problem P&I clubs have to grapple with con-cerns oil pollution liability. As the sizes of tankers have increased, so has the magnitude of oil spills. This has led to very costly clean-up operations and a growing international concern that funds should be available for these operations. Reflecting this concern, the thrust of international legislation is to place strict liability for oil spills on shipowners,[8] and for them to show proof of proper insurance coverage. Since such coverage may be prohibitively high in the insurance market, if available, it appears the P&I clubs may further expand their activities in this area.

The Underwriters

Marine insurance has a long history. While an early form of insurance was used some 3,000 years ago by the Phoenicians, today's practices are based on those of the Italian merchants who brought marine insurance to England in the thirteenth and fourteenth centuries. In those early times, the practice was for insurance on ships and cargoes to be accepted by individual, wealthy merchants as a sideline to their regular business. Each interested merchant would take a share of a particular risk and would indicate this by noting his share and signing his name on the policy. As the names were written under the policy and under each other, the insurers became known as underwriters. Both underwriters and those seeking insurance tended to favor Lloyd's Coffee House as a place to meet, exchange information, and conduct business. This practice prospered and became Lloyd's of London. But Lloyd's is not an insurance company; it is where individuals, known as underwriters, accept insurance. Lloyd's Corporation owns the premises where these activities take place and provides various services for the underwriters, but it does not itself accept insurance. However, through its services it has become an insurance market and world center for shipping intelligence. It provides a worldwide system of Lloyd's agents, a central accounting system, and departments for the checking, signing, and sealing of policies and settling claims on behalf of the underwriters.

In addition to the individual, or private, system represented by Lloyd's, there are marine insurance *companies*. These began in England in the early eighteenth century, developed rapidly in the second half of the nineteenth, and today are very extensive and still growing. The main difference between the company and the private systems is the corporate liability of the former and the personal and individual liability of the latter.

By the end of the nineteenth century, growing trade with greater risks required greater insurance coverage. To meet this need, the private underwriters, who in the past conducted their business solely on an individual basis, began to form *syndicates*. Under this system, the underwriters joined together in groups represented by agents, combining their resources so that the syndicate was able to assume the much larger risks demanded by expanding trade. Today there are in Lloyd's well over 6,000 individual underwriters grouped into some 300 syndicates.

Companies have moved toward the syndicate system as well. In the United States, syndicates were formed in 1921 in order to facilitate the sale of war-built, government-owned ships to private shipping firms. The existing marine insurance facilities were not sufficient for adequate coverage and syndication among companies was therefore encouraged by the government. Syndicated insurance is issued in one policy that names the member companies and the share of the risk each one assumes. However, the member companies do not have joint liability; a default by one does not legally obligate the others to cover it.[9] Currently, the most active development of syndicates is taking place in Australia, where the government hopes to "bring home" its insurance business by providing expanded marine insurance resources. It is likely that syndication will become more popular and receive active government support and involvement in other nations as these nations become more aware of, and able to support, what is considered a lucrative activity.[10]

With growing vessel sizes and trade volumes even syndication may not be enough to cover a major marine disaster. *Reinsurance* offers the solution to this problem. This is an old system for spreading the risks of a venture as widely as possible. If an underwriter passes on to another underwriter part of the risks he has assumed, then reinsurance has taken place. The original insurance granted to a shipowner or merchant is direct insurance; the insurance placed by the first underwriter with another underwriter is reinsurance.[11] In the late 1970s the reinsurance market grew rapidly because of escalating costs for construction and repairs and because of larger and more valuable cargo volumes. Many smaller nations are actively pursuing the reinsurance business because the capital requirements are not as large as are those for direct insurance. Some of the oil-rich Arab nations appear to be seeking a more prominent position as suppliers of reinsurance.[12] *Coinsurance* involves the placing of direct insurance with more than one underwriter. While this is not illegal, most countries have legislation preventing double payments for claims.

Current and Future Concerns[13]

The marine insurance business is obviously closely related to sea-borne trade, but there are other factors as well that affect the business cycle of the industry. After some ups and downs during the 1960s, the industry went into a steep decline in the 1970s. The reasons given are numerous. Part of the decline is attributed to internal factors such as increased competition within the industry, which is felt during and after a peak period. When business is good, claims settlements tend to be more generous and underwriters less risk averse. New underwriters enter the field, and rate-cutting practices reach greater than normal levels. This, together with the increasing settlements, leads to declining profits. The conditions gain momentum because recognition of the situation is slow to come, since profit measurement in the industry is exceptionally difficult due to outstanding claims and lengthy settlement procedures. When underwriters finally recognize the situation they take a harder line and withdraw or curtail previous concessions. This meets with opposition and tends to increase competitive rate shopping.[14] After a shaking out period, the situation reverses to boom conditions.

External factors have significant and more long-term effects on the insurance industry. This has been particularly evident in the depression of the late 1970s, regarded as much steeper than those in the past. The rapid changes in the world economic situation have created many problems for the industry, particularly worldwide inflation. Ship repair costs were estimated to have risen by 85 percent over the six-year period from 1968 to 1975.[15] Since insurance policies do not set specific time limits within which damaged vessels must be repaired, the estimated rates may result in losses if the repairs are delayed in a period of rising prices. One of the reasons for delay in effecting repairs is slow claims adjustment procedures, unavoidable at times because of the often lengthy process of determining causal factors.

Income from insurance policy sales has slipped because of the stagnation of the shipbuilding and shipping industries. World tonnage has increased faster than required by world trade, causing more ships to be laid up and scrapped. The lay-up of VLCCs and ULCCs is causing much concern within the industry because there are few safe deepwater harbors for these ships. This has led to concentra-tions of the ships in the same anchorages, and, as the potential for multiple losses has increased, the current rate level is seen as too low for the risks involved.[16] The early risk estimates for these vessels are now considered far too low in relation to recorded casualty rates. Formerly, the vessels were judged to be extremely safe because of their size, but two factors have emerged that dis-prove the earlier assessments. First, they are very deep-draft vessels and, because many of the existing navigational charts are out of date, are in some instances moving in virtually uncharted waters. The second factor relates to the fact that the very size of the vessels makes salvage operations impossible because there is no equipment large enough to carry out such operations for certain types of ac-cidents.

There are other problems as well. Casualty rates and absolute dollar losses have been steadily increasing, due in part to the VLCCs and the ULCCs. Also to blame is the fact that human error and negligence have increased dramatically.[17] The International Union of Marine Insurance feels that some method must be found to raise international standards relating to the training, composition, certification, and recertification of ships' crews and officers.[18]

Marine underwriters are also concerned with the effects the adoption of the 1968 Brussels Protocol might have on the industry. This protocol is intended to revise the Hague Rules. The proposed amendments do assist in the definition and valuation of container-ized shipments, a subject of much legal debate and relatively little uniformity. The protocol also proposes to extend the carrier's liabil-ity substantially, and this is meeting with strong opposition. There is a definite feeling amongst marine underwriters that increased shipowner liability would completely change the character of the cargo insurance business and result in increased transportation costs. The shipowners would need to increase their coverage through the P&I clubs, which could be more expensive than con-ventional cargo insurances.[19] The less-developed countries, on the other hand, are strongly supporting movements to increase carrier liability—even suggesting that the Brussels Protocol does not go far enough in that direction. Thus, both LDCs and shipowners oppose the protocol, but for different reasons, and the protocol, also known as the 1968 Visby Amendments, is in force without being univer-sally accepted. Reflecting more closely the LDCs view, the United Nations, through UNCTAD, proposed in 1978 its own Convention on the Carriage of Goods by Sea. The convention took place in Hamburg and will be known as the Hamburg Rules when it enters into force.[20]

Underwriters are also concerned with the increasingly technological complexity of maritime activities for which they are asked to provide insurance coverage. In addition to this technological sophistication, many maritime activities could result in types of marine disasters as yet unknown to the world. The uncer-tainty associated with the possible outcome of a marine disaster makes quantification of the risk extremely difficult. In order to en-sure that the underwriter has sufficient capital to withstand a disaster, he must be able to adequately assess risk potentials and set insurance rates at levels that will provide the income commensurate with the risk.

The inability to utilize past loss records as a guide for future losses presents the underwriter with increasingly difficult problems in the field of risk assessment and rate setting. Two examples of current concerns in this area are to be found in the increasing carriage by sea of dangerous cargoes and in offshore oil drilling activities. Liquefied natural gas carriers have already had minor accidents. The size of the LNG carriers now in operation as well as those currently under construction or ordered, has escalated considerably, so that a major disaster involving one of these ships could severely strain the resources of the marine insurance industry. The second example concerns the offshore drilling rigs that have also increased in number, size, and type. Experts in the field have frankly admitted that the dynamic stresses of the sea to which these rigs are exposed are unknown quantities and that it is not so much a question of whether these rigs will fail, but rather when it will happen.[21] The insurance underwriter is therefore faced with the task of attempting to assemble a body of expertise capable of coping with the increas-ingly complex and seemingly insurmountable task of assessing and quantifying unknown risks so that the marine insurance industry can survive and continue to provide necessary marine insurance protection.

Rising nationalism in many nations is also contributing to uncertainty within the industry. As more countries attempt to bring home their own insurance in order to retain the profits and benefits of this business, restrictions are springing up that limit the international character of the industry. Many in the insurance field see rising nationalism as contributing to decreasing competition because of barriers prohibiting the buyer from searching worldwide for the best available coverage. Insurance underwriters fear that this could lead to increased transportation costs as well as underinsurance coverage. Marine insurance may not then be as effective in the future as it has been in the past in its role as an essential facilitating service to world trade.[22]

Notes

1. This chapter draws upon five principal sources: Anne Empke, "Ocean Marine Insurance," unpublished paper, Canadian Marine Transportation Centre, Dalhousie University, 1978; E. Gold, *Canadian Admiralty Law: Introductory Materials,* 2nd ed. (Halifax: Dalhousie University, Faculty of Law, 1978); John Nuckles, "Marine Insurance: Its Legal and Economic Attributes," unpublished paper, Graduate School of International Studies, University of Denver, 1978; H. A. Turner, *The Principles of Marine Insurance* (London: Stone & Cox Publications, 1971); and W. Winter, *Marine Insurance—Its Principles and Practice,* 3rd ed. (New York: McGraw-Hill, 1952).

2. Nuckles, "Marine Insurance," p. 12.

3. Turner, *Principles of Marine Insurance,* p. 22.

4. Nuckles, "Marine Insurance," p. 13.

5. Winter, *Marine Insurance,* p. 175.

6. Empke, "Ocean Marine Insurance," pp. 13–14.

7. *Shipping World and Shipbuilding,* January 1977.

8. In 1975 IMCO adopted an International Convention on Civil Liability for Oil Pollution Damage.

9. Winter, *Marine Insurance,* pp. 28, 281–83.

10. Empke, "Ocean Marine Insurance," p. 23.

11. Winter, *Marine Insurance,* p. 348.

12. Empke, "Ocean Marine Insurance," p. 22.

13. Ibid., pp. 24–29.

14. V. Dover, *A Handbook to Marine Insurance*, 5th ed. (London: H. F. & G. Witherby, 1957), p. 29.

15. *Shipping World and Shipbuilding*, January 1975.

16. Ibid., March 1975.

17. Ibid., August 1976 (comments by R. Taylor, retired chairman of the Salvage Association).

18. Ibid., March 1975.

19. *Fairplay International Shipping Weekly*, December 11, 1975, p. 156.

20. Gold, *Canadian Admiralty Law*, pp. 539–41, app. 2.

21. *Shipping World and Shipbuilding*, January 1977.

22. *Fairplay International Shipping Weekly*, September 18, 1975, p. 58.

9

Rate Determination: The Tramp and Liner Markets

Demand for and Supply of Shipping

The common approach when discussing demand for shipping is to present statistical time series of the quantities of different kinds of seaborne goods together with a description of the major trade routes on which they move. The supply of tonnage is similarly presented in terms of numbers, types, and sizes of available ships. While this approach does provide information on past developments, identifies changes, and gives useful insight into various causal relationships, it is not suitable for our purposes. We seek general principles to aid in the understanding of the demand and supply sides in shipping. These principles, in turn, may serve as the basic points of departure for detailed and specific studies that are necessary if the interest is on particular commodities or trade routes.[1]

Demand

Demand for ocean transport, as for all modes, is derived demand. It is derived from world trade which, in turn, is a function of the growth in the gross national products (GNP) of the countries participating in such trade.[2] The relationship between a country's GNP and international trade is expressed in its *marginal propensity to import* – that is, that fraction of its income growth that is spent on imports. Since one country's imports must be another country's exports, and these have a strong impact on the GNP, it follows that a large economic power can affect world trade substantially by its growth policies. Therefore, a basic factor in determining demand for shipping is the economic expansion in major economies like the United States, Japan, and the European Economic Community (EEC). The periodic entry of the USSR and China into some trades, notably grain, has had significant short-term effects, and their permanent participation in international trade would affect long-term demand. For specific commodities and trades, the GNPs and growth policies of the trading partners are relevant.

Any change in either the *volume* or *distance* of transportation will affect the demand for tonnage. Hence, statistics are most meaningfully expressed in both weight carried and ton-miles, where one ton-mile is defined as one ton transported one mile. An increase in volume, given the distance, will necessitate more, not larger, ships, because the optimal ship size is mainly a function of the transport distance. Conversely, an increase in distance, with the volume given, or an increase in both volume and distance, will result in an increase in the size of the optimal ship. It follows that the *location of sources* closer to markets, as with North Sea oil, increases the demand for smaller ships, but, for example, the closing of the Suez Canal resulted in demand for larger ships. It should be noted that although it is technically feasible to build tankers of up to one million dwt, both volumes and distances—not to mention port facilities—must be such that this size is optimum.

Political and *natural factors* also exert influence on demand. For example, crop failures in one part of the world lead to increased grain shipments, with repercussions in the tramp market both when these countries enter the market and when they withdraw. That is, a demand "bulge" has occurred: in the first instance, demand increases sharply, only to decrease as sharply when the transport is completed. The needs of the USSR, China, and India provided several examples of this during the 1970s. A major increase in political tensions between the "superpowers" may lead to stockpiling with increased demand for shipping. Again, this results in a demand "bulge." This is also the case when tensions arise in an area that supplies important commodities such as oil. If industrial management expects supplies to be cut off or prices to rise significantly, private stockpiling is likely to occur.

Finally, *technological relationships* are important. For example, there is a certain relationship between GNP and energy consumption. While this is not a rigidly fixed relationship, a growing GNP requires more energy, and this has effects on the oil, gas, and coal trades. Similarly, the production of steel requires iron ore and coal. Hence, trades in these two commodities are dependent on steel production, which in turn depends on numerous domestic and international factors. The coal trade is particularly affected by these aspects. Steel production requires low-sulphur coal, of which the United States has for some time been the world's largest exporter. Because of the oil crisis and air pollution standards in the United States, domestic demand for coal may affect exports. This would in turn affect trade routes and demand for shipping as new sources may have to fill the gap. Also, as mentioned earlier, the consumer of raw materials needs a certain flow of these inputs depending on his production processes and overall purchasing and distribution system. On the whole, demand for bulk and neo-bulk cargoes, both dry and liquid, have a tendency to fluctuate more than demand for general cargo, which is primarily manufactured goods. The most important bulk cargoes today are, in descending order, oil, iron ore, coal, grain, bauxite and aluminum, and phosphate rock. The first three groups, and particularly iron ore and coal, are closely related in terms of demand for shipping. Demand for grain transport is dependent on natural forces, while bauxite and aluminum, as well as phosphate, reflect general growth factors. There are several other minor bulk commodities, including neo-bulk, each of which responds to various economic factors before becoming part of the demand for shipping.[3]

It is important to note, however, that various transport demands for different commodities affect to some extent freight rates in all markets because there are links between the various submarkets. For example, the multipurpose vessel, or tween-decker, can be chartered away from tramp service by a liner operator and vice versa. The various specialized ships, some of which are neo-bulk carriers, also have effects on the general cargo market. Most pronounced, however, is the linkage between dry and liquid bulk carriage provided by the OBO carrier and the periodic entry of tankers into the grain trade.

Although the volume of general cargo can fluctuate widely from year to year, the direction of the trade – the trade routes – is slow to change. In the bulk trade, however, trade routes change often and markedly as shifts occur in both sources of supply and markets. As such shifts occur, volumes and distances change, and this affects demand for tonnage.

Supply

The total supply of world tonnage is usually expressed in terms of the number of ships of different types and their deadweight capacities. Thus, at the end of 1977 there was a total supply of some 22,000 ships representing about 625 million dwt. This fleet carried close to 3.5 billion metric tons of various cargoes. (See Appendix A.) Obviously, each deadweight ton of capacity carried an average of about 6 cargo tons during the year. In other words, the *operational capacity* of the existing tonnage is substantially greater than the deadweight capacity indicates. (In economic terminology, the deadweight capacity is a stock concept, and operational capacity is a flow.) At the end of a time period we can calculate what operational capacity the fleet has shown itself capable of during that period. But whether this is a complete or partial utilization of that capacity cannot be ascertained, because, for any particular ship, it clearly depends on its speed and size, since these determine the number of trips and carrying capacity on each trip. The only thing that can be said with any degree of certainty is that the operational capacity is flexible and allows a relatively elastic response of total supply to changing market conditions.

The main factors determining operational capacity are the *speed* and *size* of a ship. As we have seen, these are also the two major aspects of choosing an *optimal ship* (see Chapters 5 and 6) and are determined by considering service characteristics and economic and technical factors. Factors that would tend toward larger ships would include port improvements with faster turn-around, longer distances, long-term availability of cargoes, as well as large seasonal fluctuations. Also, large cargo volumes in one direction only with no back-hauls available would tend to make the optimal ship larger, as would low frequency of service and the carriage of low-value cargoes.

With respect to speed, there are both economic and technological aspects to consider. Higher speeds are encouraged by the transport of high-value cargoes. Cheaper fuel, shorter turn-around, and high freight rates are also incentives toward higher speeds. With such speeds, high capital charges for the operator can be spread over more voyages per year, and if there are high daily costs the productivity of the ship per unit of time increases. Also, conditions of growing trade and keen competition would incline the operator toward higher-speed vessels. Technological factors that facilitate these tendencies include lower fuel consumption and machinery weight per horse power, as well as improved hull and propeller designs. Each ship is designed for a certain *service speed* that utilizes the machinery most efficiently. The ship can exceed this speed by "forced steaming," but the fuel costs increase substantially. However, as ship sizes have grown over the years, the tendency has also been toward higher service speeds. On the whole, therefore, the operational capacity of the world fleet has increased and must be assumed to be large.

At any one time, the *existing stock* of tonnage is either actively trading, seeking employment, or in lay-up. Ships in lay-up are simply those that at existing freight rates are unable to cover even variable costs. The stock increases over time by new buildings and decreases through scrappings and casualties (strandings and losses at sea). If there is a demand bulge, supply increases in the very short run by increased speeds, fuller space utilization, and fewer and shorter trips in ballast—that is, a greater utilization of operational capacity occurs. Next, as freight rates rise, the most efficient ships in lay-up are put into operation until the total stock of tonnage is employed; this is the short-run response. Thereafter, there is a time lag until new ships come into operation, i.e., the long run. New orders placed in response to the high freight market materialize with a time lag of nine to eighteen months, which is often when the demand bulge has eased. A tonnage surplus now emerges with pressures on the freight rates, and supply responds by decreasing the utilization of its operational capacity. Ships cut speeds ("slow-steaming"), sail less frequently with less than full cargoes, and ballast voyages increase. In due time, laying-up begins again and orders for new buildings decline. These peaks and valleys of demand for new ships affect the shipyards. (This process is well illustrated by the expanding "cobweb" analysis.)

The shipping cycles have given rise to tonnage stabilization schemes, shipping conferences, and arguments as well as agreements over cargo preferences. As mentioned, overall supply responds very quickly with adjustments in speed. However, there are costs connected with the laying-up of ships, keeping them there, and bringing them back into service. Therefore, this short-run supply response is relatively slow in taking effect, and this means that, in depressed times, the oversupply is likely to last for some time. Similarly, if the market picks up quickly, the shortage of tonnage will last until layups are activated. How quickly laid-up ships enter the picture depends on the operators' cost structures and some other considerations. Depending on flag and type of operations, a shipowner must consider such things as the goodwill of his customers and his social responsibilities to the crew and other employees. This means that ships with similar cost structures may still have different lay-up points. Once in lay-up, the question is how long to keep the ship there. The answer depends on expectations for the future. If the freight rates are expected to last for a short term only, then the decision may be to wait for an improving market. If expectations are for a long-term depression, then there is the possibility that obsolescence may overtake the ship, leaving a choice of selling or scrapping it. Secondhand ship prices are directly related to the freight market, so in a long-term depression this choice may not offer much attraction. Scrapping, on the other hand, depends partly on demand for scrap, which, in turn, is dependent on the steel industry's position—and one factor here may be the demand of shipyards for new construction material. Whatever action is taken, it has effects on the future supply situation, since selling merely changes the ownership of the tonnage, while scrapping decreases the existing stock.

Supply in the various submarkets is affected by the above and by the connection the markets have with each other. Conventional liner tonnage is affected by the availability of tween-deck tramps, and vice versa. Tanker and bulk carriage are closely related through the combination carriers. Only specialty carriage and the sophisticated container vessel are largely insulated from the other markets. However, a decline on one trade route would prompt these ships to relocate, thus affecting supply on other routes. Through such "spillover" effects, the adjustment in the supply of special tonnage on one route is soon shared by similar special ships on other routes.

The supply of tonnage in the tramp market, which includes both dry and liquid bulk, is also affected by chartering arrangements.

Ships on time charter are obviously not available to meet an increase in demand, so the change in demand interacts only with the free tonnage, which may be a large or a small amount at any given time.[4] As ships go off charter, they affect the free supply, but there is no relationship between a demand bulge and the increase in free tonnage due to the expiring of charters. Hence, short-term demand and supply can fluctuate widely and independently of each other causing wide fluctuations in the freight rates.

Rate Setting

The Tramp Market

Tramp rates are agreed rates, and there are no classifications or tariffs for this type of service. The structure of the tramp market (the conditions under which the rates are negotiated) is commonly regarded as freely competitive with rates set by market forces, i.e., the free interplay of demand and supply. In general, tramp rates, be they spot or time, tend to fluctuate rapidly and violently in response to even marginal developments in demand for and supply of tonnage.

To recapitulate what has been said earlier, tramps are general purpose ships and usually carry bulky, homogeneous primary products of low unit value. For such products, low transportation costs are of major importance while speed and regularity of service are of minor importance. The tramps carry cargoes whenever they are available to and from whatever ports demand and supply them. They operate under charter parties that are largely standardized. It is interesting to note that this standardization is the outcome of attempts to control competition in the tramp market. The first such attempt was the Sailing Ship Owners' International Union, formed in 1905 for the purpose of setting minimum rates on long trade routes such as the wheat trade from Australia. The Baltic and White Sea Conference was formed the same year in Copenhagen to set minimum rates on the wood trade from Russia and Scandinavia. Adherence to the rates was on a voluntary basis. Because of widespread disregard of the rules, both attempts were soon abandoned, and the latter was replaced by the Baltic and International Maritime Conference (BIMCO) formed in 1936.

In 1934 European tanker owners formed the International Tanker Owners' Association (INTERTANKO) and introduced the Schier-water plan. Named for INTERTANKO's president, the plan did not attempt direct rate regulations; instead, an *international pool* was established. A certain percentage of total revenues was set aside for the pool for distribution to the owners of tankers with-drawn from the markets—i.e., tankers laid up. The pool was quite successful in keeping tanker rates at a profitable level. Partly as a result of the pool's success, the English Parliament passed, in 1935, the British Shipping Assistance Act, which made provisions for sub-sidies to British tramp shipping and gave low-interest loans for modernizing the fleet. The subsidies gave British ships an advantage in the world markets, and when the Tramp Shipping Administrative Committee put forth a plan for international cooperation in keeping freight rates up, most maritime nations responded positively. Minimum rates were set for the grain trades from Australia, River Plate, and U.S. Gulf and Atlantic ports to Europe. There were problems, but the regulation of tramp rates in these trades worked satisfactorily until war broke out in 1939.

The Tramp Shipping Administrative Committee controlled only three of the most important grain trades, but this had some effects on the nonregulated trades. If the demand for transport in the regulated trades fell as a result of the higher rates, some ships became unemployed in these trades and were forced to move into other trades. This should have resulted in falling rates in these trades, but since there was no control on supply of ships in either the regulated or unregulated trades, there could not, in a competi-tive market, be different rates in the two areas. To a certain extent, it would be worth the carrier's time to wait for cargoes in the regulated ports. As long as the average return in the regulated ports equalled the average revenue in the nonregulated trades, no ships would move from the former trades to the latter. But if the waiting time and costs of the former were large, so that the average revenue in the nonregulated market exceeded that of the regulated, then there would be a movement to the nonregulated market and rates would fall there. Should waiting time and costs decrease, the op-posite would occur and rates would rise in the nonregulated market. That this actually happened has been shown by W. A. Lewis.[5]

The low tramp rates in the 1950s again brought about proposals for some control schemes. The International Chamber of Shipping suggested in 1958 the formation of a compensation pool scheme that, like the tanker pool, would compensate owners for laying-up ships. This particular proposal had no success, but at the end of 1962 tramp and tanker owners again got together on an international basis to consider the possibilities of a worldwide "stabilization scheme"—i.e., some kind of rate regulation. The tanker owners revived INTERTANKO to administer a new International Tanker Recovery Scheme, which went into operation in 1963. It operated on the same principles as the prewar tanker pool described above, but contributions were based on deadweight rather than gross profits. The scheme was not successful and both it and INTERTANKO were dissolved at the end of 1969. Two years later, however, a new group was formed, called the International Association of Independent Tanker Owners—again abbreviated INTERTANKO.

The scheme for the dry cargo trades did not materialize. But market forces have brought about a different type of international cooperation in tramp trades in the form of *bulk shipping pools*. These developed in the 1960s in response to the tonnage demands of very large shippers. Large exporters and importers of raw materials began to pool their purchasing and shipping requirements, thereby gaining bargaining power with respect to carriers.[6] The latter responded by forming carrier groups—the bulk shipping pools—which gave them both a stronger bargaining position and the means to allocate and utilize their tonnage more efficiently to meet the large shippers' requirements. The members of these pools manage their own ships under their own flags, but the pool itself coordinates the scheduling, does the marketing, and signs the contracts of affreightment.

The various schemes of the past contributed to the standardization of charter parties, which in turn made it easier for the market participants to digest more information. Inasmuch as the access to available information is one measure of a market's degree of competition, it can be said that the final outcome was a more perfect market than previously. Information on demand and supply is spread through the market by means of central freight markets and a well-established network of brokers and agents. The most important central market is the Baltic Mercantile and Shipping Exchange in London where chartering brokers, supervised by the Institute of

Chartered Shipbrokers, specialize in various trades. The *fixtures*, i.e., sales of space, and their terms are published and easily available in trade journals such as *Lloyd's List and Shipping Gazette, Fairplay International Shipping Weekly, Hansa,* and the *Daily Freight Register,* which also provide general market information. All ships are classified by the various independent classification agencies as to insurance and carriage characteristics, thus making it possible to close a contract without actually seeing the ship. All of these factors bring alternative sources of supply of tramp tonnage to the attention of any prospective shipper, and account for a high degree of mobility and elasticity in the market.

On balance, aside from some questions about the bulk shipping pools,[7] the tramp market evidences all the characteristics of a highly competitive market: there are many buyers and sellers; exit and entry are relatively easy, for example by bareboat charters (although financial barriers are becoming important); products shipped and services rendered are largely homogeneous; and information is easily and quickly available. Consequently, the freight rates are considered set primarily by market forces. However, it should be kept in mind that only about 10 percent of the tramp tonnage is at any one time available for spot fixing and these are the rates reported. Time charters and contracts of affreightment are usually fixed through direct negotiations and not normally reported. Hence, it is difficult to say unequivocally that this is a free market–or that it is not–although it is commonly regarded as such.

The same comments apply to the tanker market, where about 35 percent of the tonnage is owned by the major oil companies. They charter another 40–45 percent on very long terms from the private owners, leaving 20–25 percent of tanker tonnage for spot fixing. This portion of the fleet, known as the swing factor, is the tonnage for which fixtures are reported. In dry cargo fixtures, the rates are reported in actual money per ton of capacity or cargo carried, but the rates in the tanker trades are given in *Worldscale* (WS), which is a differential rate. This type of rate has been used for a long time under different names: The British Ministry of Transport (MOT) scale and the U.S. Maritime Commission (USMC) scale were both replaced by the International Scale (Intascale), which was replaced in 1969 by the present Worldscale. Rates reported as WS express a certain proportion of the standard rate–WS30 means that the rate is 30 percent of the standard. The standard itself is constructed in such a way that the daily revenue is the same for a given ship on all routes at a given WS. For example, using completely fictitious figures, a 100,000-dwt tanker is fixed at WS100 from Rastanura to Rotterdam with a round trip taking 60 days. The daily revenue for this ship should be the same as if it had gone at WS100 from Curaçao to Helsinki which takes, say, 40 days. If WS100 for the first trip is given in scale as $20 per ton, then total revenue on that trip is $2 million, or $33,333 per day. The same daily earnings should apply to the Curaçao-Helsinki trip; therefore, if these were real figures, the WS100 rate for this latter route would be $13.33.

These rates pertain to the swing tonnage. However, the actual transport cost of oil during any particular time period is the weighted average of these rates plus the various previous spot and time charters that are in effect during this period. Such a rate, the monthly average freight rate assessment (AFRA), is calculated by a panel of the Tanker Brokers Association in London and is expressed in WS and for different size tankers. This rate is not a proper shipping rate but rather a pricing tool used exactly in the manner implied by the name. Oil companies use this rate to assess what transport cost should be added to each ton of oil transported during the next month.[8] The AFRA rate is also used by the oil companies as the rate for their own ships, which, as integrated carriers, would otherwise require some alternate procedure for transfer pricing.

At the end of 1977, INTERTANKO was again considering a stabilization scheme for the tanker market. Past schemes attempted to affect rates by controlling the supply through the laying-up of tonnage, but the new prospective plan takes a more direct approach. Owners would coordinate their chartering policies, possibly by forming a tanker cartel, and simply set a minimum WS under which they would refuse to charter any VLCC.[9] Whether such a scheme may work depends on the operational capacity of the tonnage owned and already under charter to the oil companies. This capacity must be large because the ships have been voyaging at much less than service speed—i.e., slow-steaming—since early 1974.

The Liner Market

The very nature of liner service—that is, scheduled service on fixed routes—makes this an oligopolistic market. There are relatively few sellers of a service that is homogeneous or only slightly differentiated, and there is substantial lack of information for both sellers and buyers. Collusion is a common occurrence in such markets and, in shipping, would be manifested in such practices as administrative pricing, market sharing, and outright cartels.[10] In these respects, shipping is not different from other industries. The cartels in the liner trades are known as *shipping conferences*. Whether these conferences are "good" or "bad" institutions is a complex and hotly debated policy issue, but in keeping within the format of this book, we will attempt only to clarify the principles and concepts of the conference system. (However, because of the importance of the system and the controversies surrounding it, we will briefly cover the main issues and discussions in an appendix to this chapter.)

Conferences use classifications and tariffs. The rates are of the kinds described in Chapter 4 and are set within the conference system. The first conference was the Transatlantic Shipping Conference formed in 1868 for the trade between New York and Europe.[11] However, since this conference did not reach an agreement to control rates until 1902, the first real price-setting conference was the Calcutta Conference, formed in 1875 for the trade between England and India. The conference was a logical development in the liner trade, which, itself, was a logical outcome of trading patterns.

As the Western world became industrialized and trade grew, the transportation of goods by sea became increasingly separated from the ownership of the goods traded and shipped. That is, vertical disintegration occurred and shipping became a separate service industry. As long as trading was dominated by large companies and the ships were small, there was no difficulty for such a company to charter and load a whole ship. However, social and commercial developments such as increased urbanization and use of money led to a greater number of small traders. At the same time technological progress led to the building of larger ships. The smaller traders were not able to ship in full shiploads and, to keep inventories low, there was an increased demand for regular, dependable service. The growth of international trade provided the economic basis for the establishment of such services,[12] and the introduction of steam made them possible.

Continued growth and trade led to the proliferation of liner services and fierce competition on high volume routes. Since liner service entails relatively high fixed cost, competition can force the
rates far below average costs. That is to say, the liner company has
very small marginal costs and can, therefore, accept goods at a very
low rate rather than let them go to a competitor. A price war between liners themselves or between liners and tramps can drive
rates down to very low levels and lead to the elimination of the
financially weak carriers. This is what happened, and the result was
the first conference and a continuing tendency in the liner market
toward concentration and agreements to restrict unbridled competition. This development must also be seen in the light of the difference between the domestic and international common carriers. In
domestic transportation, the common carrier has an obligation to
serve, but also the right to be properly compensated. Both the
obligation and the right are implemented through *domestic regulations* of services, rates, and competition. In other words, while the
carrier is subject to regulated obligations because of the public interest, that same public interest also ensures him of some advantageous rights in terms of competition and rates. An example is his
right to a "reasonable" rate of return, countered by his obligation to
continue service until permitted to quit. In *international shipping* it is
different. Except for U.S.-subsidized lines and some state-owned
companies, the liner operator has no regulatory obligation to serve
any trade for any particular time. It is for the ship operator to decide
when and where to begin and terminate his liner services. Corresponding to the lack of obligation, there are no rights with respect
to rates of return, freight rates, and competitive circumstances. (It is
this lack of service obligation that gives rise to fears that a country
may be deprived of scheduled shipping services unless it has its own
merchant marine.) In the absence of publicly regulated rights and
obligations, the industry has developed a system of *self-regulation* by
means of shipping conferences.

In most countries, liner shipping is concentrated into relatively
few large companies, often with active government encouragement.
This has facilitated the formation of effective conferences, most
often organized with a chairman, headquarters, and secretariat to
administer the agreements. The members meet to discuss conference issues at owners' or principals' meetings several times a year

as conditions require. There is, however, a great deal of secrecy surrounding the actual proceedings.

A conference can be *open* or *closed*. In the former case, any appli-
cant able and willing to comply with the rules is admitted. Such conferences are, by law, the only ones allowed in U.S. and Canadian
trades. In most other trades they are closed, which means that admission is at the discretion of the current members of the conference. A shipping company can be a *member* or an *associate
member*. In the latter case he has no voting rights, but he has committed himself to adhere to all rules of the conference. A liner carrier
who is neither a member nor an associate is known as an *independent*.

Agreements to control competition range from "gentlemen's
agreements" to formal cartels, the latter being the shipping conference. They are organized by formal agreement, and the basic purpose is to stabilize conditions by setting freight rates and sailing
schedules on the relevant trade routes. The rate setting takes the
form of either fixed or minimum tariff rates. Some go beyond price
fixing and include pooling agreements, in which each member is
guaranteed a share of the cargoes or the revenues. In a price-fixing
conference there is scope for service competition – i.e., the cargo
goes to the best-equipped and fastest ships – but in a pooling agreement there is no competitive element and earnings are apportioned
according to a formula agreed upon by the participants. The argument for pooling is that some carriers, through service competition,
may be left with a disproportionate share of low-rated cargoes.
They would then tend to curtail their service unless they have a
share of the revenues from the more desirable carriage.

Conferences operate between two ports, two ranges, one port to
one range, or one range to one port. Hence, blankets are commonly
used. There are usually different conferences for inbound and outbound routes. Sometimes it may be possible for the shipper to ship
overland from one conference territory to that of another. For example, in the mid-1960s it was possible to ship cargo from northern
Italy to the United States via northern European ports at a lower
rate (including the cost of rail transport) than from Italian ports.
The natural response from the conferences involved was to reach an
interconference agreement.[13] Later, the very same problem, this time
occasioned by the ease with which containers can be transshipped,

prompted the concerned conferences to attempt, unsuccessfully, to expand their territory – to become, in effect, a *superconference*.[14] Interconferences as well as superconference agreements do exist in several trades,[15] the latter appearing to be conferences of conferences.

Where service competition is possible, it often leads to higher costs, giving the carrier an incentive to attempt to increase his load factor by evading the agreement. This can be done by accepting false commodity classifications and secret rebates. Hence, conferences often have control agencies to inspect and ensure proper classification. Also, to ensure compliance, conferences require a good faith or performance bond from the members. Service competition also gives an incentive to provide excess capacity and this, seemingly an inevitable consequence of the conferences, is one of the major arguments against the system.

In addition to some competition from other conferences, particularly in container trades, there is competition from tramps who occasionally top up with general cargo or containers. Independent liner services also pose powerful competition because they are often able to "skim the cream" off the traffic, thus inviting rate wars. Conferences have in the past used fighting ships to meet such competition. Now considered illegal in most countries, a fighting ship is a vessel that, regardless of cost, would duplicate or do better than the independent in terms of sailings, service, and rates. The costs of the fighting ship are borne by all members of the conference. However, another method of meeting outside competition (and providing a long-term basis for conference services) is for conferences to rely on *tying arrangements,* designed to tie the shippers to the use of conference ships. There are two such arrangements, the *dual rate* and the *deferred rebate* systems, both of which were described in Chapter 7. The rate setting itself is problematic: Since the members are different with respect to financial strength, cost structure, and trade interests, their optimum rate level is also different, making it technically difficult to establish the most rational rates for the conference as a whole. From the theoretical point of view, the solution would be to find the optimum rate level for the whole conference and combine this with an equalization fund to compensate the members losing by such an arrangement. This is essentially the procedure for pooling agreements. However, since detailed cost

analyses are required and this necessitates access to abundant confidential information from the firms, it is doubtful that optimal rates
exist even in these conferences.

Considering all the above, it is clear that rate setting is based on
the principle of "what the traffic will bear," with the difference between this and the value of service principle being as described in
Chapter 3. The tariff structure entails cross-subsidization, or discrimination, among shippers and commodities. Because of shipping's
international character, such discrimination also applies to trade
routes—that is, nations—and as a result conferences, their rates,
and rate-setting principles have become the subject of much controversy (see the addendum).

While tramp rates tend to fluctuate widely, liner rates are relatively stable—that is, their level rises, but there are no violent fluctuations.[16] One explanation lies in the operations ratio—the ratio of
operation costs to total revenue. Shipowners try to maintain an "acceptable" operations ratio.[17] If, over a certain period, the ratio has
increased, the solution is to lower costs or increase revenue. In an
inflationary period, and with high fixed costs, there is relatively little opportunity to affect the costs. Hence, the operator fairly rapidly
reaches the point of applying to the conference for a rate increase.
As more and more of the members move into this situation, rates are
finally raised. Conference rates are, therefore, more sensitive to
changes in costs than in demand. This means that rates tend to rise
over time as costs increase, but also tend to be stable in periods of
fluctuating demand.

As a final point, it should be noted that each conference serves its
own particular route. Therefore, while some generalizations can be
made, it must also be recognized that each conference operates
under its own agreement with policies and problems dictated by the
trade it serves.

Addendum: Conferences

There has always been a great deal of controversy connected with
the conference system. Conferences are often referred to as
monopolies, but a more appropriate term is oligopolies, because their
behavior must always allow for the possibility of outside competition if freight rates are too high. However, the potential monopoly

power is a concern that has been with us from the very beginning of the system. Professor Marx, in his classic study of conferences,[18] mentions a British Blue Book of 1897 that complains about differential rates injuring British trade. Regardless of the originally defensive reasons for forming conferences, the increased complaints raised the question of the abuse of monopoly power. The argument was that if conferences were strong enough to prevent rates from falling in a slump, then they were probably also strong enough to take advantage of a boom.

In 1902 the first official investigation into conferences took place when the Straits Settlements appointed a commission to investigate the effects of the conferences on the trade of the colony. The findings were that secret rebates and substantial rate increases had occurred since the conferences began operating. Several investigations followed, the most important of which were the Royal Commission on Shipping Rings (1906) in England and the Alexander Committee (1912) in the United States. The findings of the two groups were essentially the same: The conferences exhibited monopoly characteristics, but were nevertheless accepted as useful institutions because there were competitive elements as well. The power of conferences was limited by outside competition from tramps and new lines. Within the conferences, competition was maintained by the provision of services and facilities. The British commission, however, recommended collective bargaining between associations of shippers (as representatives for the whole trade) and the conferences as a means of counteracting the latter's monopoly power. The U.S. committee, on the other hand, stressed governmental regulations. Later investigations in both countries reaffirmed their respective approaches to conferences: regulation in the United States and shippers' councils in the United Kingdom.[19] The approach of relying on shippers' councils has also been accepted by UNCTAD and appears to have been effective, particularly when backed by governments (e.g., in India).

However, there has been mounting criticism of the conference system in recent years. Although all official investigations have found elements of monopoly in the system, they have also found sufficient competition, or potential competition, to counteract possible abuses. UNCTAD, which represents the interests of the less-developed countries has for the most part accepted these conclusions.[20] The basic arguments in favor of conferences are that they provide regular, reliable service with stable rates. The main arguments against them are abuse of monopoly power with misallocation of resources, excess capacity with unnecessarily high freight rates, and, particularly, price discrimination. There are numerous studies of the system, both by official agencies and academicians.[21] Some findings are for the system, others against. The most recent studies in both the United States and Canada call for the abandoning of conferences.[22] The U.S. study has been extensively criticized,[23] but is likely to have some impact on U.S. shipping policies.

On balance, we have regulation of conference practices in the United States and, to a minor extent, in Canadian trades. Consultations by shippers' councils are prominent in other trades. In the traditional maritime nations, the Committee of European and Japanese National Shipowners' Associations (CENSA) and the European Shippers' Council (ESC) attempted to set a framework for consultations in a Note of Understanding in 1963. This was followed in 1971 by a Code of Conference Conduct, intended particularly to meet the demands of the LDCs. However, the following year UNCTAD issued its own code, which was accepted as an international convention in April 1974.

As mentioned in Chapter 1, the convention will soon enter into force. The inroads made by the Russian fleet seem to have caused some of the maritime nations to ratify the code in order to secure a cargo base for their own flag ships. The convention calls for a system of international control of shipping based on the principles that:

1. Governments will have a major role in all relations between shippers and shipowners.
2. Admission to conferences should include noncommercial criteria, one of which should be the development of national shipping lines.
3. Flag discrimination to aid national shipping is accepted in principle, the guideline being for trading partners to carry 40 percent each with the remainder left for cross traders. This is the so-called 40-40-20 rule.

(It is interesting to note that the 40-40-20 rule is not entirely new; it has been practiced for several years in the U.S.-Brazil trade.)

Although the code accepts the conference system, indeed, seems to favor it, there are questions about the future. As mentioned in Chapter 1, official investigations into conferences have, in the past, concluded that there are several forces preventing conferences from assuming and abusing monopoly power. These forces were: competition between conferences; real or potential competition from tramps and independents; large conference membership, making collusion difficult and adding a competitive element within the conference; counterbalancing shippers' councils; and threat of national legislation and national fleets. However, most of these countervailing forces have disappeared or weakened. Superconferences and interconference agreements reduce the power of competition between conferences. Technological progress resulting in differentiation between tramp and liner services removes much of both real and potential competition from tramps. The international container consortia and the high capital barrier to entry into this trade reduce the threat from independents, although to some extent, the capital barrier is mitigated by the development of companies leasing containerships and equipment. In addition, shippers' councils have relied on government support for effective bargaining. The final outcome is that national regulation of conferences as the only remaining counterforce has become a major issue today. There is much uncertainty as to the future trend, but it seems clear that international shipping is moving toward some form of national or international regulation, bilateral agreements, and a much more political environment than in the past.

Notes

1. For examples of specific traffic studies, see L. C. Kendall, *The Business of Shipping* (Cambridge, Md.: Cornell Maritime Press, 1976), chap. 13.

2. See *Maritime Transport 1972* (OECD), chap. 2. The same publication for 1973, chap. 5, contains a very informative report on the role of shipping in the OECD economies. There has been very little empirical research on

the elasticity of demand for ocean transport, but useful information can be found in the OECD study *Ocean Freight Rates as Part of Total Transport Costs* (1967), and an elasticity formula is given in E. Bennathan and A. A. Walters in *The Economics of Ocean Freight Rates* (New York: Praeger, 1969).

3. It is very difficult to draw a sharp line between bulk and neo-bulk, but these minor commodities would include: ammonium, potash, and urea, which, together with phosphate rocks, are raw materials for the fertilizer industry; and cement, sugar, salt, sulphur, gypsum, tapioca, pyrites, mineral sands, manganese and nonferrous ores, petroleum coke, pig iron, steel products, lumber and wood products, and cars.

4. It has been estimated that, on the average, only about 10 percent of the tramp tonnage is "free." (*Merchant Fleet Development,* UNC-TAD/SHIP/127).

5. W. Arthur Lewis, *Overhead Costs* (London: Allen & Unwin, 1949), p. 112.

6. Export cartels have long held the dominant position in the world trade of sulphur, carbon black, phosphate, and potash. For examples of export cartels and their products, see OECD, *Export Cartels, 1974.*

7. There is undoubtedly an element of, or possibility for, price fixing in the bulk shipping pools, although the very large size of the shippers may prevent it. Under any circumstances, the arrangement is a departure from the free, competitive market structure usually ascribed to the tramp market.

8. AFRA is given for five categories of size: "general purpose," which is 16,500–24,999 dwt; "medium range," covering 25–44,999 dwt; "large range 1" for 45–79,999 dwt; "large range 2" for 80–159,999 dwt; and "large range 3," covering in excess of 160,000 dwt.

9. *Seatrade,* November 1977. An interesting inside account of INTER-TANKO's activities, and particularly the economic and political factors involved, are given by Erling Naess, *Autobiography of a Shipping Man* (Colchester, England: Seatrade Publications, 1977).

10. See K. W. Rothschild, "Price Theory and Oligopoly," *Economic Journal* 57 (1947), reprinted in AEA, *Readings in Price Theory* (Homewood, Ill.: R. D. Irwin, 1952). Also, see W. Fellner, *Competition Among the Few* (New York: Augustus M. Kelley, 1960).

11. J. R. Smith, "Ocean Freight Rates," *Political Science Quarterly,* no. 2, 1906.

12. C. E. Fayle, *A Short History of the World's Shipping Industry* (London: Allen & Unwin, 1933), chaps. 8–12.

13. U.S., Congress, Joint Economic Committee, *Discriminatory Ocean Freight Rates and the Balance of Payments,* 89th Cong., 1st sess., January 6, 1965.

14. R. Larner, "Public Policy in the Ocean Freight Industry," in *Promoting Competition in Regulated Markets,* ed. A. Phillips (Washington, D.C.: Brookings Institution, 1975).

15. U.S., Congress, Joint Economic Committee, *Discriminatory Ocean Freight Rates;* and U.S., Department of Justice, *The Regulated Ocean Shipping Industry,* Report, January 1977.

16. For the relationship between these rates, see the author's "Liner and Tramp Rates," *The Journal of the Israel Shipping Research Institute,* winter 1972.

17. See D. L. McLachlen, "The Price Policy of Liner Conferences," *Scottish Journal of Political Economy,* November 1963.

18. D. Marx, *International Shipping Cartels* (Princeton: Princeton University Press, 1953), p. 48.

19. In the U.S., the latest report to support the conference system, but with appropriate regulations, was the Bonner Report, properly titled *Steamship Conference and Dual Rate Contracts,* 87th Cong., 1st sess., S.R. 860, August 31, 1961. In Britain, it was the Rochdale Report, or *Committee on Inquiry into Shipping,* Cmnd. 4337 (HMSO), 1970.

20. *The Liner Conference System,* UNCTAD TD/B/C.4/62/Rev (1970); and *Convention on a Code of Conduct for Liner Conferences,* April 6, 1974, UN Doc. TD/CODE/11/Rev. (1974).

21. Some of the more interesting works, apart from that of Marx and the various official investigations, are: A. R. Ferguson et al., *The Economic Value of the U.S. Merchant Marine* (Evanston, Ill.: Northwestern University, 1961); E. Bennathan and A. A. Walters, *The Economics of Ocean Freight Rates* (New York: Praeger, 1969); B. M. Deakin and T. Seward, *Shipping Conferences: A Study of Their Origins, Development and Economic Practices* (Cambridge, England: Cambridge University Press, 1973); and U.S., Congress, Joint Economic Committee, *Discriminatory Ocean Freight Rates.*

22. U.S., Department of Justice, *The Regulated Ocean Shipping Industry;* and I. Bryan and Y. Kotowitz, *Shipping Conferences in Canada,* Research Monograph no. 2, Research Branch, Bureau of Competition Policy, Consumer and Corporate Affairs, Canada, 1978.

23. "Liner Shipping in the U.S. Trades," special issue of *Maritime Policy and Management,* July 1978.

10

Flags of Registry

All ships are registered in a particular country and fly that country's flag. The laws of the flag country apply to the shipowner in all his operations and to the maintenance of law and order aboard the ship. It is useful to distinguish between the regulated and the open flag registries. Under the *regulated flags*, the flag-state has sovereign *control* of the ships. To make certain of that control there are strict conditions governing the registration, particularly with respect to nationality of owners and crew. Most nations fall into this category. However, in the postwar period, and particularly in the last ten to fifteen years, one can discern a distinct division of these flags into three groups: those of the "traditional" shipping nations, the state owned (mainly that of the USSR), and LDCs.

The traditional shipping nations, which account for the major part of the world's fleet, are the OECD members. They have encountered much competition in liner trades from the Russian fleet, which has expanded rapidly during the last ten years.[1] Similarly, but not equally successfully, the LDCs have attempted to build up their national merchant marines. The aim of UNCTAD for the United Nations' Second Development Decade was for the LDCs to account for at least 10 percent of the world's deadweight tonnage by 1980.[2] This goal had not been reached by late 1978: The tonnage of these countries increased substantially from 1970, but their share of the fleet remained at about 7 percent.

The interests of these subgroups are partly conflicting and partly congruent. The state-owned fleets, operating independent liner services, pose a serious threat to the conference system, which is the backbone of shipping in the traditional shipping nations.[3] This threat has added force to the argument that these states ought to accede to the UNCTAD code in order to secure a future base for their shipping and the maintenance of the conference system. This is clearly congruent with the interests of the LDCs, who also see in the code the means for securing cargoes, justifying the expansion of their fleets, and participating in the conferences. These broad tendencies have implications for the second category of registry, the flags of convenience.

The *flags of convenience* differ from other flags in the sense that they are basically *open* to anyone satisfying minimal conditions. They have been defined as those in which the "government sees registration not as a procedure necessary in order to impose sovereignty, and hence control, over its shipping, but as a service which can be sold to foreign shipowners wishing to escape the fiscal and other consequences of registration under their own flag."[4] (*Quasi flags of convenience* exhibit some, but not all, of the characteristics common to flags of convenience. They are defined as those that offer "convenience" advantages in order to attract tonnage to their registries, but have substantial national requirements for some of the shipping under their flag.[5])

The use of foreign flags is not a new phenomenon,[6] but their current importance is certainly unprecedented: Their share of the world's deadweight tonnage has risen continuously from 6 percent in the early 1950s to about 20 percent in the late 1960s and one third in 1977.[7] The reasons for this development are to be found in the economic development and increasing prosperity experienced in the traditional shipping nations. To keep pace with these developments ashore there were demands for better wages and social conditions aboard ships. Additional demands were made on shipowners by the need to comply with international conventions on safety and pollution controls. As a result, taxation and financial as well as social and other conditions affecting the cost of ship operations developed differently in various countries. Thus, depending on the flag of registry, shipowners faced different cost conditions, which affected their international competitiveness. The owners' search for alternatives led to the rapid development of today's open, or convenience, registries.

The characteristics of the open registry are obviously those the regulated flags lack and have been identified as follows:[8]

1. The country of registry allows noncitizens to own and control its merchant ships.
2. Access to the registry is easy, as is transfer from it. Both transactions can usually be handled by the country's consulate abroad.
3. Ship income is taxed at low rates or is tax exempt. A registry fee and an annual tonnage fee are normally the only charges made.
4. Manning by nonnationals is freely permitted.

There are also two features identifying the type of country that usually has such a registry.[9] First, it is a small power with no national requirement, under any foreseeable circumstances, for all the tonnage registered under its flag. However, the receipts from very small charges on a large tonnage may have a substantial effect on its national income and balance of payments. Second, the country has neither the power nor the administrative machinery to impose effectively any government or international regulations, nor has the country the wish or the power to control the companies themselves.

The main flags of convenience in 1977 were, in descending order of importance, Liberia, Panama, Singapore, Cyprus, Lebanon, Somalia, and Honduras. The major quasi flags are Greece and the United Kingdom, the latter through the registries of Hong Kong, Bermuda, and Gibraltar. The Liberian fleet, which in 1977 comprised about two thirds of the convenience deadweight tonnage and a quarter of that of the world, is mainly composed of large ships, i.e., oil tankers and bulk carriers.[10] Its ships also tend to be newer and larger than world average. Other convenience fleets have a higher proportion of general cargo ships, often smaller than world average and, usually, considerably older (except for Singapore, where relatively new ships have appeared). The Cyprus flag seems particularly attractive to small ships, and the Somalian flag was until early 1977 the "home" of a large number of ships owned by the People's Republic of China.[11]

Much of the opposition to flags of convenience comes from labor, who oppose both the loss of employment under domestic flags and the inferior social conditions made possible by open registry. Since these flags do not restrict the use of nonnational crews, the employment loss is not considered as serious an effect as are the low wages and the standards of other social conditions. The social conditions have improved as a result of the so-called blue certificate, which certifies that a particular ship conforms to the standards of employment and safety issued by the International Transport Workers Federation (ITF). As charterers increasingly demand this certificate, improved social conditions become a prerequisite for business.[12] With respect to ITF wage scales, however, there are problems. By raising the salaries of Third World seamen to a level approaching that of the developed fleets, the competitive position of the former decreases. Also, this wage scale would put crew members from Bangladesh, Pakistan, and India on a par with high government officials in their own countries.[13] Hence, there is some LDC support for existing convenience wages, although on the whole, the attitude of LDCs is opposed to open registries because they are seen as competing with the development of national merchant marines.[14] In this context, the issue of the "genuine link" arises. This concept, introduced in the 1958 Convention on the High Seas, states that there should be a genuine link between the ship and its flag. Particularly, the flag state should control and administer technical and social matters on the ships. However, no uniform interpretation of this concept has emerged and the issue, with all its implications for flags of convenience, is still open.[15]

Perhaps more importantly, the study by Doganis and Metaxas found that convenience ships have higher accident rates that are not reflected in their insurance rates, so that the insurance of these ships is subsidized by other flag ships. The study also found that this high accident rate is, at least partly, a consequence of shipowners' attempts to keep costs down by deferment and negligence in ship repair and maintenance. This has, in turn, affected the safety rules and requirements of classification agencies. What appears to have happened is that other operators attempt also to minimize repair and maintenance costs, but unless the rules of official classification agencies allow it, there is little opportunity to do so under regulated flags. In their competition to attract new ships to their registers and prevent older ones from transferring out, classification agencies have, over time, relaxed their safety standards and rules, resulting in overall downgrading of international safety standards.[16] Criticism of the safety record of convenience ships prompted Liberia to set up a ship inspection service in 1971. Although this service has so far been ineffective, it appears that the conditions for convenience registry may become somewhat higher, at least in the major countries. At the same time there may be a continuing easing of requirements for some traditional flags—that is, the quasi-convenience flags. In the future there may, therefore, be some convergence of registry conditions.

So far there have been no discernible effects of these developments on the convenience tonnage. Not only has it increased rapidly in recent years, but there appear to be increasingly more small nations offering the service of open registry. But in the light of possible bilateralism under the UNCTAD code, there may be future problems for the convenience flags. Since these countries do not have much trade of their own, the question is how to arrange for a share of the trade of the owners' real home country. However these issues may be resolved, open registries will be an important area for future shipping policies.

Notes

1. See U.S., Congress, House, Committee on Merchant Marine and Fisheries, *Third Flag: Hearings* before the Subcommittees on the Merchant Marine, 94th Cong., 1st and 2d sess., no. 94–35, 1976.

2. UNCTAD Resolution 70 (III), May 19, 1972.

3. "The World Shipping Cartels Begin to Crumble," *Economist,* July 19, 1975.

4. K. Grundey, *Flags of Convenience in 1978,* Discussion Paper no. 8, November 1978 (London: Transport Studies Group, Polytechnic of Central London, 1978), p. 2. This definition is an extension of the one given in R. S. Doganis and B. N. Metaxas, *The Impact of Flags of Convenience,* Research Report no. 3, September 1976 (London: Transport Studies Group, Polytechnic of Central London, 1976).

5. The identification, name, and definition of this phenomenon is one result of the research done by Doganis and Metaxas.

6. Erling Naess, *The Great PanLibHon Controversy* (London: Gower Press, 1972). See also Doganis and Metaxas, *The Impact of Flags of Convenience.*

7. Grundey, *Flags of Convenience*.

8. The Rochdale Report, *Committee on Inquiry into Shipping*, Cmnd. 4337 (CHMSO), 1970.

9. The Rochdale Report included these in its identification of character-istics common to all flags of convenience. However, we feel that for clarity of exposition it is better to list these as features of a country that may open its registry on the terms identified earlier.

10. For details on the various fleets, see Doganis and Metaxas, *The Impact of Flags of Convenience;* and Grundey, *Flags of Convenience*.

11. Eighty of these ships, said to amount to about half of China's ships under the Somalian flag, were transferred in 1977 to Panamanian registry. (*Fairplay International Shipping Weekly,* February 24, 1977).

12. See Doganis and Metaxas, *The Impact of Flags of Convenience,* pp. 25–37.

13. Grundey, *Flags of Convenience,* pp. 47–48.

14. "During the decade, every effort should be made to discourage in-vestment in open registry vessels, and correspondingly to encourage development of national regional shipping lines" (*Global Strategy for the Implementation of the UN Transport and Communications Decade in Africa 1978–88; Maritime Transport: Goals and Objectives* [E/CN/ECO/138/Rev. 1], p. 14). The fifth UNCTAD meeting (May 1979, Manila) passed proposals for the phasing out of convenience flags; when these pro-posals may result in action is uncertain.

15. See Grundey, *Flags of Convenience,* for a concise discussion of this issue, its history, and its current status. Also see UNCTAD, *Economic Consequences of the Existence or Lack of a Genuine Link Between Vessel and Flag of Registry* (TD/B/C.4/168), March 10, 1977.

16. Doganis and Metaxas, *The Impact of Flags of Convenience,* pp. 105–114.

11

International Organizations

One inevitable consequence of the international character of shipping has been the emergence of various international organizations to deal with common problems. As seaborne trade grew, so did the need for international agreements on commercial, safety, and other matters and on both governmental and private levels. Some were for a short-term specific purpose, for instance, tonnage allocations in war times. Others remained and new ones have been created in response to current problems, for example, the liner conferences and bulk-shipping pools. As a result, there are today numerous international organizations, both old and new, concerned with specific shipping issues and interests. Although the very specific focus of these organizations makes it difficult to give an overall view of their place and role in shipping, a student of the industry ought to be familiar with some of the names of these organizations and their major purposes. They are presented here in two categories, *international governmental organizations* (IGOs) and *nongovernmental organizations* (NGOs). (No claim is made for this being an exhaustive listing.)

Among the more important IGOs are the Intergovernmental Maritime Consultative Organization (IMCO), the Shipping Division of the United Nations Conference on Trade and Development (UNCTAD), the Maritime Committee of OECD, the International Labor Organization (ILO), the United Nations Commission on International Trade Law (UNCITRAL), the Diplomatic Conference on Maritime Law, and the International Hydrographic Organization (IHO).

IMCO is a special agency of the UN. The convention calling for its establishment was accepted in 1948 and went into effect ten

years later, in 1958. With headquarters in London, its major purposes are to promote international cooperation in all technical matters affecting shipping, to discourage discriminatory and restrictive
shipping practices, and to promote the freest possible availability of
tonnage to meet the needs of seaborne trade. While it has not actively pursued these latter objectives, IMCO has become an important force in providing for the exchange of technical information,
particularly pertaining to safety of life at sea and marine pollution
control.

IMCO's functions are to serve as a machinery for consultation
among its members and for advising other UN agencies dealing with
marine-related aspects of labor, telecommunications, meteorology,
oceanography, aviation, atomic energy, and health. In addition, it is
responsible for, and has been very active in, the convening of international conventions on shipping matters. It is composed of an
assembly, a council, several work committees, and a secretariat for
the overall administration of the organization. The assembly is the
main body that must approve any action taken by IMCO. Each
member has an equal vote in this body. Membership in the council
and the various committees is limited and by election and should
represent the interests of the major shipping nations and the major
users of their services as well as geographic distribution. There is no
doubt that IMCO has played, and will continue to play, an important role in world shipping.[1]

UNCTAD, located in Geneva, was established in 1964 as a permanent organ of the UN General Assembly. Its purpose is to promote international trade, particularly between LDCs, in order to
further and accelerate economic development. The Conference's im-
plementing organ is the Trade and Development Board, which has a
Shipping Division concerned primarily with the shipping problems of
the LDCs. This division prepares the annual UNCTAD publication
Review of Maritime Transport. UNCTAD has been influential in
moving international shipping policies toward new directions, most
prominently seen in its Code of Conduct and in the growth of national merchant marines. Its future role in world shipping is likely to
grow.

OECD's Maritime Committee, located in Paris, began work
shortly after World War II. It provides basic data on and analyses of
the shipping scene for the organization's members—i.e., the "tradi-

tional" shipping nations. The committee prepares OECD's annual publication, *Maritime Transport,* which, together with UNCTAD's *Review,* gives very useful economic data and analyses of current developments.

ILO was originally founded as a part of the League of Nations, but since 1946 has been an independent special agency of the UN with headquarters in Geneva. Its purpose is to improve working and liv-ing conditions for workers in general. It has a Joint Maritime Com-mittee (JMC) that represents both shipowners and seamen. The organization has done much to set standards and improve training and, in general, to raise living conditions for seamen, particularly on flag of convenience ships.

Also within the United Nations is *UNCITRAL,* which, since its creation in 1966, has had the mandate to further the unification and harmonization of the international trade laws of trading nations. Within UNCITRAL is a separate Commission on International Shipping Legislation, which is particularly concerned with bills of lading.

The *Diplomatic Conference on Maritime Law* was founded in 1905 and is located in Brussels. Its purpose is to provide a forum for dis-cussions of the legal implications and ramifications entailed in the ratification of various measures and conventions. Hence, the organization initiates and sponsors conferences on maritime law. Membership is open to all nations with which Belgium has diplomatic relations.

The *IHO* is located in Monaco and was founded in 1921. Its pur-pose is to coordinate hydrographic work to make navigation safer on all seas for all nations.

Among the more important NGOs are the Baltic and Interna-tional Maritime Conference (BIMCO), the International Cargo Handling Coordination Association (ICHCA), Comité Maritime In-ternational (CMI), the International Chamber of Shipping (ICS), the International Shipping Federation (ISF), the Permanent Interna-tional Association of Navigation Congresses (PIANC), the Interna-tional Association of Ports and Harbors (IAPH), Comité Inter-national Radio Maritime (CIRM), the International Association of Lighthouse Authorities (IALA), the International Federation of Freight Forwarders (FIATA),[2] the International Union of Marine Insurance (IUMI), and the Committee of European and Japanese

National Shipowners' Associations (CENSA).

BIMCO was formed in 1936 as the successor to the Baltic and White Sea Conference created in 1905. BIMCO is a commercial organization with the objective of keeping the members informed about developments in shipping. The members consist of ship-owners (owner members), agents and brokers (broker members), and trade organizations (club members).[3] The organization publishes a confidential monthly *Bulletin*, an open *Weekly Circular*, and an *Annual Report*. The members' interests are promoted by reporting on chartering and developments in trade, such as credit and pay-ment problems, in various parts of the world. Other information per-tains to navigational problems and port conditions such as conges-tion and turn-around times. Most of this information is found in the *Weekly Circular*, but there is also an information bureau that advises on specific port costs, loading and unloading conditions, and com-mercial and legal problems. It is undoubtedly the most important trade organization in the industry.

ICHCA was formed in 1952 to improve cargo handling through international cooperation and dissemination of information. There are local chapters throughout the world that organize meetings and exchange information. The organization publishes a monthly report and *Cargo Systems International*. There is also an information service at the London headquarters.

CMI was founded by the International Law Association in 1897 for the purpose of providing an organization to deal exclusively with the laws of merchant shipping. CMI's function is to follow, pro-mote, and develop maritime law as it applies to international trade. An important aspect of the organization's work pertains to documentation and the preparation of draft conventions. The members of *ICS* are shipowners' associations from several countries. Founded in London in 1921, the purpose of the organization is to further the interests of the members—i.e., it is mainly a lobby to in-fluence shipping policies. The London-based *ISF* was originally formed in 1909 as a tool for shipowners to break the unions of seafarers. Its functions changed in 1919 to the seeking of negotiated changes in relations between management and labor. Today, this is the organization that represents the owners in the Joint Maritime Committee of ILO. *PIANC* is located in Brussels. Founded in 1900, its purpose is to support the development of both inland and ocean shipping through improved navigation and waterways. It publishes a *Bulletin* twice a year. The purpose of *IAPH* is to promote solutions to general port problems through, particularly, rationalization and specialization of procedures and equipment. It was founded in 1952 with headquarters in Tokyo.

London-based *CIRM* was created in 1928 to further radio communications at sea with particular reference to safety at sea and news information. The *IALA* is located in Paris. Formed in 1957, its objective is to coordinate and promote discussion of technical questions concerning safe navigation in approaches. Such questions may be of general or special interest. Of particular importance are IALA's current efforts aimed at the development of a standardized buoyage system. *FIATA* was founded in 1926 in Copenhagen to represent the interests of freight forwarders at various international conferences. It has done much to promote and develop the procedures of its members. The *IUMI* is headquartered in Zurich. It was founded in 1874 to promote and safeguard the interest of marine insurers. It represents these interests at IMCO. The function of *CENSA* is to further the interests of shipowners. It does negotiate and settle rate matters between the European liner conferences and various shippers' councils, particularly the European Shippers' Council (ESC).

There are also two major shipping organizations in the COMECON[4] countries. One, founded in 1961 and located in Warsaw, is the *Permanent Commission for COMECON Transport Policy*. Although its purpose is to promote common transport policies in general, there is also a section for shipping. The other organization, located in Moscow and created in 1962, has a direct impact on international shipping. The function of the *Bureau for the Coordination of Ship Chartering* is to utilize chartered tonnage at the optimum. This means the chartering and reletting of tonnage as conditions require and may have substantial effects on the market.

There are today more NGOs than IGOs in international shipping. However, the situation may be reversed in the future if, indeed, shipping becomes more bilateral, regulated, and politicized.

Notes

1. Harvey B. Silverstein, *Superships and Nation-States: The Transnational Politics of the Intergovernmental Maritime Consultative Organization*

(Boulder, Colo.: Westview Press, 1978).

2. FIATA stands for Fédération Internationale des Associations de Transitaires et Assimilés.

3. In 1976 there were some 2,300 members from 87 countries, including the Communist nations, representing about 45 percent of world tonnage.

4. Also known as the Council for Mutual Economic Assistance (CMEA), this is the common market of the Eastern bloc countries.

Appendixes

Appendix A: Statistics

Demand for shipping is derived from world seaborne trade, which is given in Table 1. Because the data come from different sources, they are not entirely compatible. This is true also for other tables presented here. However, no attempt has been made to reconcile the data as the purpose is to merely provide a frame of reference. The main characteristics are clear. Bulk cargoes account for the major share of world trade. Of the dry cargo volume they account for roughly 45 percent. Crude oil is the major commodity in the overall picture.

The volumes of major dry bulk commodities are given in Table 2, where it can be seen that the tonnages moving by sea are large and growing. The world fleet available to carry this trade at the end of 1977 is shown in Table 3. These ships were distributed among the world's nations, as given in Table 4. Not all of this tonnage was actively employed during the year. At any particular time, there is some tonnage laid up, as indicated in Table 5. The size distribution of this fleet is given in Table 6, which clearly shows the concentration of tankers in the large sizes. Most of the 1977 world fleet consisted of motorships, that is, diesel powered vessels, with the remainder being steamships. The majority of the latter are tankers, while most of the motorships are dry cargo vessels. This is shown in Table 7, with some details for 1976 and 1977 given in Table 8. In Table 9 are given the fleets of convenience flags or, as they are also called, open registries. The countries in Group A are those most commonly considered flags of convenience, while Greece together with Group B are the "quasi-convenience flags."

TABLE 1

World Seaborne Trade (in million metric tons)

Year	World Total Volume	Dry Cargo Total	Of which Bulk	Oil Total	Of which Products
1950	525	300	-	225	-
1955	800	450	-	350	-
1960	1080	540	-	540	-
1965	1640	780	-	860	-
1970	2530	1110	504	1420	245
1971	2640	1120	505	1520	247
1972	2830	1180	524	1650	261
1973	3215	1350	622	1865	274
1974	3250	1450	668	1800	264
1975	3020	1380	635	1640	233
1976	3250	1540	646	1710	260
1977	3415	1675	645	1740	273

Source: U.N. Monthly Bulletin of Statistics. Figures for bulk
and products are from Fearnley and Egers Chartering Co., as given
in OECD Maritime Transport 1978.

TABLE 2

Main Bulk Commodities (in million metric tons)

Year	Iron Ore	Grains	Coal	Bauxites & Alumina	Phosphate Rock
1970	247	73	101	34	33
1971	250	76	94	35	35
1972	247	89	96	35	38
1973	298	139	104	38	43
1974	329	130	119	42	48
1975	292	137	127	41	38
1976	294	146	127	42	37
1977	276	147	132	46	44

Source: Fearnley & Egers as given in Maritime Transport 1978

TABLE 3

World Tonnage at end of 1977

	No. of Ships	DWT (in millions)
Oil Tankers[1]	3301	331.9
Combined carriers	419	48.3
Bulk carriers	3826	129.6
All others of which:[2]	14495	114.8
General cargo	11584	88.5
Full containerships	508	7.4
Partial containerships	597	6.5
Ro-Ro vessels	205	1.4
Barge carriers	29	1.0
World Total	22041	624.6

Source: [1]Fearnley & Egers, <u>Review 1978</u>. The ships included as "all others" are seagoing vessels over 1,000 grt, while the other categories include only ships over 10,000 dwt. If <u>all</u> ships over 100 grt are included, the number of ships becomes some 35,000, while the dwt figure rises to almost 649 million.

[2]<u>Merchant Fleets of the World</u>, U.S.Dept. of Commerce, December, 1977, provides the break-down of "all others" into specific types.

TABLE 4
World Merchant Fleets, mid-1977 (in thousands of grt and dwt)

| | Total | | Tankers | |
	grt	dwt	grt	dwt
Liberia	79983	155951	50772	105013
Japan	40036	65870	17117	32485
UK	31646	51722	14834	20043
Greece	29517	49323	9725	18041
Norway	27802	49193	14401	28103
Panama	19458	31593	6524	12470
USSR	21438	23042	4386	6746
USA	15300	22135	5977	11030
France	11614	20052	7513	14505
Italy	11111	17733	4685	8679
Germany	9592	15584	3534	6799
Sweden	7429	12617	3713	7265
Spain	7186	11712	4271	7815
Singapore	6791	11352	3104	5912
India	5482	8746	1147	2045
Denmark	5331	8567	2683	5127
Netherlands	5294	8055	2286	4208
China (P.R.)	4245	6257	996	1673
Brazil	3330	5336	1202	2122
Poland	3448	4892	572	1029
Total	346033	579732	154805	301110
Rest of World	47645	69111	19319	34145
World Total	393678	648843	174124	335255

Source: Lloyd's Register of Shipping. All ships over 100 grt as
well as the Great Lakes fleets and the U.S. reserve fleet are included.

TABLE 5
Active World Fleet (in million grt; ships over 100 grt)

	TOTAL				TANKERS			
	Total	U.S. Reserve Fleet	Laid-up Tonnage	Active Fleet	Total	U.S. Reserve Fleet	Laid-up Tonnage	Active Fleet
1970	227.5	6.2	0.3	221.0	86.1	0.2	0.1	85.8
1971	247.2	5.2	0.8	241.2	96.1	0.2	0.1	95.8
1972	268.3	4.2	4.8	215.8	105.1	0.2	2.4	102.5
1973	289.9	2.5	1.0	286.4	115.4	0.2	0.3	114.9
1974	311.3	2.0	0.6	308.7	129.5	0.2	0.1	129.2
1975	342.2	2.0	18.3	321.9	150.0	0.2	14.6	264.4
1976	372.0	1.7	26.5	343.8	168.2	0.2	22.2	145.8
1977	393.7	1.7	19.7	372.3	174.1	0.2	16.1	157.8

Source: Various as given in <u>OECD Maritime Transport, 1978</u>, p. 134.

TABLE 6
Size Distribution of World Fleet, as of mid-1977 (ships over 100 grt)

Size group (grt)	Percentage of total	Percentage of dry cargo	Percentage of tankers
1000	3.4	5.6	0.6
1-2000	1.9	3.0	0.5
2-4000	4.3	7.1	0.8
4-6000	3.3	5.6	0.3
6-8000	3.9	6.5	0.6
8-10000	6.9	12.0	0.5
10-15000	10.3	15.0	4.5
15-20000	8.1	10.8	4.7
20-30000	8.1	8.8	7.1
30-40000	7.5	7.8	7.1
40-50000	5.1	3.7	6.9
50-100000	14.7	12.1	18.0
100-120000	8.6	0.8	18.4
120-140000	8.6	0.8	18.5
140,000 & over	5.3	0.4	11.5

Source: Lloyd's Register of Shipping.

TABLE 7
Propulsion Methods, at mid-year (in 1000 grt for ships over 100 grt)

	1975	1976	1977
Motorships	215978	235685	253579
of which tankers	54601	61998	64392
Steamships	126184	136315	140100
of which tankers	95456	106163	109733
World total	342162	372000	393679
of which tankers	150057	168161	174125

Source: Lloyd's Register of Shipping.

TABLE 8

Propulsion Methods for New Vessels, 1976, 1977 (in million dwt for ships over 2000 dwt)

	Total No. of Ships	dwt	Motor No. of Ships	dwt	Steam No. of Ships	dwt
1976	1064	55.7	951	28.9	113	27.0
1977	1014	37.8	964	25.9	50	11.9

Source: The Motor Ship, Jan., 1978

TABLE 9

Flags of Convenience, 1977 (in percent of world totals)

	No. of Vessels	grt	dwt
A.			
Liberia	3.85	20.32	24.03
Panama	4.81	4.94	4.87
Honduras	0.09	0.03	0.02
Lebanon	0.24	0.06	0.05
Cyprus	1.18	0.71	0.62
Somalia	0.04	0.04	0.03
Singapore	1.28	1.72	1.75
Total	11.49	27.82	31.37
B.			
Bahamas	0.16	0.03	0.02
Bermuda	0.13	0.44	0.47
Seychelles	0.01	0.01	0.01
Cayman	0.16	0.03	0.03
Maldives	0.07	0.03	0.02
Total	12.02	28.36	31.92
Greece	4.92	7.50	7.60

Source: K. Grundey, Flags of Convenience in 1978

Appendix B: International Conventions on Bills of Lading

The first international convention on bills of lading was the 1924 Hague Rules. These were generally adopted and included in domestic legislations pertaining to the carriage of goods by sea. To meet the needs of changing circumstances, the rules were amended by the 1968 Visby Rules, also known as the 1968 Brussels Protocol. These are not universally accepted at this time. It is possible, indeed probable, that these rules will be superseded by the 1978 Hamburg Rules that have been proposed by the United Nations.

The 1924 Hague Rules

International Convention
for the unification of certain rules
of law relating to bills of lading

(Brussels, August 25th, 1924)

(Translation)

The President of the German Republic, the President of the Argentine Republic, ... etc.

Having recognized the utility of fixing by agreement certain uniform rules of law relating to bills of lading,

Have decided to conclude a convention with this object and have appointed the following Plenipotentiaries :

(Follows the list of Plenipotentiaries)

Who, duly authorized thereto, have agreed as follows :

Article 1

In this Convention the following words are employed with the meanings set out below :

a) « Carrier » includes the owner or the charterer who enters into a contract of carriage with a shipper.

b) « Contract of carriage » applies only to contracts of carriage covered by a bill of lading or any similar document of title, in so far as such document relates to the carriage of goods by sea, including any bill of lading or any similar document as aforesaid issued under or pursuant to a charter party from the moment at which such bill of lading or similar document of title regulates the relations between a carrier and a holder of the same.

c) « Goods » includes goods, wares, merchandise and articles of every kind whatsoever except live animals and cargo which by the contract of carriage are stated as being carried on deck and are so carried.

d) « Ship » means any vessel used for the carriage of goods by sea.

e) « Carriage of goods » covers the period from the time when the goods are loaded on to the time they are discharged from the ship.

Article 2

Subject to the provisions of Article 6. under every contract of carriage of goods by sea the carrier, in relation to the loading. handling. stowage. carriage. custody. care and discharge of such goods. shall be subject to the responsibilities and liabilities, and entitled to the rights and immunities hereinafter set forth.

Article 3

1. The carrier shall be bound before and at the beginning of the voyage to exercise due diligence to :

a) Make the ship seaworthy;
b) Properly man, equip and supply the ship;

c) Make the holds, refrigerating and cool chambers, and all other parts of the ship in which goods are carried, fit and safe for their reception, carriage and preservation.

2. Subject to the provisions of Article 4. the carrier shall properly and carefully load, handle, stow, carry, keep, care for, and discharge the goods carried.

3. After receiving the goods into his charge the carrier or the master or agent of the carrier shall, on demand of the shipper, issue to the shipper a bill of lading showing among other things :

a) The leading marks necessary for identification of the goods as the same are furnished in writing by the shipper before the loading of such goods starts, provided such marks are stamped or otherwise shown clearly upon the goods if uncovered, or on the cases or coverings in which such goods are contained. in such a manner as should ordinarily remain legible until the end of the voyage;

b) Either the number of packages or pieces, or the quantity, or weight, as the case may be. as furnished in writing by the shipper;
c) The apparent order and condition of the goods.

Provided that no carrier, master or agent of the carrier shall be bound to state or show in the bill of lading any marks, number, quantity, or weight which he has reasonable ground for suspecting not accurately to represent the goods actually received, or which he has had no reasonable means of checking.

4. Such a bill of lading shall be *prima facie* evidence of the receipt by the carrier of the goods as therein described in accordance with § 3, *a, b* and *c.*

5. The shipper shall be deemed to have guaranteed to the carrier the accuracy at the time of shipment of the marks, number, quantity and weight, as furnished by him, and the shipper shall indemnify the carrier against all loss, damages and expenses arising or resulting from inaccuracies in such particulars. The right of the carrier to such indemnity shall in no way limit his responsibility and liability under the contract of carriage to any person other than the shipper.

6. Unless notice of loss or damage and the general nature of such loss or damage be given in writing to the carrier or his agent at the port of discharge before or at the time of the removal of the goods into the custody of the person entitled to delivery thereof under the contract of carriage, or, if the loss or damage be not apparent, within three days, such removal shall be *prima facie* evidence of the delivery by the carrier of the goods as described in the bill of lading.

If the loss or damage is not apparent, the notice must be given within three days of the delivery of the goods.

The notice in writing need not be given if the state of the goods has, at the time of their receipt, been the subject of joint survey or inspection.

In any event the carrier and the ship shall be discharged from all liability in respect of loss or damage unless suit is brought within one year after delivery of the goods or the date when the goods should have been delivered.

In the case of any actual or apprehended loss or damage the carrier and the receiver shall give all reasonable facilities to each other for inspecting and tallying the goods.

7. After the goods are loaded the bill of lading to be issued by the carrier. master, or agent of the carrier, to the shipper shall, if the shipper so demands, be a « shipped » bill of lading, provided that if the shipper shall have previously taken up any document of title to such goods, he shall surrender the same as against the issue of the « shipped » bill of lading, but at the option of the carrier such document of title may be noted at the port of shipment by the carrier, master, or agent with the name or names of the ship or ships upon which the goods have been shipped and the date or dates of shipment, and when so noted, if it shows the particulars mentioned in § 3 of Article 3. shall for the purpose of this Article be deemed to constitute a « shipped » bill of lading.

8. Any clause, covenant, or agreement in a contract of carriage relieving the carrier or the ship from liability for loss or damage to, or in connexion with, goods arising from negligence, fault, or failure in the duties and obligations provided in this Article or lessening such liability otherwise than as provided in this Convention. shall be null and void and of no effect. A benefit of insurance in favour of the carrier or similar clause shall be deemed to be a clause relieving the carrier from liability.

Article 4

1. Neither the carrier nor the ship shall be liable for loss or damage arising or resulting from unseaworthiness unless caused by want of due diligence on the part of the carrier to make the ship seaworthy and to secure that the ship is properly manned, equipped and supplied, and to make the holds. refrigerating and cool chambers and all other parts of the ship in which goods are carried fit and safe for their reception, carriage and preservation in accordance with the provisions of § 1 of Article 3. Whenever loss or damage has resulted from unseaworthiness the burden of proving the exercise of due diligence shall be on the carrier or other person claiming exemption under this Article.

2. Neither the carrier nor the ship shall be responsible for loss or damage arising or resulting from :

a) Act, neglect, or default of the master, mariner, pilot, or the servants of the carrier in the navigation or in the management of the ship;
b) Fire, unless caused by the actual fault or privity of the carrier;
c) Perils, dangers and accidents of the sea or other navigable waters;
d) Act of God;
e) Act of war;
f) Act of public enemies;
g) Arrest or restraint of princes, rulers or people, or seizure under legal process;
h) Quarantine restrictions;
i) Act or omission of the shipper or owner of the goods. his agent or representative;
j) Strikes or lockouts or stoppage or restraint of labour from whatever cause, whether partial or general;

k) Riots and civil commotions;
l) Saving or attempting to save life or property at sea;

m) Wastage in bulk or weight or any other loss or damage arising from inherent defect, quality or vice of the goods;
n) Insufficiency of packing;
o) Insufficiency or inadequacy of marks;
p) Latent defects not discoverable by due diligence;

q) Any other cause arising without the actual fault or privity of the carrier, or without the actual fault or neglect of the agents or servants of the carrier, but the burden of proof shall be on the person claiming the benefit of this exception to show that neither the actual fault or privity of the carrier nor the fault or neglect of the agents or servants of the carrier contributed to the loss or damage.

3. The shipper shall not be responsible for loss or damage sustained by the carrier or the ship arising or resulting from any cause without the act, fault or neglect of the shipper, his agents or his servants.

4. Any deviation in saving or attempting to save life or property at sea or any reasonable deviation shall not be deemed to be an infringement or breach of this Convention or of the contract of carriage, and the carrier shall not be liable for any loss or damage resulting therefrom.

5. Neither the carrier nor the ship shall in any event be or become liable for any loss or damage to or in connexion with goods in an amount exceeding 100 pounds sterling per package or unit, or the equivalent of that sum in other currency unless the nature and value of such goods have been declared by the shipper before shipment and inserted in the bill of lading.

This declaration if embodied in the bill of lading shall be *prima facie* evidence, but shall not be binding or conclusive on the carrier.

By agreement between the carrier, master or agent of the carrier and the shipper another maximum amount than that mentioned in this paragraph may be fixed, provided that such maximum shall not be less than the figure above named.

Neither the carrier nor the ship shall be responsible in any event for loss or damage to, or in connexion with, goods if the nature or value thereof has been knowingly misstated by the shipper in the bill of lading.

6. Goods of an inflammable, explosive or dangerous nature to the shipment whereof the carrier, master or agent of the carrier has not consented with knowledge of their nature and character, may at any time before discharge be landed at any place, or destroyed or rendered innocuous by the carrier without compensation, and the shipper of such goods shall be liable for all damage and expenses directly or indirectly arising out of or resulting from such shipment. If any such goods shipped with such knowledge and consent shall become a danger to the ship or cargo, they may in like manner be landed at any place, or destroyed or rendered innocuous by the carrier without liability on the part of the carrier except to general average, if any.

Article 5

A carrier shall be at liberty to surrender in whole or in part all or any of his rights and immunities or to increase any of his responsibilities and obligations under this Convention, provided such surrender or increase shall be embodied in the bill of lading issued to the shipper.

The provisions of this Convention shall not be applicable to charter parties, but if bills of lading are issued in the case of a ship under a charter party they shall comply with the terms of this Convention. Nothing in these rules shall be held to prevent the insertion in a bill of lading of any lawful provision regarding general average.

Article 6

Notwithstanding the provisions of the preceding Articles, a carrier, master or agent of the carrier and a shipper shall in regard to any particular goods be at liberty to enter into any agreement in any terms as to the responsibility and liability of the carrier for such goods, and as to the rights and immunities of the carrier in respect of such goods, or his obligation as to seaworthiness, so far as this stipulation is not contrary to public policy, or the care or diligence of his servants or agents in regard to the loading, handling, stowage, carriage, custody, care and discharge of the goods carried by sea, provided that in this case no bill of lading has been or shall be issued and that the terms agreed shall be embodied in a receipt which shall be a non-negotiable document and shall be marked as such.

Any agreement so entered into shall have full legal effect :
Provided that this Article shall not apply to ordinary commercial shipments made in the ordinary course of trade, but only to other shipments where the character or condition of the property to be carried or the circumstances, terms and conditions under which the carriage is to be performed are such as reasonably to justify a special agreement.

Article 7

Nothing herein contained shall prevent a carrier or a shipper from entering into any agreement, stipulation, condition, reservation or exemption as to the responsibility and liability of the carrier or the ship for the loss or damage to, or in connexion with, the custody and care and handling of goods prior to the loading on, and subsequent to, the discharge from the ship on which the goods are carried by sea.

Article 8

The provisions of this Convention shall not affect the rights and obligations of the carrier under any statute for the time being in force relating to the limitation of the liability of owners of sea-going vessels.

Article 9

The monetary units mentioned in this Convention are to be taken to be gold value.
Those contracting States in which the pound sterling is not a monetary unit reserve to themselves the right of translating the sums indicated in this Convention in terms of pound sterling into terms of their own monetary system in round figures.
The national laws may reserve to the debtor the right of discharging his debt in national concurrency according to the rate of exchange prevailing on the day of the arrival of the ship at the port of discharge of the goods concerned.

Article 10

The provisions of this Convention shall apply to all bills of lading issued in any of the contracting States.

Article 11

After an interval of not more than two years from the day of which the Convention is signed, the Belgian Government shall place itself in communication with the Governments of the High Contracting Parties which have declared themselves prepared to ratify the Convention, with a view to deciding whether it shall be put into force. The ratifications shall be deposited at Brussels at a date to be fixed by agreement among the said Governments. The first deposit of ratifications shall be recorded in a procès-verbal signed by the representatives of the Powers which take part therein and by the Belgian Minister for Foreign Affairs.

The subsequent deposit of ratifications shall be made by means of a written notification, addressed to the Belgian Government and accompanied by the instrument of ratification.

A duly certified copy of the procès-verbal relating to the first deposit of ratifications, of the notifications referred to in the previous paragraph, and also of the instruments of ratification accompanying them, shall be immediately sent by the Belgian Government through the diplomatic channel to the Powers who have acceded to it. In the cases contemplated in the preceding paragraph, the said Government shall inform them at the same time of the date on which it received the notification.

Article 12

Non-signatory States may accede to the present Convention whether or not they have been represented at the International Conference at Brussels.

A State which desires to accede shall notify its intention in writing to the Belgian Government, forwarding to it the document of accession, which shall be deposited in the archives of the said Government.

The Belgian Government shall immediately forward to all the States which have signed or acceded to the Convention a duly certified copy of the notification and of the act of accession, mentioning the date on which it received the notification.

Article 13

The High Contracting Parties may at the time of signature, ratification or accession declare that their acceptance of the present Convention does not include any or all of the self-governing dominions, or of the colonies, overseas possessions, protectorates or territories under their sovereignty or authority, and they may subsequently accede separately on behalf of any self-governing dominion, colony, overseas possession, protectorate or territory excluded in their declaration. They may also denounce the Convention separately in accordance with its provisions in respect of any self-governing dominion, or any colony, overseas possession, protectorate or territory under their sovereignty or authority.

Article 14

The present Convention shall take effect, in the case of the States which have taken part in the first deposit of ratification, one year after the date of the protocol recording such deposit.

As respects the States which ratify subsequently or which accede, and also in cases in which the Convention is subsequently put into effect in accordance with Article 13, it shall take effect six months after the notifica-

tions specified in paragraph 2 of Artcile 11 and paragraph 2 of Article 12 have been received by the Belgian Government.

Article 15

In the event of one of the contracting States wishing to denounce the present Convention, the denunciation shall be notified in writing to the Belgian Government, which shall immediately communicate a duly certified copy of the notification to all the other States, informing them of the date on which it was received.

The denunciation shall only operate in respect of the State which made the notification, and on the expiry of one year after the notification has reached the Belgian Government.

Article 16

Any one of the contracting States shall have the right to call for a fresh conference with a view to considering possible amendments.

A State which would exercise this right should notify its intention to the other States through the Belgian Government, which would make arrangements for convening the Conference.

Done at Brussels, in a single copy, August 25th, 1924.

(Follow the signatures)

PROTOCOL OF SIGNATURE

At the time of signing the International Convention for the unification of certain rules of law relating to bills of lading the Plenipotentiaries whose signatures appear below have adopted this Protocol, which will have the same force and the same value as if its provisions were inserted in the text of the Convention to which it relates.

The High Contracting Parties may give effect to this Convention either by giving it the force of law or by including in their national legislation in a form appropriate to that legislation the rules adopted under this Convention.

They may reserve the right :

1. To prescribe that in the cases referred to in paragraph 2 *c* to *p* of Article 4 the holder of a bill of lading shall be entitled to establish responsibility for loss or damage arising from the personal fault of the carrier or the fault of his servants which are not covered by paragraph *a*.

2. To apply Article 6 in so far as the national coasting trade is concerned to all classes of goods without taking account of the restriction set out in the last paragraph of that Article.

Done at Brussels, in a single copy, August 25th, 1924.

(Follow the signatures)

Protocol
to amend
the International Convention
for the unification
of certain rules of law
relating to bills of lading,
signed at Brussels
on 25th August 1924

(Brussels, February 23rd, 1968)

The Contracting Parties.

Considering that it is desirable to amend the International Convention for the unification of certain rules of law relating to bills of lading, signed at Brussels on 25th August 1924,

Have agreed as follows :

Article 1

1. In Article 3, paragraph 4, shall be added :

« However, proof to the contrary shall not be admissible when the bill of lading has been transferred to a third party acting in good faith. »

2. In Article 3, paragraph 6, sub-paragraph 4 shall be deleted and replaced by :

« Subject to paragraph 6*bis* the carrier and the ship shall in any event be discharged from all liability whatsoever in respect of the goods, unless suit is brought within one year of their delivery or of the date when they should have been delivered. This period may, however, be extended if the parties so agree after the cause of action has arisen. »

3. In Article 3, after paragraph 6, shall be added the following paragraph 6*bis* :

« An action for indemnity against a third person may be brought even after the expiration of the year provided for in the preceding paragraph if brought within the time allowed by the law of the Court seized of the case. However, the time allowed shall be not less than three months, commencing from the day when the person bringing such action for indemnity has settled the claim or has been served with process in the action against himself. »

Article 2

Article 4, paragraph 5, shall be deleted and replaced by the following :

« *a)* Unless the nature and value of such goods have been declared by the shipper before shipment and inserted in the bill of lading, neither the carrier nor the ship shall in any event be or become liable for any loss or damage to or in connection with the goods in an amount exceeding the equivalent of 10.000 francs per package or unit or 30 francs per kilo of gross weight of the goods lost or damaged, wichever is the higher.

b) The total amount recoverable shall be calculated by reference to the value of such goods at the place and time at which the goods are discharged from the ship in accordance with the contract or should have been so discharged.

The value of the goods shall be fixed according to the commodity exchange price, or, if there be no such price, according to the current market price, or, if there be no commodity exchange price or current market price, by reference to the normal value of goods of the same kind and quality.

c) Where a container, pallet or similar article of transport is used to consolidate goods, the number of packages or units enumerated in the bill of lading as packed in such article of transport shall be deemed the number of packages or units for the purpose of this paragraph as far as these packages or units are concerned. Except as aforesaid such article of transport shall be considered the package or unit.

d) A franc means a unit consisting of 65.5 milligrammes of gold of millesimal fineness 900'. The date of conversion of the sum awarded into national currencies shall be governed by the law of the Court seized of the case.

e) Neither the carrier nor the ship shall be entitled to the benefit of the limitation of liability provided for in this paragraph if it is proved that the damage resulted from an act or omission of the carrier done with intent to cause damage, or recklessly and with knowledge that damage would probably result.

f) The declaration mentioned in sub-paragraph a) of this paragraph, if embodied in the bill of lading, shall be prima facie evidence, but shall not be binding or conclusive on the carrier.

g) By agreement between the carrier, master or agent of the carrier and the shipper other maximum amounts than those mentioned in sub-paragraph a) of this paragraph may be fixed, provided that no maximum amount so fixed shall be less than the appropriate maximum mentioned in that sub-paragraph.

h) Neither the carrier nor the ship shall be responsible in any event for loss or damage to, or in connection with, goods if the nature or value thereof has been knowingly mis-stated by the shipper in the bill of lading. »

Article 3

Between Articles 4 and 5 of the Convention shall be inserted the following Article 4*bis* :

« 1. The defences and limits of liability provided for in this Convention shall apply in any action against the carrier in respect of loss or damage to goods covered by a contract of carriage whether the action be founded in contract or in tort.

2. If such an action is brought against a servant or agent of the carrier (such servant or agent not being an independent contractor), such servant or agent shall be entitled to avail himself of the defences and limits of liability which the carrier is entitled to invoke under this Convention.

3. The aggregate of the amounts recoverable from the carrier, and such servants and agents, shall in no case exceed the limit provided for in this Convention.

4. Nevertheless, a servant or agent of the carrier shall not be entitled to avail himself of the provisions of this Article, if it is proved that the damage resulted from an act or omission of the servant or agent done with intent to cause damage or recklessly and with knowledge that damage would probably result. »

Article 4

Article 9 of the Convention shall be deleted and replaced by the following :

« This Convention shall not affect the provisions of any international Convention or national law governing liability for nuclear damage. »

Article 5

Article 10 of the Convention shall be deleted and replaced by the following :

« The provisions of this Convention shall apply to every bill of lading relating to the carriage of goods between ports in two different States if :

a) the bill of lading is issued in a Contracting State, or

b) the carriage is from a port in a Contracting State, or

c) the contract contained in or evidenced by the bill of lading provides that the rules of this Convention or legislation of any State giving effect to them are to govern the contract,
whatever may be the nationality of the ship, the carrier, the shipper, the consignee, or any other interested person.

Each Contracting State shall apply the provisions of this Convention to the bills of lading mentioned above.

This Article shall not prevent a Contracting State from applying the Rules of this Convention to bills of lading not included in the preceding paragraphs. »

Article 6

As between the Parties to this Protocol the Convention and the Protocol shall be read and interpreted together as one single instrument.

A Party to this Protocol shall have no duty to apply the provisions of this Protocol to bills of lading issued in a State which is a Party to the Convention but which is not a Party to this Protocol.

Article 7

As between the Parties to this Protocol, denunciation by any of them of the Convention in accordance with Article 15 thereof, shall not be construed in any way as a denunciation of the Convention as amended by this Protocol.

Article 8

Any dispute between two or more Contracting Parties concerning the interpretation or application of the Convention which cannot be settled through negotiation, shall, at the request of one of them, be submitted to arbitration. If within six months from the date of the request for arbitration the Parties are unable to agree on the organization of the arbitration, any one of those Parties may refer the dispute to the International Court of Justice by request in conformity with the Statute of the Court.

Article 9

1. Each Contracting Party may at the time of signature or ratification of this Protocol or accession thereto, declare that it does not consider itself bound by Article 8

of this Protocol. The other Contracting Parties shall not be bound by this Article with respect to any Contracting Party having made such a reservation.

2. Any Contracting Party having made a reservation in accordance with paragraph 1 may at any time withdraw this reservation by notification to the Belgian Government.

Article 10

This Protocol shall be open for signature by the States which have ratified the Convention or which have adhered thereto before the 23rd February 1968, and by any State represented at the twelfth session (1967-1968) of the Diplomatic Conference on Maritime Law.

Article 11

1. This Protocol shall be ratified.

2. Ratification of this Protocol by any State which is not a Party to the Convention shall have the effect of accession to the Convention.

3. The instruments of ratification shall be deposited with the Belgian Government.

Article 12

1. States, Members of the United Nations or Members of the specialized agencies of the United Nations, not represented at the twelfth session of the Diplomatic Conference on Maritime Law, may accede to this Protocol.

2. Accession to this Protocol shall have the effect of accession to the Convention.

3. The instruments of accession shall be deposited with the Belgian Gouvernment.

Article 13

1. This Protocol shall come into force three months after the date of the deposit of ten instruments of ratification or accession, of which at least five shall have been deposited by States that have each a tonnage equal or superior to one million gross tons of tonnage.

2. For each State which ratifies this Protocol or accede thereto after the date of deposit of the instrument of ratification or accession determining the coming into force such as is stipulated in § 1 of this Article, this Protocol shall come into force three months after the deposit of its instrument of ratification or accession.

Article 14

1. Any Contracting State may denounce this Protocol by notification to the Belgian Government.

2. This denunciation shall have the effect of denunciation of the Convention.

3. The denunciation shall take effect one year after the date on which the notification has been received by the Belgian Government.

Article 15

1. Any Contracting State may at the time of signature, ratification or accession or at any time thereafter declare by written notification to the Belgian Government which among the territories under its sovereignty or for whose international relations it is responsible, are those to which the present Protocol applies.

The Protocol shall three months after the date of the receipt of such notification by the Belgian Government extend to the territories named therein, but not before the date of the coming into force of the Protocol in respect of such State.

2. This extension also shall apply to the Convention if the latter is not yet applicable to those territories.

3. Any Contracting State which has made a declaration under § 1 of this Article, may at any time thereafter declare by notification given to the Belgian Government that the Protocol shall cease to extend to such territory.

This denunciation shall take effect one year after the date on which notification thereof has been received by the Belgian Government: it also shall apply to the Convention.

Article 16

The Contracting Parties may give effect to this Protocol either by giving it the force of law or by including in their national legislation in a form appropriate to that legislation the rules adopted under this Protocol.

Article 17

The Belgian Government shall notify the States represented at the twelfth session (1967-1968) of the Diplomatic Conference on Maritime Law, the acceding States to this Protocol, and the States Parties to the Convention, of the following :

1. The signatures, ratifications and accessions received in accordance with Articles 10, 11 and 12.

2. The date on which the present Protocol will come into force in accordance with Article 13.

3. The notifications with regard to the territorial application in accordance with Article 15.

4. The denunciations received in accordance with Article 14.

In witness whereof the undersigned Plenipotentiaries, duly authorized, have signed this Protocol.

Done at Brussels, this 23rd day of February 1968, in the French and English languages, both texts being equally authentic, in a single copy, which shall remain deposited in the archives of the Belgian Government, which shall issue certified copies.

(Follow the signatures)

THE 1978 HAMBURG RULES

UNITED NATIONS CONVENTION ON THE CARRIAGE OF GOODS BY SEA, 1978

Preamble

THE STATES PARTIES TO THIS CONVENTION,

HAVING RECOGNIZED the desirability of determining by agreement certain rules relating to the carriage of goods by sea,
HAVE DECIDED to conclude a Convention for this purpose and have thereto agreed as follows:

PART I.   GENERAL PROVISIONS

Article 1.   Definitions

In this Convention:
1.   "Carrier" means any person by whom or in whose name a contract of carriage of goods by sea has been concluded with a shipper.
2.   "Actual carrier" means any person to whom the performance of the carriage of the goods, or of part of the carriage, has been entrusted by the carrier, and includes any other person to whom such performance has been entrusted.
3.   "Shipper" means any person by whom or in whose name or on whose behalf a contract of carriage of goods by sea has been concluded with a carrier, or any person by whom or in whose name or on whose behalf the goods are actually delivered to the carrier in relation to the contract of carriage by sea.
4.   "Consignee" means the person entitled to take delivery of the goods.
5.   "Goods" includes live animals; where the goods are consolidated in a container, pallet or similar article of transport or where they are packed, "goods" includes such article of transport or packaging if supplied by the shipper.
6.   "Contract of carriage by sea" means any contract whereby the carrier undertakes against payment of freight to carry goods by sea from one port to another; however, a contract which involves carriage by sea and also carriage by some other means is deemed to be a contract of carriage by sea for the purposes of this Convention only in so far as it relates to the carriage by sea.
7.   "Bill of lading" means a document which evidences a contract of carriage by sea and the taking over or loading of the goods by the carrier, and by which the carrier undertakes to deliver the goods against surrender of the document. A provision in the document that the goods are to be delivered to the order of a named person, or to order, or to bearer, constitutes such an undertaking.
8.   "Writing" includes, _inter alia_, telegram and telex.

Article 2. Scope of application

1. The provisions of this Convention are applicable to all contracts of carriage by sea between two different States, if:

(a) the port of loading as provided for in the contract of carriage by sea is located in a Contracting State, or

(b) the port of discharge as provided for in the contract of carriage by sea is located in a Contracting State, or

(c) one of the optional ports of discharge provided for in the contract of carriage by sea is the actual port of discharge and such port is located in a Contracting State, or

(d) the bill of lading or other document evidencing the contract of carriage by sea is issued in a Contracting State, or

(e) the bill of lading or other document evidencing the contract of carriage by sea provides that the provisions of this Convention or the legislation of any State giving effect to them are to govern the contract.

2. The provisions of this Convention are applicable without regard to the nationality of the ship, the carrier, the actual carrier, the shipper, the consignee or any other interested person.

3. The provisions of this Convention are not applicable to charter-parties. However, where a bill of lading is issued pursuant to a charter-party, the provisions of the Convention apply to such a bill of lading if it governs the relation between the carrier and the holder of the bill of lading, not being the charterer.

4. If a contract provides for future carriage of goods in a series of shipments during an agreed period, the provisions of this Convention apply to each shipment. However, where a shipment is made under a charter-party, the provisions of paragraph 3 of this article apply.

Article 3. Interpretation of the Convention

In the interpretation and application of the provisions of this Convention regard shall be had to its international character and to the need to promote uniformity.

PART II. LIABILITY OF THE CARRIER

Article 4. Period of responsibility

1. The responsibility of the carrier for the goods under this Convention covers the period during which the carrier is in charge of the goods at the port of loading, during the carriage and at the port of discharge.

2. For the purpose of paragraph 1 of this article, the carrier is deemed to be in charge of the goods

    (a) from the time he has taken over the goods from:
        (i)   the shipper, or a person acting on his behalf; or
       (ii)   an authority or other third party to whom, pursuant
            to law or regulations applicable at the port of
            loading, the goods must be handed over for
            shipment;
    (b) until the time he has delivered the goods:
        (i)   by handing over the goods to the consignee; or
       (ii)   in cases where the consignee does not receive the
            goods from the carrier, by placing them at the
            disposal of the consignee in accordance with the
            contract or with the law or with the usage of
            the particular trade, applicable at the port of
            discharge; or
      (iii)   by handing over the goods to an authority or
            other third party to whom, pursuant to law or
            regulations applicable at the port of discharge,
            the goods must be handed over.

3.   In paragraphs 1 and 2 of this article, reference to the
carrier or to the consignee means, in addition to the carrier
or the consignee, the servants or agents, respectively of the
carrier or the consignee.

Article 5. Basis of liability

1.   The carrier is liable for loss resulting from loss of
or damage to the goods, as well as from delay in delivery, if
the occurrence which caused the loss, damage or delay took
place while the goods were in his charge as defined in article
4, unless the carrier proves that he, his servants or agents
took all measures that could reasonably be required to avoid
the occurrence and its consequences.

2.   Delay in delivery occurs when the goods have not been
delivered at the port of discharge provided for in the contract
of carriage by sea within the time expressly agreed upon or, in
the absence of such agreement, within the time which it would
be reasonable to require of a diligent carrier, having regard
to the circumstances of the case.

3.   The person entitled to make a claim for the loss of
goods may treat the goods as lost if they have not been delivered as required by article 4 within 60 consecutive days
following the expiry of the time for delivery according to
paragraph 2 of this article.

    4. (a) The carrier is liable
        (i)   for loss of or damage to the goods or delay
            in delivery caused by fire, if the claimant
            proves that the fire arose from fault or
            neglect on the part of the carrier, his
            servants or agents;
       (ii)   for such loss, damage or delay in delivery
            which is proved by the claimant to have

resulted from the fault or neglect of the
carrier, his servants or agents, in taking
all measures that could reasonably be required to put out the fire and avoid or
mitigate its consequences.

(b) In case of fire on board the ship affecting the
goods, if the claimant or the carrier so desires, a survey in
accordance with shipping practices must be held into the cause
and circumstances of the fire, and a copy of the surveyor's
report shall be made available on demand to the carrier and
the claimant.

5. With respect to live animals, the carrier is not liable
for loss, damage or delay in delivery resulting from any
special risks inherent in that kind of carriage. If the
carrier proves that he has complied with any special instructions
given to him by the shipper respecting the animals and that, in
the circumstances of the case, the loss, damage or delay in
delivery could be attributed to such risks, it is presumed that
the loss, damage or delay in delivery was so caused, unless there
is proof that all or a part of the loss, damage or delay in
delivery resulted from fault or neglect on the part of the
carrier, his servants or agents.

6. The carrier is not liable, except in general average,
where loss, damage or delay in delivery resulted from measures
to save life or from reasonable measures to save property at sea.

7. Where fault or neglect on the part of the carrier, his
servants or agents combines with another cause to produce loss,
damage or delay in delivery the carrier is liable only to the
extent that the loss, damage or delay in delivery is attributable
to such fault or neglect, provided that the carrier proves the
amount of the loss, damage or delay in delivery not attributable
thereto.

Article 6. Limits of liability

1. (a) The liability of the carrier for loss resulting
from loss of or damage to goods according to the provisions of
article 5 is limited to an amount equivalent to 835 units of
account per package or other shipping unit or 2.5 units of
account per kilogramme of gross weight of the goods lost or
damaged, whichever is the higher.

(b) The liability of the carrier for delay in delivery
according to the provisions of article 5 is limited to an
amount equivalent to two and a half times the freight payable
for the goods delayed, but not exceeding the total freight
payable under the contract of carriage of goods by sea.

(c) In no case shall the aggregate liability of the
carrier, under both subparagraphs (a) and (b) of this paragraph,
exceed the limitation which would be established under sub-
paragraph (a) of this paragraph for total loss of the goods
with respect to which such liability was incurred.

2. For the purpose of calculating which amount is the higher in accordance with paragraph 1(a) of this article, the following rules apply:

(a) Where a container, pallet or similar article of transport is used to consolidate goods, the package or other shipping units enumerated in the bill of lading, if issued, or otherwise in any other document evidencing the contract of carriage by sea, as packed in such article of transport are deemed packages or shipping units. Except as aforesaid the goods in such article of transport are deemed one shipping unit.

(b) In cases where the article of transport itself has been lost or damaged, that article of transport, if not owned or otherwise supplied by the carrier, is considered one separate shipping unit.

3. Unit of account means the unit of account mentioned in article 26.

4. By agreement between the carrier and the shipper, limits of liability exceeding those provided for in paragraph 1 may be fixed.

Article 7. Application to non-contractual claims

1. The defences and limits of liability provided for in this Convention apply in any action against the carrier in respect of loss or damage to the goods covered by the contract of carriage by sea, as well as of delay in delivery whether the action is founded in contract, in tort or otherwise.

2. If such an action is brought against a servant or agent of the carrier, such servant or agent, if he proves that he acted within the scope of his employment, is entitled to avail himself of the defences and limits of liability which the carrier is entitled to invoke under this Convention.

3. Except as provided in article 8, the aggregate of the amounts recoverable from the carrier and from any persons referred to in paragraph 2 of this article shall not exceed the limits of liability provided for in this Convention.

Article 8. Loss of right to limit responsibility

1. The carrier is not entitled to the benefit of the limitation of liability provided for in article 6 if it is proved that the loss, damage or delay in delivery resulted from an act or omission of the carrier done with the intent to cause such loss, damage or delay, or recklessly and with knowledge that such loss, damage or delay would probably result.

2. Notwithstanding the provisions of paragraph 2 of article 7, a servant or agent of the carrier is not entitled to the benefit of the limitation of liability provided for in article 6 if it is proved that the loss, damage or delay in delivery resulted from an act or omission of such servant or agent, done with the intent to cause such loss, damage or delay,

or recklessly and with knowledge that such loss, damage or delay would probably result.

Article 9. Deck cargo

1. The carrier is entitled to carry the goods on deck only if such carriage is in accordance with an agreement with the shipper or with the usage of the particular trade or is required by statutory rules or regulations.

2. If the carrier and the shipper have agreed that the goods shall or may be carried on deck, the carrier must insert in the bill of lading or other document evidencing the contract of carriage by sea a statement to that effect. In the absence of such a statement the carrier has the burden of proving that an agreement for carriage on deck has been entered into; however, the carrier is not entitled to invoke such an agreement against a third party, including a consignee, who has acquired the bill of lading in good faith.

3. Where the goods have been carried on deck contrary to the provisions of paragraph 1 of this article or where the carrier may not under paragraph 2 of this article invoke an agreement for carriage on deck, the carrier, notwithstanding the provisions of paragraph 1 of article 5, is liable for loss of or damage to the goods, as well as for delay in delivery, resulting solely from the carriage on deck, and the extent of his liability is to be determined in accordance with the provisions of article 6 or article 8 of this Convention, as the case may be.

4. Carriage of goods on deck contrary to express agreement for carriage under deck is deemed to be an act or omission of the carrier within the meaning of article 8.

Article 10. Liability of the carrier and actual carrier

1. Where the performance of the carriage or part thereof has been entrusted to an actual carrier, whether or not in pursuance of a liberty under the contract of carriage by sea to do so, the carrier nevertheless remains responsible for the entire carriage according to the provisions of this Convention. The carrier is responsible, in relation to the carriage performed by the actual carrier, for the acts and omissions of the actual carrier and of his servants and agents acting within the scope of their employment.

2. All the provisions of this Convention governing the responsibility of the carrier also apply to the responsibility of the actual carrier for the carriage performed by him. The provisions of paragraphs 2 and 3 of article 7 and of paragraph 2 of article 8 apply if an action is brought against a servant or agent of the actual carrier.

3. Any special agreement under which the carrier assumes obligations not imposed by this Convention or waives rights

conferred by this Convention affects the actual carrier only if
agreed to by him expressly and in writing. Whether or not the
actual carrier has so agreed, the carrier nevertheless remains
bound by the obligations or waivers resulting from such special
agreement.

4. Where and to the extent that both the carrier and the
actual carrier are liable, their liability is joint and several.

5. The aggregate of the amounts recoverable from the
carrier, the actual carrier and their servants and agents shall
not exceed the limits of liability provided for in this Convention.

6. Nothing in this article shall prejudice any right of
recourse as between the carrier and the actual carrier.

Article 11. Through carriage

1. Notwithstanding the provisions of paragraph 1 of
article 10, where a contract of carriage by sea provides
explicitly that a specified part of the carriage covered by the
said contract is to be performed by a named person other than
the carrier, the contract may also provide that the carrier is
not liable for loss, damage or delay in delivery caused by an
occurrence which takes place while the goods are in the charge
of the actual carrier during such part of the carriage. Nevertheless, any stipulation limiting or excluding such liability
is without effect if no judicial proceedings can be instituted
against the actual carrier in a court competent under paragraph
1 or 2 of article 21. The burden of proving that any loss,
damage or delay in delivery has been caused by such an occurrence
rests upon the carrier.

2. The actual carrier is responsible in accordance with
the provisions of paragraph 2 of article 10 for loss, damage or
delay in delivery caused by an occurrence which takes place
while the goods are in his charge.

PART III. LIABILITY OF THE SHIPPER

Article 12. General rule

The shipper is not liable for loss sustained by the carrier
or the actual carrier, or for damage sustained by the ship, unless such loss or damage was caused by the fault or neglect of
the shipper, his servants or agents. Nor is any servant or agent
of the shipper liable for such loss or damage unless the loss or
damage was caused by fault or neglect on his part.

Article 13. Special rules on dangerous goods

1. The shipper must mark or label in a suitable manner
dangerous goods as dangerous.

2. Where the shipper hands over dangerous goods to the carrier or an actual carrier, as the case may be, the shipper must inform him of the dangerous character of the goods and, if necessary, of the precautions to be taken. If the shipper fails to do so and such carrier or actual carrier does not otherwise have knowledge of their dangerous character:

(a) the shipper is liable to the carrier and any actual carrier for the loss resulting from the shipment of such goods; and

(b) the goods may at any time be unloaded, destroyed or rendered innocuous, as the circumstances may require, without payment of compensation.

3. The provisions of paragraph 2 of this article may not be invoked by any person if during the carriage he has taken the goods in his charge with knowledge of their dangerous character.

4. If, in cases where the provisions of paragraph 2, subparagraph (b), of this article do not apply or may not be invoked, dangerous goods become an actual danger to life or property, they may be unloaded, destroyed or rendered innocuous, as the circumstances may require, without payment of compensation except where there is an obligation to contribute in general average or where the carrier is liable in accordance with the provisions of article 5.

PART IV. TRANSPORT DOCUMENTS

Article 14. Issue of bill of lading

1. When the carrier or the actual carrier takes the goods in his charge, the carrier must, on demand of the shipper, issue to the shipper a bill of lading.

2. The bill of lading may be signed by a person having authority from the carrier. A bill of lading signed by the master of the ship carrying the goods is deemed to have been signed on behalf of the carrier.

3. The signature on the bill of lading may be in handwriting, printed in facsimile, perforated, stamped, in symbols, or made by any other mechanical or electronic means, if not inconsistent with the law of the country where the bill of lading is issued.

Article 15. Contents of bill of lading

1. The bill of lading must include, *inter alia*, the following particulars:

(a) the general nature of the goods, the leading marks necessary for identification of the goods, an express statement, if applicable, as to the dangerous character of the goods, the number of packages or pieces, and the weight of the goods or

their quantity otherwise expressed, all such particulars as
furnished by the shipper;

    (b)   the apparent condition of the goods;

    (c)   the name and principal place of business of the
carrier;

    (d)   the name of the shipper;

    (e)   the consignee if named by the shipper;

    (f)   the port of loading under the contract of carriage
by sea and the date on which the goods were taken over by the
carrier at the port of loading;

    (g)   the port of discharge under the contract of carriage
by sea;

    (h)   the number of originals of the bill of lading, if
more than one;

    (i)   the place of issuance of the bill of lading;

    (j)   the signature of the carrier or a person acting on
his behalf;

    (k)   the freight to the extent payable by the consignee or
other indication that freight is payable by him;

    (l)   the statement referred to in paragraph 3 of
article 23;

    (m)   the statement, if applicable, that the goods shall or
may be carried on deck;

    (n)   the date or the period of delivery of the goods at the
port of discharge if expressly agreed upon between the parties;
and

    (o)   any increased limit or limits of liability where
agreed in accordance with paragraph 4 of article 6.

    2. After the goods have been loaded on board, if the
shipper so demands the carrier must issue to the shipper a
"shipped" bill of lading which, in addition to the particulars
required under paragraph 1 of this article, must state that the
goods are on board a named ship or ships, and the date or dates
of loading. If the carrier has previously issued to the shipper
a bill of lading or other document of title with respect to any
of such goods, on request of the carrier, the shipper must surrender such document in exchange for a "shipped" bill of lading.
The carrier may amend any previously issued document in order to
meet the shipper's demand for a "shipped" bill of lading if, as
amended, such document includes all the information required to
be contained in a "shipped" bill of lading.

    3. The absence in the bill of lading of one or more
particulars referred to in this article does not affect the
legal character of the document as a bill of lading provided
that it nevertheless meets the requirements set out in paragraph
7 of article 1.

Article 16. Bills of lading: reservations and evidentiary effect

    1. If the bill of lading contains particulars concerning

the general nature, leading marks, number of packages or pieces, weight or quantity of the goods which the carrier or other person issuing the bill of lading on his behalf knows or has reasonable grounds to suspect do not accurately represent the goods actually taken over or, where a "shipped" bill of lading is issued, loaded, or if he had no reasonable means of checking such particulars, the carrier or such other person must insert in the bill of lading a reservation specifying these inaccuracies, grounds of suspicion or the absence of reasonable means of checking.

2. If the carrier or other person issuing the bill of lading on his behalf fails to note on the bill of lading the apparent condition of the goods, he is deemed to have noted on the bill of lading that the goods were in apparent good condition.

3. Except for particulars in respect of which and to the extent to which a reservation permitted under paragraph 1 of this article has been entered:

(a) the bill of lading is <u>prima facie</u> evidence of the taking over or, where a "shipped" bill of lading is issued, loading, by the carrier of the goods as described in the bill of lading; and

(b) proof to the contrary by the carrier is not admissible if the bill of lading has been transferred to a third party, including a consignee, who in good faith has acted in reliance on the description of the goods therein.

4. A bill of lading which does not, as provided in paragraph 1, subparagraph (k) of article 15, set forth the freight or otherwise indicate that freight is payable by the consignee or does not set forth demurrage incurred at the port of loading payable by the consignee, is <u>prima facie</u> evidence that no freight or such demurrage is payable by him. However, proof to the contrary by the carrier is not admissible when the bill of lading has been transferred to a third party, including a consignee, who in good faith has acted in reliance on the absence in the bill of lading of any such indication.

Article 17. Guarantees by the shipper

1. The shipper is deemed to have guaranteed to the carrier the accuracy of particulars relating to the general nature of the goods, their marks, number, weight and quantity as furnished by him for insertion in the bill of lading. The shipper must indemnify the carrier against the loss resulting from inaccuracies in such particulars. The shipper remains liable even if the bill of lading has been transferred by him. The right of the carrier to such indemnity in no way limits his liability under the contract of carriage by sea to any person other than the shipper.

2. Any letter of guarantee or agreement by which the shipper undertakes to indemnify the carrier against loss resulting from the issuance of the bill of lading by the carrier, or by a person acting on his behalf, without entering

a reservation relating to particulars furnished by the shipper
for insertion in the bill of lading, or to the apparent condition of the goods, is void and of no effect as against any
third party, including a consignee, to whom the bill of lading
has been transferred.

3.   Such letter of guarantee or agreement is valid as
against the shipper unless the carrier or the person acting on
his behalf, by omitting the reservation referred to in paragraph
2 of this article, intends to defraud a third party, including
a consignee, who acts in reliance on the description of the
goods in the bill of lading.   In the latter case, if the reservation omitted relates to particulars furnished by the shipper for
insertion in the bill of lading, the carrier has no right of
indemnity from the shipper pursuant to paragraph 1 of this
article.

4.   In the case of intended fraud referred to in paragraph
3 of this article the carrier is liable, without the benefit of
the limitation of liability provided for in this Convention, for
the loss incurred by a third party, including a consignee,
because he has acted in reliance on the description of the goods
in the bill of lading.

Article 18. Documents other than bills of lading

Where a carrier issues a document other than a bill of lading
to evidence the receipt of the goods to be carried, such a document is *prima facie* evidence of the conclusion of the contract of
carriage by sea and the taking over by the carrier of the goods
as therein described.

PART V.   CLAIMS AND ACTIONS

Article 19. Notice of loss, damage or delay

1.   Unless notice of loss or damage, specifying the general
nature of such loss or damage, is given in writing by the
consignee to the carrier not later than the working day after
the day when the goods were handed over to the consignee, such
handing over is *prima facie* evidence of the delivery by the
carrier of the goods as described in the document of transport
or, if no such document has been issued, in good condition.

2.   Where the loss or damage is not apparent, the provisions
of paragraph 1 of this article apply correspondingly if notice
in writing is not given within 15 consecutive days after the day
when the goods were handed over to the consignee.

3.   If the state of the goods at the time they were handed
over to the consignee has been the subject of a joint survey or
inspection by the parties, notice in writing need not be given of
loss or damage ascertained during such survey or inspection.

4. In the case of any actual or apprehended loss or damage the carrier and the consignee must give all reasonable facilities to each other for inspecting and tallying the goods.

5. No compensation shall be payable for loss resulting from delay in delivery unless a notice has been given in writing to the carrier within 60 consecutive days after the day when the goods were handed over to the consignee.

6. If the goods have been delivered by an actual carrier, any notice given under this article to him shall have the same effect as if it had been given to the carrier, and any notice given to the carrier shall have effect as if given to such actual carrier.

7. Unless notice of loss or damage, specifying the general nature of the loss or damage, is given in writing by the carrier or actual carrier to the shipper not later than 90 consecutive days after the occurrence of such loss or damage or after the delivery of the goods in accordance with paragraph 2 of article 4, whichever is later, the failure to give such notice is prima facie evidence that the carrier or the actual carrier has sustained no loss or damage due to the fault or neglect of the shipper, his servants or agents.

8. For the purpose of this article, notice given to a person acting on the carrier's or the actual carrier's behalf, including the master or the officer in charge of the ship, or to a person acting on the shipper's behalf is deemed to have been given to the carrier, to the actual carrier or to the shipper, respectively.

Article 20. Limitation of actions

1. Any action relating to carriage of goods under this Convention is time-barred if judicial or arbitral proceedings have not been instituted within a period of two years.

2. The limitation period commences on the day on which the carrier has delivered the goods or part thereof or, in cases where no goods have been delivered, on the last day on which the goods should have been delivered.

3. The day on which the limitation period commences is not included in the period.

4. The person against whom a claim is made may at any time during the running of the limitation period extend that period by a declaration in writing to the claimant. This period may be further extended by another declaration or declarations.

5. An action for indemnity by a person held liable may be instituted even after the expiration of the limitation period provided for in the preceding paragraphs if instituted within the time allowed by the law of the State where proceedings are instituted. However, the time allowed shall not be less than 90 days commencing from the day when the persons instituting

such action for indemnity has settled the claim or has been
served with process in the action against himself.

Article 21. Jurisdiction

1. In judicial proceedings relating to carriage of goods
under this Convention the plaintiff, at his option, may institute an action in a court which, according to the law of the
State where the court is situated, is competent and within the
jurisdiction of which is situated one of the following places:
(a) the principal place of business or, in the absence
thereof, the habitual residence of the defendant; or
(b) the place where the contract was made provided that
the defendant has there a place of business, branch or agency
through which the contract was made; or
(c) the port of loading or the port of discharge; or
(d) any additional place designated for that purpose in
the contract of carriage by sea.
2. (a) Notwithstanding the preceding provisions of this
article, an action may be instituted in the courts by any port
or place in a Contracting State at which the carrying vessel or
any other vessel of the same ownership may have been arrested
in accordance with applicable rules of the law of that State
and of international law. However, in such a case, at the
petition of the defendant, the claimant must remove the action,
at his choice, to one of the jurisdictions referred to in
paragraph 1 of this article for the determination of the claim,
but before such removal the defendant must furnish security
sufficient to ensure payment of any judgement that may subsequently be awarded to the claimant in the action.
(b) All questions relating to the sufficiency or otherwise
of the security shall be determined by the court of the port
or place of the arrest.
3. No judicial proceedings relating to carriage of goods
under this Convention may be instituted in a place not specified
in paragraph 1 or 2 of this article. The provisions of this
paragraph do not constitute an obstacle to the jurisdiction of
the Contracting States for provisional or protective measures.
4. (a) Where an action has been instituted in a court
competent under paragraph 1 or 2 of this article or where judgement has been delivered by such a court, no new action may be
started between the same parties on the same grounds unless the
judgement of the court before which the first action was
instituted is not enforceable in the country in which the new
proceedings are instituted;
(b) for the purpose of this article the institution of
measures with a view to obtaining enforcement of a judgement
is not to be considered as the starting of a new action;
(c) for the purpose of this article, the removal of an
action to a different court within the same country, or to a
court in another country, in accordance with paragraph 2(a) of

this article, is not to be considered as the starting of a new action.

5. Notwithstanding the provisions of the preceding paragraphs, an agreement made by the parties, after a claim under the contract of carriage by sea has arisen, which designates the place where the claimant may institute an action, is effective.

Article 22. Arbitration

1. Subject to the provisions of this article, parties may provide by agreement evidenced in writing that any dispute that may arise relating to carriage of goods under this Convention shall be referred to arbitration.

2. Where a charter-party contains a provision that disputes arising thereunder shall be referred to arbitration and a bill of lading issued pursuant to the charter-party does not contain a special annotation providing that such provision shall be binding upon the holder of the bill of lading, the carrier may not invoke such provision as against a holder having acquired the bill of lading in good faith.

3. The arbitration proceedings shall, at the option of the claimant, be instituted at one of the following places:

   (a) a place in a State within whose territory is situated:

      (i) the principal place of business of the defendant or, in the absence thereof, the habitual residence of the defendant; or

      (ii) the place where the contract was made, provided that the defendant has there a place of business, branch or agency through which the contract was made; or

     (iii) the port of loading or the port of discharge; or

   (b) any place designated for that purpose in the arbitration clause or agreement.

4. The arbitrator or arbitration tribunal shall apply the rules of this Convention.

5. The provisions of paragraphs 3 and 4 of this article are deemed to be part of every arbitration clause or agreement, and any term of such clause or agreement which is inconsistent therewith is null and void.

6. Nothing in this article affects the validity of an agreement relating to arbitration made by the parties after the claim under the contract of carriage by sea has arisen.

PART VI. SUPPLEMENTARY PROVISIONS

Article 23. Contractual stipulations

1. Any stipulation in a contract of carriage by sea, in a bill of lading, or in any other document evidencing the contract

of carriage by sea is null and void to the extent that it
derogates, directly or indirectly, from the provisions of this
Convention. The nullity of such a stipulation does not affect
the validity of the other provisions of the contract or document
of which it forms a part. A clause assigning benefit of insurance of the goods in favour of the carrier, or any similar
clause, is null and void.
    2. Notwithstanding the provisions of paragraph 1 of this
article, a carrier may increase his responsibilities and obligations under this Convention.
    3. Where a bill of lading or any other document evidencing
the contract of carriage by sea is issued, it must contain a
statement that the carriage is subject to the provisions of
this Convention which nullify any stipulation derogating therefrom to the detriment of the shipper or the consignee.
    4. Where the claimant in respect of the goods has incurred
loss as a result of a stipulation which is null and void by
virtue of the present article, or as a result of the omission
of the statement referred to in paragraph 3 of this article, the
carrier must pay compensation to the extent required in order
to give the claimant compensation in accordance with the provisions of this Convention for any loss of or damage to the
goods as well as for delay in delivery. The carrier must, in
addition, pay compensation for costs incurred by the claimant
for the purpose of exercising his right, provided that costs
incurred in the action where the foregoing provision is invoked
are to be determined in accordance with the law of the State
where proceedings are instituted.

Article 24. General average

    1. Nothing in this Convention shall prevent the application
of provisions in the contract of carriage by sea or national law
regarding the adjustment of general average.
    2. With the exception of article 20, the provisions of this
Convention relating to the liability of the carrier for loss of
or damage to the goods also determine whether the consignee may
refuse contribution in general average and the liability of the
carrier to indemnify the consignee in respect of any such
contribution made or any salvage paid.

Article 25. Other conventions

    1. This Convention does not modify the rights or duties
of the carrier, the actual carrier and their servants and
agents, provided for in international conventions or national
law relating to the limitation of liability of owners of
seagoing ships.
    2. The provisions of articles 21 and 22 of this Convention
do not prevent the application of the mandatory provisions of

any other multilateral convention already in force at the date
of this Convention relating to matters dealt with in the said
articles, provided that the dispute arises exclusively between
parties having their principal place of business in States
members of such other convention. However, this paragraph does
not affect the application of paragraph 4 of article 22 of this
Convention.

3. No liability shall arise under the provisions of this
Convention for damage caused by a nuclear incident if the
operator of a nuclear installation is liable for such damage:

(a) under either the Paris Convention of 29 July 1960 on
Third Party Liability in the Field of Nuclear Energy as amended
by the Additional Protocol of 28 January 1964 or the Vienna
Convention of 21 May 1963 on Civil Liability for Nuclear Damage,
or

(b) by virtue of national law governing the liability for
such damage, provided that such law is in all respects as
favourable to persons who may suffer damage as either the Paris
or Vienna Conventions.

4. No liability shall arise under the provisions of this
Convention for any loss of or damage to or delay in delivery of
luggage for which the carrier is responsible under any international convention or national law relating to the carriage of
passengers and their luggage by sea.

5. Nothing contained in this Convention prevents a
Contracting State from applying any other international convention which is already in force at the date of this Convention
and which applies mandatorily to contracts of carriage of goods
primarily by a mode of transport other than transport by sea.
This provision also applies to any subsequent revision or
amendment of such international convention.

Article 26. Unit of account

1. The unit of account referred to in article 6 of this
Convention is the Special Drawing Right as defined by the
International Monetary Fund. The amounts mentioned in article 6
are to be converted into the national currency of a State according to the value of such currency at the date of judgement or the
date agreed upon by the parties. The value of a national currency,
in terms of the Special Drawing Right, of a Contracting State
which is a member of the International Monetary Fund is to be
calculated in accordance with the method of valuation applied by
the International Monetary Fund in effect at the date in question
for its operations and transactions. The value of a national
currency in terms of the Special Drawing Right of a Contracting
State which is not a member of the International Monetary Fund
is to be calculated in a manner determined by that State.

2. Nevertheless, those States which are not members of the
International Monetary Fund and whose law does not permit the

application of the provisions of paragraph 1 of this article
may, at the time of signature, or at the time of ratification,
acceptance, approval or accession or at any time thereafter,
declare that the limits of liability provided for in this
Convention to be applied in their territories shall be fixed as:
    12,500 monetary units per package or other shipping unit
or 37.5 monetary units per kilogramme of gross weight of the
goods.
    3. The monetary unit referred to in paragraph 2 of this
article corresponds to sixty-five and a half milligrammes of
gold of millesimal fineness nine hundred. The conversion of
the amounts referred to in paragraph 2 into the national
currency is to be made according to the law of the State
concerned.
    4. The calculation mentioned in the last sentence of
paragraph 1 and the conversion mentioned in paragraph 3 of this
article is to be made in such a manner as to express in the
national currency of the Contracting State as far as possible
the same real value for the amounts in article 6 as is expressed
there in units of account. Contracting States must communicate
to the depositary the manner of calculation pursuant to paragraph 1 of this article, or the result of the conversion mentioned in paragraph 3 of this article, as the case may be, at
the time of signature or when depositing their instruments of
ratification, acceptance, approval or accession, or when
availing themselves of the option provided for in paragraph 2
of this article and whenever there is a change in the manner
of such calculation or in the result of such conversion.

PART VII. FINAL CLAUSES

Article 27. Depositary

The Secretary-General of the United Nations is hereby
designated as the depositary of this Convention.

Article 28. Signature, ratification, acceptance, approval, accession

1. This Convention is open for signature by all States
until 30 April 1979 at the Headquarters of the United Nations,
New York.
    2. This Convention is subject to ratification, acceptance
or approval by the signatory States.
    3. After 30 April 1979, this Convention will be open for
accession by all States which are not signatory States.
    4. Instruments of ratification, acceptance, approval and
accession are to be deposited with the Secretary-General of
the United Nations.

Article 29. Reservations

No reservations may be made to this Convention.

Article 30. Entry into force

1. This Convention enters into force on the first day of the month following the expiration of one year from the date of deposit of the 20th instrument of ratification, acceptance, approval or accession.

2. For each State which becomes a Contracting State to this Convention after the date of the deposit of the 20th instrument of ratification, acceptance, approval or accession, this Convention enters into force on the first day of the month following the expiration of one year after the deposit of the appropriate instrument on behalf of that State.

3. Each Contracting State shall apply the provisions of this Convention to contracts of carriage by sea concluded on or after the date of the entry into force of this Convention in respect of that State.

Article 31. Denunciation of other conventions

1. Upon becoming a Contracting State to this Convention, any State party to the International Convention for the Unification of Certain Rules relating to Bills of Lading signed at Brussels on 25 August 1924 (1924 Convention) must notify the Government of Belgium as the depositary of the 1924 Convention of its denunciation of the said Convention with a declaration that the denunciation is to take effect as from the date when this Convention enters into force in respect of that State.

2. Upon the entry into force of this Convention under paragraph 1 of article 30, the depositary of this Convention must notify the Government of Belgium as the depositary of the 1924 Convention of the date of such entry into force, and of the names of the Contracting States in respect of which the Convention has entered into force.

3. The provisions of paragraphs 1 and 2 of this article apply correspondingly in respect of States parties to the Protocol signed on 23 February 1968 to amend the International Convention for the Unification of Certain Rules relating to Bills of Lading signed at Brussels on 25 August 1924.

4. Notwithstanding article 2 of this Convention, for the purposes of paragraph 1 of this article, a Contracting State may, if it deems it desirable, defer the denunciation of the 1924 Convention and of the 1924 Convention as modified by the 1968 Protocol for a maximum period of five years from the entry into force of this Convention. It will then notify the Government of Belgium of its intention. During this transitory period, it must apply to the Contracting States this Convention to the exclusion of any other one.

Article 32.   Revision and amendment

1.   At the request of not less than one-third of the Contracting States to this Convention, the depositary shall convene a conference of the Contracting States for revising or amending it.

2.   Any instrument of ratification, acceptance, approval or accession deposited after the entry into force of an amendmend to this Convention, is deemed to apply to the Convention as amended.

Article 33.   Revision of the limitation amounts and unit of account or monetary unit

1.   Notwithstanding the provisions of article 32, a conference only for the purpose of altering the amount specified in article 6 and paragraph 2 of article 26, or of substituting either or both of the units defined in paragraphs 1 and 3 of article 26 by other units is to be convened by the depositary in accordance with paragraph 2 of this article. An alteration of the amounts shall be made only because of a significant change in their real value.

2.   A revision conference is to be convened by the depositary when not less than one-fourth of the Contracting States so request.

3.   Any decision by the conference must be taken by a two-thirds majority of the participating States. The amendment is communicated by the depositary to all the Contracting States for acceptance and to all the States signatories of the Convention for information.

4.   Any amendment adopted enters into force on the first day of the month following one year after its acceptance by two-thirds of the Contracting States. Acceptance is to be effected by the deposit of a formal instrument to that effect, with the depositary.

5.   After entry into force of an amendment a Contracting State which has accepted the amendment is entitled to apply the Convention as amended in its relations with Contracting States which have not within six months after the adoption of the amendment notified the depositary that they are not bound by the amendment.

6.   Any instrument of ratification, acceptance, approval or accession deposited after the entry into force of an amendment to this Convention, is deemed to apply to the Convention as amended.

Article 34.   Denunciation

1.   A Contracting State may denounce this Convention at any time by means of a notification in writing addressed to the depositary.

2. The denunciation takes effect on the first day of the month following the expiration of one year after the notification is received by the depositary. Where a longer period is specified in the notification, the denunciation takes effect upon the expiration of such longer period after the notification is received by the depositary.

DONE at Hamburg, this thirty-first day of March one thousand nine hundred and seventy-eight, in a single original, of which the Arabic, Chinese, English, French, Russian and Spanish texts are equally authentic.

IN WITNESS WHEREOF the undersigned plenipotentiaries, being duly authorized by their respective Governments, have signed the present Convention.

ANNEX III

RESOLUTION ADOPTED BY THE UNITED NATIONS CONFERENCE
ON THE CARRIAGE OF GOODS BY SEA

"The United Nations Conference on the Carriage of Goods by Sea,

"Noting with appreciation the kind invitation of the Federal Republic of Germany to hold the Conference in Hamburg,

"Being aware that the facilities placed at the disposal of the Conference and the generous hospitality bestowed on the participants by the Government of the Federal Republic of Germany and by the Free and Hanseatic City of Hamburg, have in no small measure contributed to the success of the Conference,

"Expresses its gratitude to the Government and people of the Federal Republic of Germany, and

"Having adopted the Convention on the Carriage of Goods by Sea on the basis of a draft Convention prepared by the United Nations Commission on International Trade Law at the request of the United Nations Conference on Trade and Development,

"Expresses its gratitude to the United Nations Commission on International Trade Law and to the United Nations Conference on Trade and Development for their outstanding contribution to the simplification and harmonization of the law of the carriage of goods by sea, and

"Decides to designate the Convention adopted by the Conference as the: 'UNITED NATIONS CONVENTION ON THE CARRIAGE OF GOODS BY SEA, 1978', and

"Recommends that the rules embodied therein be known as the 'HAMBURG RULES'."

ANNEX II

COMMON UNDERSTANDING ADOPTED BY THE UNITED NATIONS
CONFERENCE ON THE CARRIAGE OF GOODS BY SEA

It is the common understanding that the liability of the
carrier under this Convention is based on the principle of
presumed fault or neglect. This means that, as a rule, the
burden of proof rests on the carrier but, with respect to
certain cases, the provisions of the Convention modify this
rule.

Appendix C:
International Conventions on Marine Pollution Controls

The protection of the marine environment is a major international concern that affects all marine-based activities, particularly shipping. The major conventions in this area are the 1954 Convention for the Prevention of
Pollution of the Sea by Oil, the 1969 Convention on Civil Liability for Oil
Pollution Damage, and the proposed 1973 Convention for the Prevention
of Pollution from Ships. The 1954 convention was amended in 1962 and
1969. These amendments, which entered into force in 1978, are not included here, but in essence they provide for a reduction in the amount of
oil a ship can discharge at sea during the course of its operations. This convention will be superseded when the convention of 1973 enters into force.
The civil liability convention entered into force in 1975.

THE 1954 INTERNATIONAL CONVENTION FOR THE PREVENTION OF POLLUTION OF THE SEA BY OIL

MULTILATERAL

International Convention for the Prevention of Pollution
of the Sea by Oil, 1954

Opened for signature at London May 12, 1954;
Ratification advised by the Senate of the United States
of America, subject to an understanding, reservations, and a recommendation, May 16, 1961;
Ratified, and acceptance declared, by the President of
the United States of America, subject to the said

From R. Churchill and M. Nordquist, eds., *New Directions in the Law of the Sea,* vols. 2 (1973)
and 4 (1975) (Dobbs Ferry, N.Y.: Oceana Publications). Used by permission.

understanding, reservations, and recommendation,
   May 29, 1961;
Acceptance deposited with the Intergovernmental Maritime
   Consultative Organization, subject to the said under-
   standing, reservations, and recommendation,
   September 8, 1961;
Proclaimed by the President of the United States of America
   December 8, 1961;
Entered into force for the United States of America
   December 8, 1961.

THE INTERNATIONAL CONVENTION FOR THE PREVENTION OF POLLUTION OF THE SEA BY OIL, 1954

The Governments represented at the International Conference
on Pollution of the Sea by Oil held in London from 26th April,
1954, to 12th May, 1954,
   Desiring to take action by common agreement to prevent pollution of the sea by oil discharged from ships, and considering that this end may best be achieved by the conclusion of a
Convention,

Have accordingly appointed the undersigned plenipotentiaries, who, having communicated their full powers, found in good
and due form, have agreed as follows:-

Article I

(1) For the purposes of the present Convention, the following expressions shall (unless the context otherwise requires)
have the meanings hereby respectively assigned to them, that
is to say:-

"The Bureau" has the meaning assigned to it by Article XXI:
"Discharge" in relation to oil or to an oily mixture means
   any discharge or escape howsoever caused;

"Heavy diesel oil" means marine diesel oil, other than those
   distillates of which more than 50 per cent. by volume
   distils at a temperature not exceeding 340° C. when
   tested by A.S.T.M. Standard Method D.158/53;
"Mile" means a nautical mile of 6080 feet or 1852 metres;
"Oil" means crude oil, fuel oil, heavy diesel oil and lubricating oil, and "oily" shall be construed accordingly.

(2) For the purposes of the present Convention the territories of a Contracting Government mean the territory of the
country of which it is the Government and any other territory
for the international relations of which the Government is responsible and to which the Convention shall have been extended
under Article XVIII.

Article II

The present Convention shall apply to sea-going ships registered in any of the territories of a Contracting Government, except

    (i)   ships for the time being used as naval auxiliaries;

    (ii) ships of under 500 tons gross tonnage;

    (iii) ships for the time being engaged in the whaling industry;

    (iv) ships for the time being navigating the Great Lakes of North America and their connecting and tributary waters as far east as the lower exit of the Lachine Canal at Montreal in the Province of Quebec, Canada.

Article III

(1) Subject to the provisions of Articles IV and V, the discharge from any tanker, being a ship to which the Convention applies, within any of the prohibited zones referred to in Annex A to the Convention in relation to tankers of-

    (a) oil;

    (b) any oily mixture the oil in which fouls the surface of the sea, shall be prohibited.

For the purposes of this paragraph the oil in an oily mixture of less than 100 parts of oil in 1,000,000 parts of the mixture shall not be deemed to foul the surface of the sea.

(2) Subject to the provisions of Articles IV and V, any discharge into the sea from a ship, being a ship to which the Convention applies and not being a tanker, of oily ballast water or tank washings shall be made as far as practicable from land. As from a date three years after the date on which the Convention comes into force, paragraph (1) of this Article shall apply to ships other than tankers as it applies to tankers, except that:-

    (a) the prohibited zones in relation to ships other than tankers shall be those referred to as such in Annex A to the Convention; and

    (b) the discharge of oil or of an oily mixture from such a ship shall not be prohibited when the ship is proceeding to a port not provided with such reception facilities as are referred to in Article VIII.

(3) Any contravention of paragraphs (1) and (2) of this Article shall be an offence punishable under the laws of the territory in which the ship is registered.

Article IV

(1) Article III shall not apply to:-

(a) the discharge of oil or of an oily mixture from a ship
for the purpose of securing the safety of the ship,
preventing damage to the ship or cargo, or saving life
at sea; or

(b) the escape of oil, or of an oily mixture, resulting
from damage to the ship or unavoidable leakage, if all
reasonable precautions have been taken after the occurrence of the damage or discovery of the leakage for the
puspose of preventing or minimising the escape;

(c) the discharge of sediment:-

    (i)   which cannot be pumped from the cargo tanks of
tankers by reason of its solidity; or

    (ii) which is residue arising from the purification
or clarification of oil fuel or lubricating oil,
provided that such discharge is made as far from land
as is practicable.

(2) In the event of such discharge or escape as is referred
to in this Article a statement shall be made in the oil record
book required by Article IX of the circumstances of and reason
for the discharge.

Article V

Article III shall not apply to the discharge from the bilges
of a ship:-

(a) of any oily mixture during the period of twelve months
following the date on which the Convention comes into force in
respect of the territory in which the ship is registered;

(b) after the expiration of such period, of an oily mixture
containing no oil other than lubricating oil.

Article VI

The penalties which may be imposed in pursuance of Article
III under the law of any of the territories of a Contracting
Government in respect of the unlawful discharge from a ship of
oil or of an oily mixture into waters outside the territorial
waters of that territory shall not be less than the penalties
which may be imposed under the law of that territory in respect
of the unlawful discharge of oil or of an oily mixture from a
ship into such territorial waters.

Article VII

As from a date twelve months after the present Convention comes into force in respect of any of the territories of a Contracting Government all ships registered in that territory shall be required to be so fitted as to prevent the escape of fuel oil or heavy diesel oil into bilges the contents of which are discharged into the sea without being passed through an oily-water separator.

Article VIII

As from a date three years after the present Convention comes into force in respect of any of the territories of a Contracting Government, that Government shall ensure the provision in each main port in that territory of facilities adequate for the reception, without causing undue delay to ships, of such residues from oily ballast water and tank washings as would remain for disposal by ships, other than tankers, using the port, if the water had been separated by the use of an oily-water separator, a settling tank or otherwise. Each Contracting Government shall from time to time determine which ports are the main ports in its territories for the purposes of this Article, and shall notify the Bureau in writing accordingly indicating whether adequate reception facilities have been installed.

Article IX

(1) There shall be carried in every ship to which the Convention applies an oil record book (whether as part of the ship's official logbook or otherwise) in the form specified in Annex B to the present Convention. The appropriate entries shall be made in that book, and each page of the book, including any statement under paragraph (2) of Article IV, shall be signed by the officer or officers in charge of the operations concerned and by the master of the ship. The written entries in the oil record book shall be in an official language of the territory in which the ship is registered, or in English or French.

(2) The competent authorities of any of the territories of a Contracting Government may inspect on board any such ship while within a port in that territory the oil record book required to be carried in the ship in compliance with the provisions of the Convention, and may make a true copy of any entry in that book and may require the master of the ship to certify that the copy is a true copy of such entry. Any copy so made which purports to have been certified by the master of the ship as a true copy of an entry in the ship's oil record book shall be made admissible in any judicial proceedings as evidence of the facts stated in the entry. Any action by the competent authorities under this paragraph shall be taken as expeditiously as possible and the ship shall not be delayed.

Article X

(1) Any Contracting Government may furnish to the Contracting Government in the territory of which a ship is registered particulars in writing of evidence that any provision of the Convention has been contravened in respect of that ship, wheresoever the alleged contravention may have taken place. If it is practicable to do so, the competent authorities of the former Government shall notify the master of the ship of the alleged contravention.

(2) Upon receiving such particulars the latter Government shall investigate the matter, and may request the former Government to furnish further or better particulars of the alleged contravention. If the Government in the territory of which the ship is registered is satisfied that sufficient evidence is available in the form required by law to enable proceedings against the owner or master of the ship to be taken in respect of the alleged contravention, it shall cause such proceedings to be taken as soon as possible, and shall inform the other Contracting Government and the Bureau of the result of such proceedings.

Article XI

Nothing in the present Convention shall be construed as derogating from the powers of any Contracting Government to take measures within its jurisdiction in respect of any matter to which the Convention relates or as extending the jurisdiction of any Contracting Government.

Article XII

Each Contracting Government shall send to the Bureau and to the appropriate organ of the United Nations:-

(a) the text of laws, decrees, orders and regulations in force in its territories which give effect to the present Convention;

(b) all official reports or summaries of official reports in so far as they show the results of the application of the provisions of the Convention, provided always that such reports or summaries are not, in the opinion of that Government, of a confidential nature.

Article XIII

Any dispute between Contracting Governments relating to the interpretation or application of the present Convention which cannot be settled by negotiation shall be referred at the request of either party to the International Court of Justice for decision unless the parties in dispute agree to submit it to arbitration.

Article XIV

(1) The present Convention shall remain open for signature for three months from this day's date and shall thereafter remain open for acceptance.

(2) Governments may become parties to the Convention by-

(i) signature without reservation as to acceptance;

(ii) signature subject to acceptance followed by acceptance; or

(iii) acceptance.

(3) Acceptance shall be effected by the deposit of an instrument of acceptance with the Bureau, which shall inform all Governments that have already signed or accepted the Convention of each signature and deposit of an acceptance and of the date of such signature or deposit.

Article XV

(1) The present Convention shall come into force twelve months after the date on which not less than ten Governments have become parties to the Convention, including five Governments of countries each with not less than 500,000 gross tons of tanker tonnage.

(2)--(a) For each Government which signs the Convention without reservation as to acceptance or accepts the Convention before the date on which the Convention comes into force in accordance with paragraph (1) of this Article it shall come into force on that date. For each Government which accepts the Convention on or after that date, it shall come into force three months after the date of the deposit of that Government's acceptance.
(b) The Bureau shall, as soon as possible, inform all Governments which have signed or accepted the Convention of the date on which it will come into force.

Article XVI

(1) Upon the request of any Contracting Government a proposed amendment of the present Convention shall be communicated by the Bureau to all Contracting Governments for consideration.

(2) Any amendment communicated to Contracting Governments for consideration under paragraph (1) of this Article shall be deemed to have been accepted by all Contracting Governments and shall come into force on the expiration of a period of six months after it has been so communicated, unless any one of the

Contracting Governments shall have made a declaration not less
than two months before the expiration of that period that it
does not accept the amendment.

(3)-- (a) A conference of Contracting Governments to consider amendments of the Convention proposed by any Contracting
Government shall be convened by the Bureau upon the request of
one-third of the Contracting Governments.

(b) Every amendment adopted by such a conference by
a two-thirds majority vote of the Contracting Governments represented shall be communicated by the Bureau to all Contracting
Governments for their acceptance.

(4) Any amendment communicated to Contracting Governments
for their acceptance under paragraph (3) of this Article shall
come into force for all Contracting Governments, except those
which before it comes into force make a declaration that they
do not accept the amendment, twelve months after the date on
which the amendment is accepted by two-thirds of the Contracting Governments.

(5) Any declaration under this Article shall be made by
a notification in writing to the Bureau which shall notify
all Contracting Governments of the receipt of the declaration.

(6) The Bureau shall inform all signatory and Contracting
Governments of any amendments which come into force under this
Article, together with the date on which such amendments shall
come into force.

Article XVII

(1) The present Convention may be denounced by any Contracting Government at any time after the expiration of a period
of five years from the date on which the Convention comes into
force for that Government.

(2) Denunciation shall be effected by a notification in
writing addressed to the Bureau, which shall notify all the
Contracting Governments of any denunciation received and of
the date of its receipt.

(3) A denunciation shall take effect twelve months, or
such longer period as may be specified in the notification,
after its receipt by the Bureau.

Article XVIII

(1) -- (a) Any Government may, at the time of signature
or acceptance of the present Convention, or at any time thereafter, declare by notification in writing given to the Bureau
that the Convention shall extend to any of the territories for
whose international relations it is responsible.

(b) The Convention shall, from the date of the
receipt of the notificaiton, or from such other date as may be
specified in the notification, extend to the territories
named therein.

(2) -- (a) Any Contracting Government which has made a
declaration under paragraph (1) of this Article may, at any
time after the expiration of a period of five years from the

date on which the Convention has been so extended to any territory, give notification in writing to the Bureau, declaring
that the Convention shall cease to extend to any such territory
named in the notification.

   (b)   The Convention shall cease to extend to any
territory mentioned in such notification twelve months, or
such longer period as may be specified therein, after the
date of receipt of the notification by the Bureau.

   (3)   The Bureau shall inform all Contracting Governments
of the extension of the Convention to any territories
under paragraph (1) of this Article, and of the termination
of any such extension under paragraph (2) of this Article,
stating in each case the date from which the Convention has
been, or will cease to be, so extended.

Article XIX

   (1)   In case of war or other hostilities, a Contracting
Government which considers that it is affected, whether as
a belligerent or as a neutral, may suspend the operation of
the whole or any part of the present Convention in respect
of all or any of its territories. The suspending Government
shall immediately give notice of any such suspension to the
Bureau.

   (2)   The suspending Government may at any time terminate
such suspension and shall in any event terminate it as soon
as it ceases to be justified under paragraph (1) of this
Article. Notice of such termination shall be given immediately
to the Bureau by the Government concerned.

   (3)   The Bureau shall notify all Contracting Governments
of any suspension or termination of suspension under this
Article.

Article XX

   As soon as the present Convention comes into force it shall
be registered by the Bureau with the Secretary-General of the
United Nations.

Article XXI

   The duties of the Bureau shall be carried out by the Government of the United Kingdom of Great Britain and Northern Ire-
land unless and until the Inter-Governmental Maritime Consul-
tive Organisation comes into being and takes over the duties
assigned to it under the Convention signed at Geneva on the
6th day of March, 1948, (1) and thereafter the duties of the
Bureau shall be carried out by the said Organisation.

----

[1]TIAS 4044; 9 UST 621.

In witness whereof the undersigned plenipotentiaries have signed the present Convention.

Done in London this twelfth day of May, 1954, in English and French, both texts being equally authoritative, in a single copy, which shall be deposited with the Bureau and of which the Bureau shall transmit certified copies to all signatory and Contracting Governments.

THE PARTIES TO THE CONVENTION,

BEING CONSCIOUS of the need to preserve the human environment in general and the marine environment in particular,

RECOGNIZING that deliberate, negligent or accidental release of oil and other harmful substances from ships constitutes a serious source of pollution,

RECOGNIZING ALSO the importance of the International Convention for the Prevention of Pollution of the Sea by Oil, 1954, as being the first multilateral instrument to be concluded with the prime objective of protecting the environment, and appreciating the significant contribution which that Convention has made in preserving the seas and coastal environment from pollution,

DESIRING to achieve the complete elimination of intentional pollution of the marine environment by oil and other harmful substances and the minimization of accidental discharge of such substances,

CONSIDERING that this object may best be achieved by establishing rules not limited to oil pollution having a universal purport,

HAVE AGREED as follows:

ARTICLE 1

General Obligations under the Convention

(1) The Parties to the Convention undertake to give effect to the provisions of the present Convention and those Annexes thereto by which they are bound, in order to prevent the pollution of the marine environment by the discharge of harmful substances or effluents containing such substances in contravention of the present Convention.

(2) Unless expressly provided otherwise, a reference to the present Convention constitutes at the same time a reference to its Protocols and to the Annexes.

ARTICLE 2

Definitions

For the purposes of the present Convention, unless expressly provided otherwise:

(1) "Regulations" means the Regulations contained in the Annexes to the present Convention.

(2) "Harmful substance" means any substance which, if introduced into the sea, is liable to create hazards to human health, to harm living resources and marine life, to damage amenities or to interfere with other legitimate uses of the sea, and includes any substance subject to control by the present Convention.

(3) (a) "Discharge", in relation to harmful substances or effluents containing such substances, means any release howsoever caused from a ship and includes any escape, disposal, spilling, leaking, pumping, emitting or emptying;

(b) "Discharge" does not include:

(i) dumping within the meaning of the Convention on the Prevention of Marine Pollution by Dumping of Wastes and Other Matter, done at London on 13 November 1972; or

(ii) release of harmful substances directly arising from the exploration, exploitation and associated off-shore processing of sea-bed mineral resources; or

(iii) release of harmful substances for purposes of legitimate scientific research into pollution abatement or control.

(4) "Ship" means a vessel of any type whatsoever operating in the marine environment and includes hydrofoil boats, air-cushion vehicles, submersibles, floating craft and fixed or floating platforms.

(5) "Administration" means the Government of the State under whose authority the ship is operating. With respect to a ship entitled to fly a flag of any State, the Administration is the Government of that State. With respect to fixed or floating platforms engaged in exploration and exploitation of the sea-bed and subsoil thereof adjacent to the coast over which the coastal State exercises sovereign rights for the purposes of exploration and exploitation of their natural resources, the Administration is the Government of the coastal State concerned.

(6) "Incident" means an event involving the actual or probable discharge into the sea of a harmful substance, or effluents containing such a substance.

(7) "Organization" means the Inter-Governmental Maritime Consultative Organization.

ARTICLE 3

Application

(1) The present Convention shall apply to:

(a) ships entitled to fly the flag of a Party to the Convention; and

(b) ships not entitled to fly the flag of a Party but which operate under the authority of a Party.

(2) Nothing in the present Article shall be construed as derogating from or extending the sovereign rights of the Parties under international law over the sea-bed and subsoil thereof adjacent to their coasts for the purposes of exploration and exploitation of their natural resources.

(3) The present Convention shall not apply to any warship, naval auxiliary or other ship owned or operated by a State and used, for the time being, only on government non-commercial service. However, each Party shall ensure by the adoption of appropriate measures not impairing the operations or operational capabilities of such ships owned or operated by it, that such ships act in a manner consistent, so far as is reasonable and practicable, with the present Convention.

ARTICLE 4

Violation

(1) Any violation of the requirements of the present Convention shall be prohibited and sanctions shall be established therefor under the law of the Administration of the ship concerned wherever the violation occurs. If the Administration is informed of such a violation and is satisfied that sufficient evidence is available to enable proceedings to be brought in respect of the alleged violation, it shall cause such proceedings to be taken as soon as possible, in accordance with its law.

(2) Any violation of the requirements of the present Convention within the jurisdiction of any Party to the Convention shall be prohibited and sanctions shall be established therefor under the law of that Party. Whenever such a violation occurs, that Party shall either:

(a) cause proceedings to be taken in accordance with its law; or

(b) furnish to the Administration of the ship such information and evidence as may be in its possession that a violation has occurred.

(3) Where information or evidence with respect to any violation of the present Convention by a ship is furnished to the Administration of that ship, the Administration shall promptly inform the Party which has furnished the information or evidence, and the Organization, of the action taken.

(4) The penalties specified under the law of a Party pursuant to the present Article shall be adequate in severity to discourage violations of the present Convention and shall be equally severe irrespective of where the violations occur.

ARTICLE 5

Certificates and Special Rules on Inspection of Ships

(1) Subject to the provisions of paragraph (2) of the present Article a certificate issued under the authority of a Party to the Convention in accordance with the provisions of the Regulations shall be accepted by the other Parties and regarded for all purposes covered by the present Convention as having the same validity as a certificate issued by them.

(2) A ship required to hold a certificate in accordance with the provisions of the Regulations is subject, while in the ports or off-shore terminals under the jurisdiction of a Party, to inspection by officers duly authorized by that Party. Any such inspection shall be limited to verifying that there is on board a valid certificate, unless there are clear grounds for believing that the condition of the ship or its equipment

does not correspond substantially with the particulars of that certificate. In that case, or if the ship does not carry a valid certificate, the Party carrying out the inspection shall take such steps as will ensure that the ship shall not sail until it can proceed to sea without presenting an unreasonable threat of harm to the marine environment. That Party may, however, grant such a ship permission to leave the port or off-shore terminal for the purpose of proceeding to the nearest appropriate repair yard available.

(3)   If a Party denies a foreign ship entry to the ports or off-shore terminals under its jurisdiction or takes any action against such a ship for the reason that the ship does not comply with the provisions of the present Convention, the Party shall immediately inform the consul or diplomatic representative of the Party whose flag the ship is entitled to fly, or if this is not possible, the Administration of the ship concerned. Before denying entry or taking such action the Party may request consultation with the Administration of the ship concerned. Information shall also be given to the Administration when a ship does not carry a valid certificate in accordance with the provisions of the Regulations.

(4)   With respect to the ships of non-Parties to the Convention, Parties shall apply the requirements of the present Convention as may be necessary to ensure that no more favourable treatment is given to such ships.

ARTICLE 6

Detection of Violations and Enforcement of the Convention

(1)   Parties to the Convention shall co-operate in the detection of violations and the enforcement of the provisions of the present Convention, using all appropriate and practicable measures of detection and environmental monitoring, adequate procedures for reporting and accumulation of evidence.

(2)   A ship to which the present Convention applies may, in any port or off-shore terminal of a Party, be subject to inspection by officers appointed or authorized by that Party for the purpose of verifying whether the ship has discharged any harmful substances in violation of the provisions of the Regulations. If an   pection indicates a violation of the Convention, a report shall be forwarded to the Administration for any appropriate action.

(3)   Any Party shall furnish to the Administration evidence, if any, that the ship has discharged harmful substances or effluents containing such substances in violation of the provisions of the Regulations. If it is practicable to do so, the competent authority of the former Party shall notify the Master of the ship of the alleged violation.

(4)   Upon receiving such evidence, the Administration so informed shall investigate the matter, and may request the other Party to furnish further or better evidence of the alleged contravention. If the Administration is satisfied that sufficient evidence is available to enable proceedings to be brought in respect of the alleged violation, it shall cause such proceedings to be taken in accordance with its law as soon as possible. The Administration shall promptly inform the Party which has reported the alleged violation, as well as the Organization, of the action taken.

(5)   A Party may also inspect a ship to which the present Convention applies when it enters the ports or off-shore terminals under its jurisdiction, if a request for an

investigation is received from any Party together with sufficient evidence that the ship has discharged harmful substances or effluents containing such substances in any place. The report of such investigation shall be sent to the Party requesting it and to the Administration so that the appropriate action may be taken under the present Convention.

ARTICLE 7

Undue Delay to Ships

(1) All possible efforts shall be made to avoid a ship being unduly detained or delayed under Article 4, 5 or 6 of the present Convention.

(2) When a ship is unduly detained or delayed under Article 4, 5 or 6 of the present Convention, it shall be entitled to compensation for any loss or damage suffered.

ARTICLE 8

Reports on Incidents Involving Harmful Substances

(1) A report of an incident shall be made without delay to the fullest extent possible in accordance with the provisions of Protocol I to the present Convention.

(2) Each Party to the Convention shall:

   (a) make all arrangements necessary for an appropriate officer or agency to receive and process all reports on incidents; and

   (b) notify the Organization with complete details of such arrangements for circulation to other Parties and Member States of the Organization.

(3) Whenever a Party receives a report under the provisions of the present Article, that Party shall relay the report without delay to:

   (a) the Administration of the ship involved; and

   (b) any other State which may be affected.

(4) Each Party to the Convention undertakes to issue instructions to its maritime inspection vessels and aircraft and to other appropriate services, to report to its authorities any incident referred to in Protocol I to the present Convention. That Party shall, if it considers it appropriate, report accordingly to the Organization and to any other party concerned.

ARTICLE 9

Other Treaties and Interpretation

(1) Upon its entry into force, the present Convention supersedes the International Convention for the Prevention of Pollution of the Sea by Oil, 1954, as amended, as between Parties to that Convention.

(2)   Nothing in the present Convention shall prejudice the codification and development of the law of the sea by the United Nations Conference on the Law of the Sea convened pursuant to Resolution 2750 C(XXV) of the General Assembly of the United Nations nor the present or future claims and legal views of any State concerning the law of the sea and the nature and extent of coastal and flag State jurisdiction.

(3)   The term "jurisdiction" in the present Convention shall be construed in the light of international law in force at the time of application or interpretation of the present Convention.

ARTICLE 10

Settlement of Disputes

Any dispute between two or more Parties to the Convention concerning the interpretation or application of the present Convention shall, if settlement by negotiation between the Parties involved has not been possible, and if these Parties do not otherwise agree, be submitted upon request of any of them to arbitration as set out in Protocol II to the present Convention.

ARTICLE 11

Communication of Information

(1)   The Parties to the Convention undertake to communicate to the Organization:

   (a)   the text of laws, orders, decrees and regulations and other instruments which have been promulgated on the various matters within the scope of the present Convention;

   (b)   a list of non-governmental agencies which are authorized to act on their behalf in matters relating to the design, construction and equipment of ships carrying harmful substances in accordance with the provisions of the Regulations;

   (c)   a sufficient number of specimens of their certificates issued under the provisions of the Regulations;

   (d)   a list of reception facilities including their location, capacity and available facilities and other characteristics;

   (e)   official reports or summaries of official reports in so far as they show the results of the application of the present Convention; and

   (f)   an annual statistical report, in a form standardized by the Organization, of penalties actually imposed for infringement of the present Convention.

(2)   The Organization shall notify Parties of the receipt of any communications under the present Article and circulate to all Parties any information communicated to it under sub-paragraphs (1)(b) to (f) of the present Article.

ARTICLE 12

Casualties to Ships

(1)   Each Administration undertakes to conduct an investigation of any casualty occurring to any of its ships subject to the provisions of the Regulations if such casualty has produced a major deleterious effect upon the marine environment.

(2)   Each Party to the Convention undertakes to supply the Organization with information concerning the findings of such investigation, when it judges that such information may assist in determining what changes in the present Convention might be desirable.

ARTICLE 13

Signature, Ratification, Acceptance, Approval and Accession

(1)   The present Convention shall remain open for signature at the Headquarters of the Organization from 15 January 1974 until 31 December 1974 and shall thereafter remain open for accession. States may become Parties to the present Convention by:

   (a)   signature without reservation as to ratification, acceptance or approval; or

   (b)   signature subject to ratification, acceptance or approval, followed by ratification, acceptance or approval; or

   (c)   accession.

(2)   Ratification, acceptance, approval or accession shall be effected by the deposit of an instrument to that effect with the Secretary-General of the Organization.

(3)   The Secretary-General of the Organization shall inform all States which have signed the present Convention or acceded to it of any signature or of the deposit of any new instrument of ratification, acceptance, approval or accession and the date of its deposit.

ARTICLE 14

Optional Annexes

(1)   A State may at the time of signing, ratifying, accepting, approving or acceding to the present Convention declare that it does not accept any one or all of Annexes III, IV and V (hereinafter referred to as "Optional Annexes") to the present Convention. Subject to the above, Parties to the Convention shall be bound by any Annex in its entirety.

(2)   A State which has declared that it is not bound by an Optional Annex may at any time accept such Annex by depositing with the Organization an instrument of the kind referred to in Article 13(2) of the present Convention.

(3)   A State which makes a declaration under paragraph (1) of the present Article in respect of an Optional Annex and which has not subsequently accepted that Annex in accordance with paragraph (2) of the present Article shall not be under any obligation nor entitled to claim any privileges under the present Convention in

respect of matters related to such Annex and all references to Parties in the present Convention shall not include that State in so far as matters related to such Annex are concerned.

(4)   The Organization shall inform the States which have signed or acceded to the present Convention of any declaration under the present Article as well as the receipt of any instrument deposited in accordance with the provisions of paragraph (2) of the present Article.

ARTICLE 15

Entry into Force

(1)   The present Convention shall enter into force twelve months after the date on which not less than fifteen States, the combined merchant fleets of which constitute not less than fifty per cent of the gross tonnage of the world's merchant shipping, have become parties to it in accordance with Article 13 of the present Convention.

(2)   An Optional Annex shall enter into force twelve months after the date on which the conditions stipulated in paragraph (1) of the present Article have been satisfied in relation to that Annex.

(3)   The Organization shall inform the States which have signed the present Convention or acceded to it of the date on which it enters into force and of the date on which an Optional Annex enters into force in accordance with paragraph (2) of the present Article.

(4)   For States which have deposited an instrument of ratification, acceptance, approval or accession in respect of the present Convention or any Optional Annex after the requirements for entry into force thereof have been met but prior to the date of entry into force, the ratification, acceptance, approval or accession shall take effect on the date of entry into force of the Convention or such Annex or three months after the date of deposit of the instrument whichever is the later date.

(5)   For States which have deposited an instrument of ratification,' acceptance, approval or accession after the date on which the Convention or an Optional Annex entered into force, the Convention or the Optional Annex shall become effective three months after the date of deposit of the instrument.

(6)   After the date on which all the conditions required under Article 16 to bring an amendment to the present Convention or an Optional Annex into force have been fulfilled, any instrument of ratification, acceptance, approval or accession deposited shall apply to the Convention or Annex as amended.

ARTICLE 16

Amendments

(1)   The present Convention may be amended by any of the procedures specified in the following paragraphs.

(7)   Any amendment to a Protocol or to an Annex shall relate to the substance of that Protocol or Annex and shall be consistent with the Articles of the present Convention.

(8)   The Secretary-General of the Organization shall inform all Parties of any amendments which enter into force under the present Article, together with the date on which each such amendment enters into force.

(9)   Any declaration of acceptance or of objection to an amendment under the present Article shall be notified in writing to the Secretary-General of the Organization. The latter shall bring such notification and the date of its receipt to the notice of the Parties to the Convention.

ARTICLE 17

Promotion of Technical Co-operation

The Parties to the Convention shall promote, in consultation with the Organization and other international bodies, with assistance and co-ordination by the Executive Director of the United Nations Environment Programme, support for those Parties which request technical assistance for:

(a)   the training of scientific and technical personnel;

(b)   the supply of necessary equipment and facilities for reception and monitoring;

(c)   the facilitation of other measures and arrangements to prevent or mitigate pollution of the marine environment by ships; and

(d)   the encouragement of research;

preferably within the countries concerned, so furthering the aims and purposes of the present Convention.

ARTICLE 18

Denunciation

(1)   The present Convention or any Optional Annex may be denounced by any Parties to the Convention at any time after the expiry of five years from the date on which the Convention or such Annex enters into force for that Party.

(2)   Denunciation shall be effected by notification in writing to the Secretary-General of the Organization who shall inform all the other Parties of any such notification received and of the date of its receipt as well as the date on which such denunciation takes effect.

(3)   A denunciation shall take effect twelve months after receipt of the notification of denunciation by the Secretary-General of the Organization or after the expiry of any other longer period which may be indicated in the notification.

(2) Amendments after consideration by the Organization:

    (a) any amendment proposed by a Party to the Convention shall be submitted to the Organization and circulated by its Secretary-General to all Members of the Organization and all Parties at least six months prior to its consideration;

    (b) any amendment proposed and circulated as above shall be submitted to an appropriate body by the Organization for consideration;

    (c) Parties to the Convention, whether or not Members of the Organization, shall be entitled to participate in the proceedings of the appropriate body;

    (d) amendments shall be adopted by a two-thirds majority of only the Parties to the Convention present and voting;

    (e) if adopted in accordance with sub-paragraph (d) of this paragraph, amendments shall be communicated by the Secretary-General of the Organization to all the Parties to the Convention for acceptance;

    (f) an amendment shall be deemed to have been accepted in the following circumstances:

        (i) an amendment to an Article of the Convention shall be deemed to have been accepted on the date on which it is accepted by two-thirds of the Parties, the combined merchant fleets of which constitute not less than fifty per cent of the gross tonnage of the world's merchant fleet;

        (ii) an amendment to an Annex to the Convention shall be deemed to have been accepted in accordance with the procedure specified in sub-paragraph (f)(iii) of this paragraph unless the appropriate body, at the time of its adoption, determines that the amendment shall be deemed to have been accepted on the date on which it is accepted by two-thirds of the Parties, the combined merchant fleets of which constitute not less than fifty per cent of the gross tonnage of the world's merchant fleet. Nevertheless, at any time before the entry into force of an amendment to an Annex to the Convention, a Party may notify the Secretary-General of the Organization that its express approval will be necessary before the amendment enters into force for it. The latter shall bring such notification and the date of its receipt to the notice of Parties;

        (iii) an amendment to an Appendix to an Annex to the Convention shall be deemed to have been accepted at the end of a period to be determined by the appropriate body at the time of its adoption, which period shall be not less than ten months, unless within that period an objection is communicated to the Organization by not less than one-third of the Parties or by Parties the combined merchant fleets of which constitute not less than fifty per cent of the gross tonnage of the world's merchant fleet whichever condition is fulfilled;

        (iv) an amendment to Protocol I to the Convention shall be subject to the same procedures as for the amendments to the Annexes to the Convention, as provided for in sub-paragraphs (f)(ii) or (f)(iii) of this paragraph;

(v)   an amendment to Protocol II to the Convention shall be subject to the same procedures as for the amendments to an Article of the Convention, as provided for in sub-paragraph (f)(i) of this paragraph;

(g)   the amendment shall enter into force under the following conditions:

    (i)   in the case of an amendment to an Article of the Convention, to Protocol II, or to Protocol I or to an Annex to the Convention not under the procedure specified in sub-paragraph (f)(iii) of this paragraph, the amendment accepted in conformity with the foregoing provisions shall enter into force six months after the date of its acceptance with respect to the Parties which have declared that they have accepted it;

    (ii)   in the case of an amendment to Protocol I, to an Appendix to an Annex or to an Annex to the Convention under the procedure specified in sub-paragraph (f)(iii) of this paragraph, the amendment deemed to have been accepted in accordance with the foregoing conditions shall enter into force six months after its acceptance for all the Parties with the exception of those which, before that date, have made a declaration that they do not accept it, or a declaration under sub-paragraph (f)(ii) of this paragraph, that their express approval is necessary.

(3)   Amendment by a Conference:

(a)   Upon the request of a Party, concurred in by at least one-third of the Parties, the Organization shall convene a Conference of Parties to the Convention to consider amendments to the present Convention.

(b)   Every amendment adopted by such a Conference by a two-thirds majority of those present and voting of the Parties shall be communicated by the Secretary-General of the Organization to all Contracting Parties for their acceptance.

(c)   Unless the Conference decides otherwise, the amendment shall be deemed to have been accepted and to have entered into force in accordance with the procedures specified for that purpose in sub-paragraphs (2)(f) and (g) of the present Article.

(4)   (a)   In the case of an amendment to an Optional Annex, a reference in the present Article to a "Party to the Convention" shall be deemed to mean a reference to a Party bound by that Annex.

    (b)   Any Party which has declined to accept an amendment to an Annex shall be treated as a non-Party only for the purpose of application of that Amendment.

(5)   The adoption and entry into force of a new Annex shall be subject to the same procedures as for the adoption and entry into force of an amendment to an Article of the Convention.

(6)   Unless expressly provided otherwise, any amendment to the present Convention made under this Article, which relates to the structure of a ship, shall apply only to ships for which the building contract is placed, or in the absence of a building contract, the keel of which is laid, on or after the date on which the amendment comes into force.

ARTICLE 19

Deposit and Registration

(1)   The present Convention shall be deposited with the Secretary-General of the Organization who shall transmit certified true copies thereof to all States which have signed the present Convention or acceded to it.

(2)   As soon as the present Convention enters into force, the text shall be transmitted by the Secretary-General of the Organization to the Secretary-General of the United Nations for registration and publication, in accordance with Article 102 of the Charter of the United Nations.

ARTICLE 20

Languages

The present Convention is established in a single copy in the English, French, Russian and Spanish languages, each text being equally authentic. Official translations in the Arabic, German, Italian and Japanese languages shall be prepared and deposited with the signed original.

IN WITNESS WHEREOF the undersigned* being duly authorized by their respective Governments for that purpose have signed the present Convention.

DONE AT LONDON this second day of November, one thousand nine hundred and seventy-three.

---

* *Signatures omitted.*

The 1969 International Convention on Civil Liability for Oil Pollution Damage

The States Parties to the present Convention,

Conscious of the dangers of pollution posed by the worldwide maritime carriage of oil in bulk,

Convinced of the need to ensure that adequate compensation is available to persons who suffer damage caused by pollution resulting from the escape or discharge of oil from ships,

Desiring to adopt uniform international rules and procedures for determining questions of liability and providing adequate compensation in such cases,

Have agreed as follows:

Article I

For the purposes of this Convention:

1. "Ship" means any sea-going vessel and any seaborne craft of any type whatsoever, actually carrying oil in bulk as cargo.

2. "Person" means any individual or partnership or any public or private body, whether corporate or not, including a State or any of its constituent subdivisions.

3. "Owner" means the person or persons registered as the owner of the ship or, in the absence of registration, the person or persons owning the ship. However in the case of a ship owned by a State and operated by a company which in that State is registered as the ship's operator, "owner" shall mean such company.

4. "State of the ship's registry" means in relation to registered ships the State of registration of the ship, and in relation to unregistered ships the State whose flag the ship is flying.

5. "Oil" means any persistent oil such as crude oil, fuel oil, heavy diesel oil, lubricating oil and whale oil, whether carried on board a ship as cargo or in the bunkers of such a ship.

6. "Pollution damage" means loss or damage caused outside the ship carrying oil by contamination resulting from the escape or discharge of oil from the ship, wherever such escape or discharge may occur, and includes the costs of preventive measures and further loss or damage caused by preventive measures.

7. "Preventive measures" means any reasonable measures taken by any person after an incident has occurred to prevent or minimize pollution damage.

8. "Incident" means any occurrence, or series of occurrences having the same origin, which causes pollution damage.

9. "Organization" means the Inter-Governmental Maritime Consultative Organization.

ARTICLE II

This Convention shall apply exclusively to pollution damage caused on the territory including the territorial sea of a Contracting State and to preventive measures taken to prevent or minimize such damage.

ARTICLE III

1. Except as provided in paragraphs 2 and 3 of this Article, the owner of a ship at the time of an incident, or where the incident consists of a series of occurrences at the time of the first such occurrence, shall be liable for any pollution damage caused by oil which has escaped or been discharged from the ship as a result of the incident.

2. No liability for pollution damage shall attach to the owner if he proves that the damage:

    (a) resulted from an act of war, hostilities, civil war, insurrection or a natural phenomenon of an exceptional, inevitable and irresistible character, or

    (b) was wholly caused by an act or omission done with intent to cause damage by a third party, or

    (c) was wholly caused by the negligence or other wrongful act of any Government or other authority responsible for the maintenance of lights or other navigational aids in the exercise of that function.

3. If the owner proves that the pollution damage resulted wholly or partially either from an act or omission done with intent to cause damage by the person who suffered the damage or from the negligence of that person, the owner may be exonerated wholly or partially from his liability to such person.

4. No claim for compensation for pollution damage shall be made against the owner otherwise than in accordance with this Convention. No claim for pollution damage under this Convention or otherwise may be made against the servants or agents of the owner.

5. Nothing in this Convention shall prejudice any right of recourse of the owner against third parties.

ARTICLE IV

When oil has escaped or has been discharged from two or more ships, and pollution damage results therefrom, the owners of all the ships concerned, unless exonerated under Article III, shall be jointly and severally liable for all such damage which is not reasonably separable.

ARTICLE V

1. The owner of a ship shall be entitled to limit his liability under this Convention in respect of any one incident to an aggregate amount of 2,000 francs for each ton of the ship's tonnage. However, this aggregate amount shall not in any event exceed 210 million francs.

2. If the incident occurred as a result of the actual fault or privity of the owner, he shall not be entitled to avail himself of the limitation provided in paragraph 1 of this Article.

3. For the purpose of availing himself of the benefit of limitation provided for in paragraph 1 of this Article the owner shall constitute a fund for the total sum representing the limit of his liability with the Court or other competent authority of any one of the Contracting States in which action is brought under Article IX. The fund can be constituted either by depositing the sum or by producing a bank guarantee or other guarantee, acceptable under the legislation of the Contracting State where the fund is constituted, and considered to be adequate by the Court or another competent authority.

4. The fund shall be distributed among the claimants in proportion to the amounts of their established claims.

5. If before the fund is distributed the owner or any of his servants or agents or any person providing him insurance or other financial security has as a result of the incident in question, paid compensation for pollution damage, such person shall, up to the amount he has paid, acquire by subrogation the rights which the person so compensated would have enjoyed under this Convention.

6. The right of subrogation provided for in paragraph 5 of this Article may also be exercised by a person other than those mentioned therein in respect of any amount of compensation for pollution damage which he may have paid but only to the extent that such subrogation is permitted under the applicable national law.

7. Where the owner or any other person establishes that he may be compelled to pay at a later date in whole or in part any such amount of compensation, with regard to which such person would have enjoyed a right of subrogation under paragraphs 5 or 6 of this Article, had the compensation been paid before the fund was distributed, the Court or other competent authority of the State where the fund has been constituted may order that a sufficient sum shall be provisionally set aside to enable such person at such later date to enforce his claim against the fund.

8. Claims in respect of expenses reasonably incurred or sacrifices reasonably made by the owner voluntarily to prevent or minimize pollution damage shall rank equally with other claims against the fund.

9. The franc mentioned in this Article shall be a unit consisting of sixty-five and a half milligrams of gold of millesimal fineness nine hundred. The amount mentioned in paragraph 1 of this Article shall be converted into the national currency of the State in which the fund is being constituted on the basis of the value of that currency by reference to the unit defined above on the date of the constitution of the fund.

10. For the purpose of this Article the ship's tonnage shall be the net tonnage of the ship with the addition of the amount deducted from the gross tonnage on account of engine room space for the purpose of ascertaining the net tonnage. In the case of a ship which cannot be measured in accordance with the normal rules of tonnage measurement, the ship's tonnage shall be deemed to be 40 per cent of the weight in tons (of 2240 lbs) of oil which the ship is capable of carrying.

11. The insurer or other person providing financial security shall be entitled to constitute a fund in accordance with this Article on the same conditions and having the same effect as if it were constituted

by the owner. Such a fund may be constituted even in the event of the actual fault or privity of the owner but its constitution shall in that case not prejudice the rights of any claimant against the owner.

ARTICLE VI

1. Where the owner, after an incident, has constituted a fund in accordance with Article V, and is entitled to limit his liability,

(*a*) no person having a claim for pollution damage arising out of that incident shall be entitled to exercise any right against any other assets of the owner in respect of such claim;

(*b*) the Court or other competent authority of any Contracting State shall order the release of any ship or other property belonging to the owner which has been arrested in respect of a claim for pollution damage arising out of that incident, and shall similarly release any bail or other security furnished to avoid such arrest.

2. The foregoing shall, however, only apply if the claimant has access to the Court administering the fund and the fund is actually available in respect of his claim.

ARTICLE VII

1. The owner of a ship registered in a Contracting State and carrying more than 2,000 tons of oil in bulk as cargo shall be required to maintain insurance or other financial security, such as the guarantee of a bank or a certificate delivered by an international compensation fund, in the sums fixed by applying the limits of liability prescribed in Article V, paragraph 1 to cover his liability for pollution damage under this Convention.

2. A certificate attesting that insurance or other financial security is in force in accordance with the provisions of this Convention shall be issued to each ship. It shall be issued or certified by the appropriate authority of the State of the ship's registry after determining that the requirements of paragraph 1 of this Article have been complied with. This certificate shall be in the form of the annexed model and shall contain the following particulars:

(*a*) name of ship and port of registration;

(*b*) name and principal place of business of owner;

(*c*) type of security;

(*d*) name and principal place of business of insurer or other person giving security and, where appropriate, place of business where the insurance or security is established;

(*e*) period of validity of certificate which shall not be longer than the period of validity of the insurance or other security.

3. The certificate shall be in the official language or languages of the issuing State. If the language used is neither English nor French, the text shall include a translation into one of these languages.

4. The certificate shall be carried on board the ship and a copy shall be deposited with the authorities who keep the record of the ship's registry.

5. An insurance or other financial security shall not satisfy the requirements of this Article if it can cease, for reasons other than the expiry of the period of validity of the insurance or security specified

in the certificate under paragraph 2 of this Article, before three months have elapsed from the date on which notice of its termination is given to the authorities referred to in paragraph 4 of this Article, unless the certificate has been surrendered to these authorities or a new certificate has been issued within the said period. The foregoing provisions shall similarly apply to any modification which results in the insurance or security no longer satisfying the requirements of this Article.

6. The State of registry shall, subject to the provisions of this Article, determine the conditions of issue and validity of the certificate.

7. Certificates issued or certified under the authority of a Contracting State shall be accepted by other Contracting States for the purposes of this Convention and shall be regarded by other Contracting States as having the same force as certificates issued or certified by them. A Contracting State may at any time request consultation with the State of a ship's registry should it believe that the insurer or guarantor named in the certificate is not financially capable of meeting the obligations imposed by this Convention.

8. Any claim for compensation for pollution damage may be brought directly against the insurer or other person providing financial security for the owner's liability for pollution damage. In such case the defendant may, irrespective of the actual fault or privity of the owner, avail himself of the limits of liability prescribed in Article V, paragraph 1. He may further avail himself of the defenses (other than the bankruptcy or winding up of the owner) which the owner himself would have been entitled to invoke. Furthermore, the defendant may avail himself of the defense that the pollution damage resulted from the wilful misconduct of the owner himself, but the defendant shall not avail himself of any other defense which he might have been entitled to invoke in proceedings brought by the owner against him. The defendant shall in any event have the right to require the owner to be joined in the proceedings.

9. Any sums provided by insurance or by other financial security maintained in accordance with paragraph 1 of this Article shall be available exclusively for the satisfaction of claims under this Convention.

10. A Contracting State shall not permit a ship under its flag to which this Article applies to trade unless a certificate has been issued under paragpaph 2 or 12 of this Article.

11. Subject to the provisions of this Article, each Contracting State shall ensure, under its national legislation, that insurance or other security to the extent specified in paragraph 1 of this Article is in force in respect of any ship, wherever registered, entering or leaving a port in its territory, or arriving at or leaving an off-shore terminal in its territorial sea, if the ship actually carries more than 2,000 tons of oil in bulk as cargo.

12. Insurance or other financial security is not maintained in respect of a ship owned by a Contracting State, the provisions of this Article relating thereto shall not be applicable to such ship, but the ship shall carry a certificate issued by the appropriate authorities of the State of the ship's registry stating that the ship is owned by that State and that the ship's liability is covered within the limits pre-

scribed by Article V, paragraph 1. Such a certificate shall follow as
closely as practicable the model prescribed by paragraph 2 of this
Article.

ARTICLE VIII

Rights of compensation under this Convention shall be extinguished
unless an action is brought thereunder within three years from the
date when the damage occurred. However, in no case shall an action
be brought after six years from the date of the incident which caused
the damage. Where this incident consists of a series of occurrences,
the six years' period shall run from the date of the first such occurrence.

ARTICLE IX

1. Where an incident has caused pollution damage in the territory
including the territorial sea of one or more Contracting States, or
preventive measures have been taken to prevent or minimize pollution
damage in such territory including the territorial sea, actions for compensation may only be brought in the Courts of any such Contracting
State or States. Reasonable notice of any such action shall be given
to the defendant.

2. Each Contracting State shall ensure that its Courts possess the
necessary jurisdiction to entertain such actions for compensation.

3. After the fund has been constituted in accordance with Article
V the Courts of the State in which the fund is constituted shall be
exclusively competent to determine all matters relating to the ap-
portionment and distribution of the fund.

ARTICLE X

1. Any judgment given by a Court with jurisdiction in accordance
with Article IX which is enforceable in the State of origin where it
is no longer subject to ordinary forms of review, shall be recognized
in any Contracting State, except:

    (a) where the judgment was obtained by fraud; or

    (b) where the defendant was not given reasonable notice and
a fair opportunity to present his case.

2. A judgment recognized under paragraph 1 of this Article shall be
enforceable in each Contracting State as soon as the formalities required in that State have been complied with. The formalities shall not
permit the merits of the case to be re-opened.

ARTICLE XI

1. The provisions of this Convention shall not apply to warships or
other ships owned or operated by a State and used, for the time being,
only on Government non-commercial service.

2. With respect to ships owned by a Contracting State and used for
commercial purposes, each State shall be subject to suit in the jurisdictions set forth in Article IX and shall waive all defences based on its
status as a sovereign State.

ARTICLE XII

This Convention shall supersede any International Conventions in force or open for signature, ratification or accession at the date on which the Convention is opened for signature, but only to the extent that such Conventions would be in conflict with it; however, nothing in this Article shall affect the obligations of Contracting States to non-Contracting States arising under such International Conventions.

ARTICLE XIII

1. The present Convention shall remain open for signature until 31 December 1970 and shall thereafter remain open for accession.

2. States Members of the United Nations or any of the Specialized Agencies or of the International Atomic Energy Agency or Parties to the Statute of the International Court of Justice may become Parties to this Convention by:

(*a*) signature without reservation as to ratification, acceptance or approval;

(*b*) signature subject to ratification, acceptance or approval followed by ratification, acceptance or approval; or

(*c*) accession.

ARTICLE XIV

1. Ratification, acceptance, approval or accession shall be effected by the deposit of a formal instrument to that effect with the Secretary-General of the Organization.

2. Any instrument of ratification, acceptance, approval or accession deposited after the entry into force of an amendment to the present Convention with respect to all existing Contracting States, or after the completion of all measures required for the entry into force of the amendment with respect to those Contracting States shall be deemed to apply to the Convention as modified by the amendment.

ARTICLE XV

1. The present Convention shall enter into force on the ninetieth day following the date on which Governments of eight States including five States each with not less than 1,000,000 gross tons of tanker tonnage have either signed it without reservation as to ratification, acceptance or approval or have deposited instruments of ratification, acceptance, approval or accession with the Secretary-General of the Organization.

2. For each State which subsequently ratifies, accepts, approves or accedes to it the present Convention shall come into force on the ninetieth day after deposit by such State of the appropriate instrument.

ARTICLE XVI

1. The present Convention may be denounced by any Contracting State at any time after the date on which the Convention comes into force for that State.

2. Denunciation shall be effected by the deposit of an instrument with the Secretary-General of the Organization.

3. A denunciation shall take effect one year, or such longer period as may be specified in the instrument of denunciation, after its deposit with the Secretary-General of the Organization.

ARTICLE XVII

1. The United Nations, where it is the administering authority for a territory, or any Contracting State responsible for the international relations of a territory, shall as soon as possible consult with the appropriate authorities of such territory or take such other measures as may be appropriate, in order to extend the present Convention to that territory and may at any time by notification in writing to the Secretary-General of the Organization declare that the present Convention shall extend to such territory.

2. The present Convention shall, from the date of receipt of the notification or from such other date as may be specified in the notification, extend to the territory named therein.

3. The United Nations, or any Contracting State which has made a declaration under paragraph 1 of this Article may at any time after the date on which the Convention has been so extended to any territory declare by notification in writing to the Secretary-General of the Organization that the present Convention shall cease to extend to any such territory named in the notification.

4. The present Convention shall cease to extend to any territory mentioned in such notification one year, or such longer period as may be specified therein, after the date of receipt of the notification by the Secretary-General of the Organization.

ARTICLE XVIII

1. A Conference for the purpose of revising or amending the present Convention may be convened by the Organization.

2. The Organization shall convene a Conference of the Contracting States for revising or amending the present Convention at the request of not less than one-third of the Contracting States.

ARTICLE XIX

1. The present Convention shall be deposited with the Secretary-General of the Organization.

2. The Secretary-General of the Organization shall:

(a) inform all States which have signed or acceded to the Convention of

(i) each new signature or deposit of instrument together with the date thereof;

(ii) the deposit of any instrument of denunciation of this Convention together with the date of the deposit;

(iii) the extension of the present Convention to any territory under paragraph 1 of Article XVII and of the termination of any such extension under the provisions of paragraph 4 of that Article stating in each case the date on which the present Convention has been or will cease to be so extended;

(*b*) transmit certified true copies of the present Convention to all Signatory States and to all States which accede to the present Convention.

Article XX

As soon as the present Convention comes into force, the text shall be transmitted by the Secretary-General of the Organization to the Secretariat of the United Nations for registration and publication in accordance with Article 102 of the Charter of the United Nations.

Article XXI

The present Convention is established in a single copy in the English and French languages, both texts being equally authentic. Official translations in the Russian and Spanish languages shall be prepared and deposited with the signed original.

In witness whereof the undersigned being duly authorized by their respective Governments for that purpose have signed the present Convention.

Done at Brussels this twenty-ninth day of November 1969.

Selected Bibliography and Information Sources

There is a voluminous body of literature on both general and ocean transportation. The following sources constitute a partial list for those who wish to acquire a broader and more substantial understanding of the subject matter.

General Transportation

Baumol, William, et al. "The Role of Cost in the Minimum Pricing of Railroad Services." *Journal of Business,* October 1962.

Bonavia, M. R. *The Economics of Transport.* London: Nisbet & Co., 1954.

Calmus, Thomas W. "Full Cost versus Incremental Cost: Again." *Transportation Journal,* winter 1969.

Campbell, Thomas C. "Transport and its Impact on Developing Countries." *Transportation Journal,* fall 1972.

Currie, A. W. *Economics of Canadian Transportation.* Toronto: University of Toronto Press, 1954.

Fair, Marion L., and Williams, E. W. *Economics of Transportation and Logistics.* Dallas: Business Publications, 1973.

Fellner, W. J. *Competition Among the Few.* Reprints of Economic Classics. New York: Augustus M. Kelley, 1960.

Frederick, John H. *Commercial Air Transportation.* 5th ed. Homewood, Ill.: R. D. Irwin, 1961.

Gilmore, Harlan W. *Transportation and the Growth of Cities.* Glencoe, Ill.: Free Press of Glencoe, 1953.

Hazard, John L. *Transportation: Management, Economics, Policy.* Cambridge, Md.: Cornell Maritime Press, 1977.

Heaver, Trevor D. "Multi-Modal Ownership—The Canadian Experience." *Transportation Journal,* fall 1971.

Hille, Stanley J., and Poist, Richard. *Transportation Principles and Perspectives.* Danville, Ill.: Interstate Printers and Publishers, 1974.

Langford, John. *Transport in Transition* (The Reorganization of the Federal Transport Portfolio) [Canada]. Montreal: McGill-Queen's University Press, 1976.

Lansing, J. *Transportation and Economic Policy.* New York: Free Press, 1966.

Lewis, W. A. *Overhead Costs.* London: Allen & Unwin, 1949.

Locklin, Phillip D. *Economics of Transportation.* 7th ed. Homewood, Ill.: R. D. Irwin, 1972.

McElhiney, Paul T. "Transportation: A Developing Profession." *Transportation Journal,* fall 1964.

Moses, Leon F. "A General Equilibrium Model of Production, Interregional Trade and Location of Industry." *Review of Economics and Statistics,* November 1960.

Munby, Denis. *Transport: Selected Readings.* Baltimore: Penguin Books, 1968.

Norton, Hugh S. *Modern Transportation Economics.* 2nd ed. Columbus, Ohio: Charles E. Merrill Publishing Co., 1971.

Owen, W. *Strategy for Mobility.* Washington, D.C.: Brookings Institution, 1970.

Pegrum, Dudley F. *Transportation: Economics and Public Policy.* 3rd ed. Homewood, Ill.: R. D. Irwin, 1973.

Phillips, A., ed. *Promoting Competition in Regulated Markets.* Washington, D.C.: Brookings Institution, 1975.

Prest, A. R., and Turvey, R. "Cost-Benefit Analysis: A Survey." *Economic Journal,* December 1965.

Rose, Joseph R. "Limits on Marginal Cost Pricing." *Transportation Journal,* winter 1964.

Rothschild, K. W. "Price Theory and Oligopoly." *Economic Journal* 57 (1947). Reprinted in AEA, *Readings in Price Theory.* Homewood, Ill.: R. D. Irwin, 1952.

Sampson, Roy J. "The Pricing of Transportation Services." *Proceedings of the Colloquium Series on Transportation, 1967–68.* Winnipeg: Center for Transportation Studies, University of Manitoba, 1968.

Sampson, R., and Farris, M. *Domestic Transportation: Practice, Theory and Policy.* 4th ed. Boston: Houghton Mifflin, 1979.

Sharp, C. H. *Transport Economics.* London: Macmillan Press, 1973.

Smykay, E. W. *Physical Distribution Management.* 3rd ed. New York: Macmillan, 1973.

Steiner, H. M. "Social Benefit Cost Analysis of Transport Proposals." *Proceedings: Transportation Research Forum* 14 (1973).

Taft, Charles A. *Management of Physical Distribution and Transportation.* 6th ed. Homewood, Ill.: R. D. Irwin, 1978.

Thomson, J. M. "Some Reflections on Transport Research in Europe." *Research Seminar Series*, spring 1978. Ottawa: Canadian Transport Commission, 1978.

Vellenga, David B., and Ettlie, John E. "Technology Transfer in Transportation: Problems and Research Questions." *Proceedings: Transportation Research Forum* 16 (1975).

Vickrey, William S. "Congestion Theory and Transport Investment." *American Economic Review*, May 1969.

Walters, A. A. *The Economics of Road User Charges.* Baltimore: Johns Hopkins University Press, 1968.

Wilson, George W. "Regulation, Public Policy and Efficient Provision of Freight Transportation." *Transportation Journal*, fall 1975.

There are also numerous trade journals and other periodicals in the field. Some of the better known are:

Aviation Week and Space Technology
Canadian Transportation and Distribution Management
Containers International
Distribution Worldwide
Handling and Shipping
International Journal of Physical Distribution
Railway Age
Traffic World
Transport Topics
Transportation Research

More technical and scholarly publications are:

The I.C.C. Practitioner's Journal
Journal of Transport Economics and Policy
Traffic Quarterly
The Transportation Journal

Other journals that often have articles on transportation topics include:

The American Economic Review
Canadian Journal of Economics
Economic Geography
Geography
Journal of Industrial Economics
Land Economics
Logistics Review

Ocean Transportation

Abrahamsson, B. J. "Liner and Tramp Rates." *Journal of the Israel Shipping Research Institute,* winter 1972.

_____."The Marine Environment and Ocean Shipping: Some Implications for a New Law of the Sea." *International Organization,* spring 1977.

Abrahamsson, B. J., and Singer, M. A. "A Shipping Research Program with Particular Reference to Smaller Nations," *Journal of the Israel Shipping Research Institute,* April 1972.

Alexanderson, G., and Norstrom, G. *World Shipping.* New York: John Wiley and Sons, 1963.

Athay, Robert E. *The Economics of Soviet Merchant Shipping Policy.* Oxford: Oxford University Press, 1972.

Barker, J., and Brandwein, Robert. *The U.S. Merchant Marine in National Perspective.* Lexington, Mass.: D. C. Heath & Co., 1970.

Barros, J., and Johnston, D. M. *The International Law of Pollution.* New York: Free Press, 1974.

Bennathan, E., and Walters, A. A. *Port Pricing and Investment Policy for Developing Countries.* Oxford: Oxford University Press, 1979.

_____. *The Economics of Ocean Freight Rates.* New York: Praeger, 1969.

Berglund, A. *Ocean Transportation.* New York: Longmans, Green and Co., 1931.

Bes, J. *Chartering and Shipping Terms.* 7th ed. New York: W. S. Heinman, 1975.

_____. *Bulk Carriers.* New York: W. S. Heinman, 1975.

Blackwell, Robert J. "Implementation of the Merchant Marine Act of 1970." *Journal of Maritime Law and Commerce,* January 1974.

Boczek, B. A. *Flags of Convenience: An International Legal Study.* Cambridge, Mass.: Harvard University Press, 1962.

Branch, Alan E. *The Elements of Shipping.* 4th ed. London: Chapman and Hall, 1977.

British Shipping Laws. London: Stevens and Sons, various years. (This is a set of volumes each by a different author on a different subject. Volume 13 gives much information on international organizations and classification agencies in shipping.)

Bross, Steven. *Ocean Shipping.* Cambridge, Md.: Cornell Maritime Press, 1956.

Bryan, I. A. "The Effect of Ocean Transport Costs on the Demand for Some Canadian Exports." *Weltwirtschaftliches Archiv.,* no. 4, 1974.

Bryan, I., and Kotowitz, Y. *Shipping Conferences in Canada.* Research Monograph no. 2. Research Branch, Bureau of Competition Policy, Consumer and Corporate Affairs, Canada, 1978.

Bush, William L. "Steamship Conference Contract Rate Agreements and the Dual Rate System." *I.C.C. Practictioner's Journal,* November–December 1972.

Canadian Transport Commission. *Study of the Economic Implications of the International Convention on a Code of Conduct for Liner Conferences.* Ottawa: ESAB 76-13, February 1976.

Churchill, R., and Nordquist, M. *New Directions in the Law of the Sea.* Dobbs Ferry, N.Y.: Oceana Publications, 1973. (This set, in many volumes, gives the original texts of conventions and amendments.)

Cohen, D., and Schneerson, D. "The Domestic Resource Costs of Establishing or Expanding a National Fleet." *Maritime Studies and Management,* no. 4, 1976.

Comité Maritime International. *International Conventions on Maritime Law* (texts). Secretariat of the International Maritime Committee. (This can be obtained by writing c/o Henry Voet-Genicot, 17 Borzestraat, B2000 Antwerp, Belgium.)

Couper, A. D. *The Geography of Sea Transport.* London: Hutchinson and Co., 1972.

Croner's Directory of Freight Conferences.

Cufley, C. F. *Ocean Freights and Chartering.* London: Crosby Lockwood Staples, 1974.

Danton, G. L. *The Theory and Practice of Seamanship.* 5th ed. London: Routledge & Kegan Paul, 1974.

Darling, H. J. *The Elements of an International Shipping Policy for Canada.* Ottawa: Transport Canada Marine, 1974.

Deakin, B. M. "Shipping Conferences, Some Economic Aspects of International Regulation," *Maritime Studies and Management,* July 1974.

Deakin, B. M., and Seward, T. *Shipping Conferences: A Study of their Origins, Development and Economic Practices.* Cambridge, England: Cambridge University Press, 1973.

Devanney, J. W. *Marine Decisions under Uncertainty.* Cambridge, Md.: Cornell Maritime Press, 1971.

Devanney, J. W.; Livanos, V. M.; and Stewart, R. J. "Conference Rate Making and the West Coast of South America," *Journal of Transportation Economics and Policy,* May 1975.

DeVerchove, Rene. *International Maritime Dictionary.* 2nd ed. Princeton: D. Van Nostrand Co., 1961.

Doganis, R. S., and Metaxas, B. N. *The Impact of Flags of Convenience.* Research Report no. 3, September 1976. London: Transport Studies Group, Polytechnic of Central London, 1976. (This report was followed by a discussion paper by Ken Grundey.)

Dover, Victor. *A Handbook to Marine Insurance.* 8th ed. London: H. F. & G. Witherby, 1975.

Drewry, H. P., Shipping Consultants, Ltd. *Organization and Structure of the Dry Bulk Shipping Industry*, Study no. 63. London: 1978.
_____. *Ports and Terminals for Large Bulk Carriers*. London: 1975.
Dupuit, J. "Public Works and the Consumer." In *Transport: Selected Readings*, edited by Denis Munby. Baltimore: Penguin Books, 1968.
Evans, A. A. *Technical and Social Changes in the World's Ports*. Geneva: International Labor Office, 1969.
Fayle, C. E. *A Short History of the World's Shipping Industry*. London: Allen & Unwin, 1933.
Fearnley and Egers Chartering Co., Ltd. *Review: World Bulk Trades* (annual). Oslo.
Federal Maritime Commission. *Fact Finding Investigation No. 6: The Effect of Steamship Conference Organization, Rules, Regulations, and Practices upon the Foreign Commerce of the U.S.*, 1965.
Ferguson, A. R., et al. *The Economic Value of the U.S. Merchant Marine*. Evanston: Northwestern University Transportation Center, 1961.
Flere, W. A. *Port Economics*. London: Foxlow Publications, 1967.
Frankel, E., and Marcus, H. S. *Ocean Transportation*. Cambridge, Mass.: MIT Press, 1972.
Fuchs, John. "The Shipping Industry in Canada." Research Series no. 2. In *Strategic Factors in Industrial Relations Systems*. Geneva: International Institute for Labour Studies, 1976.
Future of Liner Shipping. International Symposium in Bremen, September 23-25, 1975. Bremen: Institute for Shipping Economics, 1975.
Garnett, H. C. "Competition between Ports and Investment Planning." *Scottish Journal of Political Economics*, November 1970.
Gilman, S. "Optimal Shipping Technologies for Routes to Developing Countries." *Journal of Transportation Economics and Policy*, January 1977.
Gold, Edgar, ed. *New Directions in Maritime Law 1978*. Halifax: Dalhousie University, Faculty of Law, 1978.
_____. *Canadian Admiralty Law: Introductory Materials*. 2nd ed. Halifax: Dalhousie University, Faculty of Law, 1978.
Goss, R. O., ed. *Studies in Maritime Economics*. Cambridge, England: Cambridge University Press, 1968.
_____. *Advances in Maritime Economics*. Cambridge, England: Cambridge University Press, 1977.
Grammenos, Costas. "Bank Finance for Ship Purchase." Bangor Occasional Papers in Economics, no. 16. Cardiff: University of Wales Press, 1979.
Grossman, W. L. *Ocean Freight Rates*. Cambridge, Md.: Cornell Maritime Press, 1956.
Grundey, K. *Flags of Convenience in 1978*. Discussion Paper no. 8,

November 1978. London: Transport Studies Group, Polytechnic of Central London, 1978. (This is a follow-up of the study by Doganis and Metaxas.)

Hanson, Phillip. "Soviet Union and World Shipping." *Journal of Soviet Studies*, July 1970.

Healy, N. J., and Sharpe, D. J. *Admiralty: Cases and Materials*. American Casebook Series. St. Paul, Minn.: West Publishing Co., 1974.

Heaver, T. D. "A Theory of Shipping Conference Pricing and Policies." *Maritime Studies and Management*, no. 1, 1973.

_____. "TransPacific Trade Liner Shipping and Conference Rates," *Transportation and Logistics Reviews*, spring 1972.

_____. "The Structure of Liner Conference Rates," *Journal of Industrial Economics*, 1973.

Hedlin, Menzies and Associates, Ltd. *Canadian Merchant Marine: Analysis of Economic Potential*. Ottawa: Canadian Transport Commission, December 1970.

Hill, J.M.M. *The Seafaring Career*. London: Tavistock Institute of Human Relations, 1972.

Horn, Johan. "Nationalism and Internationalism in Shipping." *Journal of Transportation Economics and Policy*, September 1969.

Kendall, Lane C. *The Business of Shipping*. Cambridge, Md.: Cornell Maritime Press, 1973.

Kilgour, John G. *The U.S. Merchant Marine: National Maritime Policy and Industrial Relations*. New York: Praeger, 1975.

Laing, E. T. "The Rationality of Conference Pricing and Output Policies." Part I, *Maritime Studies and Management*, no. 3, 1975. Part II, *Maritime Studies and Management*, no. 3, 1976. (See Schneerson's commentary in the latter issue.)

Larner, R. "Public Policy in the Ocean Freight Industry." In *Promoting Competition in Regulated Markets*, edited by A. Phillips. Washington, D.C.: Brookings Institution, 1975.

Lawrence, Samuel A. *U.S. Merchant Shipping Policies and Politics*. Washington, D.C.: Brookings Institution, 1966.

_____. *International Shipping: The Years Ahead*. Lexington, Mass.: Lexington Books, 1972.

"Liner Shipping in the U.S. Trades." *Maritime Policy and Management*, July 1978. (This is a special issue and is an answer to the 1977 report by the U.S. Department of Justice, *The Regulated Ocean Shipping Industry*.)

Lloyd's of London. *Lloyd's Calendar and National Yearbook* (annual). London: Lloyd's of London Press.

McLachlen, D. L. "The Price Policy of Liner Conferences." *Scottish*

Journal of Political Economy, November 1963.

Mankabady, S., ed. *The Hamburg Rules on the Carriage of Goods by Sea.* Boston/Leyden: A. W. Sijthoff, 1978.

Marcus, Henry A. *Planning Ship Replacement in the Containerization Era.* Lexington, Mass.: D. C. Heath & Co., 1974.

Marx, Daniel. *International Shipping Cartels.* Princeton: Princeton University Press, 1953.

Mayer, H. M. "Some Geographic Aspects of Technological Change in Maritime Transportation." *Economic Geography,* April 1973.

Metaxas, B. N. "Notes on the Internationalization Process in the Maritime Sectors." *Maritime Policy and Management,* January 1978.

_____. *The Economics of Tramp Shipping.* London: Athlone Press, 1971.

Moreby, David. *The Human Element in Shipping.* Colchester, England: Seatrade Publications, 1975.

Moyer, Charles. "A Critique of the Rationales for Present U.S. Maritime Programs." *Transportation Journal,* winter 1974.

Munro-Smith, R. *Merchant Ship Types.* London: Marine Media Management, 1975.

Naess, Erling D. *The Great PanLibHon Controversy.* London: Gower Press, 1972.

_____. *Autobiography of a Shipping Man.* Colchester, England: Seatrade Publications, 1977.

National Academy of Sciences. *Maritime Information Sources: A Guide to Current Statistical Data.* Washington, D.C.: Maritime Transportation Board, December 1978.

National Research Council. *The Sea-going Workforce: Implications of Technological Change.* Washington, D.C.: 1974.

Northwestern University Transportation Center Forum. *Proceedings: In Search of a Rational Liner Shipping Policy.* March 13–14, 1978. Evanston, Ill.: Northwestern University Transportation Center, 1978.

OECD. *Maritime Transport* (annual). Paris.

_____. *Ocean Freight Rates as Part of Total Transport Costs.* Paris: 1967.

_____. *Export Cartels.* Paris: 1974.

O'Loughlin, Carleen. *The Economics of Sea Transport.* London: Pergamon Press, 1967.

Pearson, Charles S. *International Marine Environment Policy: The Economic Dimension.* Baltimore: Johns Hopkins University Press, 1975.

Prescott, J.R.V. *The Political Geography of the Oceans.* Vancouver, Canada: David and Charles, 1975.

Ram, M. S. *Shipping.* New York: Asia Publishing House, 1969.

Restrictive Trade Practices Commission (Canada). *Shipping Conferences Arrangements and Practices.* Ottawa: Queen's Printers, 1966.

Rinman, T., and Linden, R. *Shipping–How it Works.* Gothenburg, Sweden: 1978.

Rochdale Report. *Committee on Inquiry into Shipping.* CHMSO, Cmd 4337, 1970.

Schenker, E., and Brockel, H. C. *Port Planning and Development as Related to the Problem of U.S. Ports and the U.S. Coastal Environment.* Cambridge, Md.: Cornell Maritime Press, 1974.

Schneerson, D. "The Rationality of Conference Pricing and Output Policies: Commentary." *Maritime Studies and Management,* no. 3, 1976.

––––––. "The Structure of Liner Freight Rates." *Journal of Transportation Economics and Policy,* January 1976.

Shipping Conferences Rate Policy and Developing Countries. Hamburg: Institute for International Economics, 1973.

Shipping Statistics Yearbook (annual). Bremen: Institute for Shipping Economics.

Singh, Nagendra. *International Conventions of Merchant Shipping.* 2nd ed. London: Stevens and Sons, 1973. (This is vol. 8 of *British Shipping Laws.*)

Smith, J. R. "Ocean Freight Rates." *Political Science Quarterly,* no. 2, 1906.

Sturmey, S. G. *British Shipping and World Competition.* London: Athlone Press, 1962.

––––––. *Shipping Economics: Collected Papers.* London: Macmillan Press, 1975.

––––––. "The Development of the Code of Conduct for Liner Conferences," *Marine Policy,* April 1979.

Taylor, L. G. *Seaports: An Introduction to Their Place and Purpose.* Glasgow: Brown, Son and Ferguson, 1974.

Thorburn, T. *The Supply and Demand of Water Transport.* Stockholm: Stockholm School of Economics, 1960.

Tozzoli, Anthony. "Containerization and its Impact on Port Development." *Journal of the Waterways,* August 1972.

Turner, H. A. *The Principles of Marine Insurance.* London: Stone & Cox Publications, 1971.

UN. *The Application of Modern Transport Technology to Mineral Development in Developing Countries.* New York: 1976.

UNCTAD. *Review of Maritime Transport* (annual).

––––––. *Level and Structure of Freight Rates Conference Practices and Adequacy of Shipping Services.* TD/B/c.4/38, 1969.

––––––. *The Liner Conference System.* TD/B/c.4/62/ Rev. 1, 1970.

––––––. *Economic Consequences of the Existence or Lack of a Genuine Link between Vessel and Flag of Registry.* TD/B/c.4/168, March 10, 1977.

––––––. *Shipping in the Seventies.* UN Sales No. 72, II. D. 15.

_____. *Convention on a Code of Conduct for Liner Conferences,* UN Document TD/CODE/11/Rev., April 6, 1974.

U.S., Congress, House. Committee on Merchant Marine and Fisheries. *Third Flag. Hearings* before the Subcommittee on the Merchant Marine. 94th Cong., 1st and 2d sess., serial no. 95-35, 1977.

_____. Judiciary Committee. *The Ocean Freight Industry.* 87th Cong., 2d sess., H.R. 1414, 1962.

U.S., Congress, Joint Economic Committee. *Discriminatory Ocean Freight Rates and the Balance of Payments.* 89th Cong., 1st sess., January 6, 1965.

U.S., Congress, Senate. Committee on Commerce, Science, and Transportation. *Illegal Rebating in the U.S. Ocean Commerce. Hearings* before the Subcommittee on Merchant Marine and Tourism. 95th Cong., 1st sess., serial no. 95-13, 1977.

_____. *Steamship Conferences and Dual Rate Contracts* (Bonner Report). 87th Cong., 1st sess., S.R. 860, August 31, 1961.

U.S., Department of Commerce, Maritime Administration (MARAD). *Annual Reports of MARAD.*

_____. *A Statistical Analysis of the World's Merchant Fleet* (annual).

_____. *Effective U.S. Control of Merchant Ships: A Statistical Study.*

_____. *Foreign Flag Ships Owned by U.S. Parent Companies* (annual).

U.S., Department of Justice, Antitrust Division. *The Regulated Ocean Shipping Industry,* Report, 1977 (stock #027-000-00474-1).

Van den Burg, G. *Containerization: A Modern Transport System.* London: Hutchinson, 1969.

Winter, W. *Marine Insurance—Its Principles and Practice.* 3rd ed. New York: McGraw-Hill, 1952.

Zannetos, Z. "Persistent Economic Misconceptions in the Transportation of Oil by Sea." *Maritime Studies and Management,* no. 1, 1973.

There are innumerable trade periodicals catering to local needs, as well as some with international coverage and distribution. Included among the latter are:

Cargo Systems International (formerly *ICHCA Journal*)
Fairplay International Shipping Weekly
Hansa
Hitachi Zosen News
IMCO News
Indian Shipping
Lloyd's Daily List

Lloyd's Shipping Economist
Marine Engineering/Log
Marine Week
The Motorship
Norwegian Shipping News
Safety at Sea
Seaports and the Shipping World
Seatrade
Shipping World and Shipbuilding
Swedish Shipping Gazette

Scholarly journals specializing in ocean-related issues and having global distribution include:

Journal of Maritime Law and Commerce
Lloyd's Maritime and Commercial Law Quarterly
Marine Policy
Marine Technology Society Journal
Maritime Policy and Management
Nautical Review
Ocean Development and International Law
Ocean Management

In addition, current research is reported in the Journal of Abstracts (published by the British Ship Research Association) and in the MRIS Abstracts (published by the U.S. National Research Council). Many studies and statistical series are also published by various UN agencies, particularly the Shipping Division of UNCTAD. Its annual Review of Maritime Transport and OECD's Maritime Transport together provide excellent coverage of current developments, issues, and prospects.

There is much information to be had from ship classification agencies, brokers and charter agents, private consulting firms, and shipping research institutes. Such information is, however, not usually available at public or university libraries. The most prominent of the private sources are Norwegian and British sources and are commonly quoted in U.S. and OECD publications. The Norwegian sources are R. S. Platou A/S and Fearnley and Egers Chartering Co., both located in Oslo. The former issues a general annual report on shipping, while the latter regularly publishes special reports on bulk trading. The British firms are located in London. H. P. Drewry (Shipping Consultants), Ltd., publishes a monthly Shipping Statistics and Economics as well as special studies. John I. Jacobs Co. issues a semiannual World Tanker Fleet Review, and The Westinform Service comes out with monthly reports as well as special reports to subscribers. Lambert Brothers (Shipping), Ltd., issues special studies on shipping in general and particularly on container shipping, and H. Clarkson and Co., Ltd., publishes a yearly register of tankers and liquid gas carriers. Maritime Research, Inc., in New York provides current freight rate data on a subscription basis.

Specialized shipping research centers have been and continue to be established throughout the world. As early as 1919, Italy formed the Instituto Universitario Navale in Naples. In Bremen, West Germany, there is an Institute for Shipping Economics, and similar institutes exist in East Germany at the universities of Rostock and Dresden. Poland has two maritime research units, the Instytut Morski in Gdansk and the School of Economics in Sopot. The USSR has a Shipping Research Institute in Moscow with branches in Leningrad, Odessa, Vladivostok, and Baku; each unit is concerned with the problems of one region under the direction of the main institute. Greece has attached an Institute for Shipping Studies to the School of Economics in Piraeus. In the Far East, there is the Japan Maritime Research Institute in Tokyo; and at Kobe University's Research Institute for Economics and Business Administration there is a section for International Economic Research, which has several positions in maritime economics. South Korea's Institute for Science and Technology has a shipping research division. The Israel Shipping Research Institute is located in Haifa. The Netherlands has a Maritime Research Center (Stichting Maritime Research), and the well-known Norwegian Institute for Shipping Research is in Bergen, Norway. There are several centers in England, but best known internationally is the one at the University of Wales Institute of Science and Technology. Another major source in England is the British Ship Research Association.

In the United States, much research is centered in the sea-grant universities, especially M.I.T.; the universities of Rhode Island, Washington, and Delaware; Virginia Polytechnic Institute; and Stevens Institute of Technology. Other major sources of information are the Transportation Center Library at Northwestern University, the Institute of Transportation Studies Library at the University of California (Berkeley), and the Society of Naval Architects and Marine Engineers (SNAME) in New York. In Canada there are, aside from government sources, the transportation division in the business school of the University of British Columbia, the Transportation Research Forum in Montreal, and the Canadian Marine Transportation Centre at Dalhousie University in Halifax. The Law Faculty at Dalhousie is also very active in shipping research, and the university is rapidly becoming a major center for marine affairs.

Index

Printed in the United States
by Baker & Taylor Publisher Services

Printed in the United States
by Baker & Taylor Publisher Services